FIELD OF SCREAMS

Haunted Tales from the Baseball
Diamond, the Locker Room, and Beyond

Mickey Bradley and Dan Gordon

LYONS PRESS
Guilford, Connecticut
An imprint of Globe Pequot Press

To our mothers, who are in a league of their own

To buy books in quantity for corporate use
or incentives, call **(800) 962-0973**
or e-mail **premiums@GlobePequot.com.**

Lyons Press is an imprint of Globe Pequot Press.

Project editor: Gregory Hyman
Layout artist: Kevin Mak

Library of Congress Cataloging-in-Publication data is available on file.

ISBN 978-1-59921-856-4

Printed in the United States of America

10 9 8 7 6 5 4 3 2 1

10|10

CONTENTS

ACKNOWLEDGMENTS

We would like to extend a warm thanks to the hundreds of ballplayers and folks working behind the scenes in baseball who were kind enough to share their firsthand stories or point us in helpful directions.

Many other people contributed their wisdom, talents, and kindness to our endeavor.

Tim Wiles at the National Baseball Hall of Fame Research Library opened his files to us. Junwei Yu provided the story on Taiwan's Chengqing Lake Stadium. Marty Kuehnert worked his magic in Japan. Hiromi Lima, Hitoshi Maruyama, and Shoko Ogata were invaluable research assistants and interpreters. *Domo arigatos* as well to Jim Allen, Garrett DeOrio, Wayne Graczyk, Ted Sato, Masayuki Tamaki, and Robert Whiting.

We are also grateful to Curtis Garfield, George Gmelch, C. Daryl Healea, Kevin Kennedy, Nathan Levan, Bruce Markusen, Greg Schwalenberg, Lee Swanson, and Carl and Joan Turin. Brian Bernardoni and Greg Underwood not only shared their own stories but also went the extra mile in connecting us to additional resources and contacts.

Special thanks to Gary Joseph for his Ruthian editorial wisdom and Jim McDonald for his unflagging support in every stage of the book's development.

As always, we are indebted to our agent Rob Wilson for his outstanding managerial skills.

Our gratitude again to the talented team at Lyons for their faith in our project.

INTRODUCTION

It's hard to believe that when we set out to research *Haunted Baseball: Ghosts, Curses, Legends, and Eerie Events*, we were crossing our fingers that we'd find enough stories to fill a book. Of course we had heard of some famous curses—the Red Sox, the Cubs—along with some talk of a few ballpark ghosts. And we were confident that an institution as rich and historic as baseball would have accrued all kinds of lore over the years. Still, we were stunned at how many stories were making their way around locker rooms, team buses, and water coolers, having never been captured in print before.

More stories, it turns out, than could be captured in one volume.

In fact, we knew when putting together *Haunted Baseball* that a second book would have to follow. We simply collected more tales than could be squeezed into one tome. In addition, new stories are added to baseball's canon every season. Before the original Yankee Stadium (for years rumored by many players to be the site of ghostly intervention on behalf of the home team) hosted its last game, its replacement was already making headlines for a new "curse" imparted on it by an ardent Red Sox fan. Which itself inspired a Yankee fan's attempt to hex Fenway Park. All of which adds some new personality to the two teams' latest battles on the ball field, new fuel—and fun—for their historic rivalry. The tale is told here in "New York's New Jersey."

Our goal with these books is to document some of the fun folklore that surrounds the game but to which—in many cases—fans have not previously had access. As much as we admire and appreciate stats and records and historic achievement on the ball field, we didn't set out to produce that kind of a book. We were more interested in the soul of the game and the stories that memorialize its legendary players and historic moments.

Take Babe Ruth. To hear many fans tell it, the Sultan of Swat is as active today as he ever was when he was alive. In "Chasing Babe Ruth," numerous people—including the Bambino's own granddaughter—regularly encounter the game's all-time greatest player. Other diamond heroes like Ty Cobb, Roberto Clemente, and Mickey Mantle also make appearances in these pages, since fans and players claim they make regular appearances in the world of the living.

With so many departed Hall of Famers still spotted in parks and training facilities and even fans' homes, it's no surprise that the Hall of Fame itself has become a repository for ghostly activity. We heard tales from museum guards and workers of strange noises and inexplicable encounters. Cooperstown itself has a rich history of apparitions and spirits, so lingering ballplayers fit right in.

And those are just some of the stories collected here. We are pleased that this volume casts a somewhat wider net than its predecessor. Although many major league teams are spotlighted with entertaining tales, we also include minor league ballparks and hotels, baseball memorabilia, and a fun look at some major-league pranks players indulge in to spook each other. In "Land of the Rising Dead," there's a look at Asian legends and "Viva La Fantasma" homes in on Latin lore, proving that while baseball may be considered America's pastime, haunted baseball stories are truly global.

As before, we take no sides in *Field of Screams*. Both true believers and skeptics have their say, and we leave it to the reader to take these anecdotes as literal truth or fanciful fiction. Either way, these supernatural stories add color to the legacies of great teams and to the game itself. As authors, our main goal is to entertain. As baseball enthusiasts, we have been most gratified to know that by presenting these tales, we've added some important, previously undocumented threads to baseball's tapestry. And hopefully helped capture the "spirit" of the game, in more ways than one.

Chapter 1
Strange Things
A-Brewin'

Baseball fans might expect the most feared site in the National League to be an imposing pitcher's park or a home-team-friendly stadium. But to hear most players tell it, the most feared site in the National League is the Pfister Hotel in Milwaukee, where many visiting teams stay while in town to play the Brewers. Dozens of big-leaguers dread their over-nights at the historic building, having suffered through some spooky encounters they can only explain one way.

"It was haunted, man," says Adrian Beltre. "I'm dead serious. I couldn't sleep for three straight nights."

The sure-handed third baseman's story is typical of many players. He stayed at the hotel in 2003 while with the Los Angeles Dodgers. "I felt some weird stuff," he attests.

For starters, there were noises. While lying in bed, Beltre heard steps as if someone were walking by him—but nobody else was in the room. He heard the sounds of someone hitting the wall. And he heard a knocking on his door. "I got up and looked out and nothing—nobody was there." He believes the room was haunted by the ghost of a woman, because "when I went into the bathroom, there was [the smell of a] woman's perfume."

If the imposing, 220-pound slugger's observations are limited to noises and odors, there's a good reason: "I didn't see nothing because I was covered under the blanket!" he admits. "But definitely some stuff was going on.

"I slept for only an hour in three days," he recalls. "I was scared. I was real scared, but I got through it."

According to teammate Alex Cora, Beltre was so upset that the entire team was affected. "The next year we switched hotels because of him."

But Beltre was not the only Dodger dodging ghosts that night. At the ballpark the next day, several players talked about their own odd experiences, including Eric Gagne ("I heard all kinds of noises," says the pitcher). Coach John Shelby—who had been staying at the hotel without incident since his playing career began in 1981—was shaken from his own encounter.

"I'm laying down, I'm sleepy, and I reach up to turn the light off—the lamp, by my bed. I turn on my back and lay down. And I hear this deep sigh, like somebody just took a deep breath." Shelby says the sound was low but unmistakable, and he's certain it wasn't just air escaping from the pillow as he lay his head down.

"So my eyes are wide open now. I'm laying there. It's dark. And now I'm real focused." He tried to convince himself he was just hearing things. "And the next thing I know, I hear it again! And it's right by my ear!

"It was scary," Shelby admits. "My heart was racing." He quickly turned on the light. "I looked at my bed. Didn't see anybody. I looked around the room. Didn't see anybody.

"And I've been sleeping with the light on in the bathroom ever since when we go to the Pfister."

•◆•

Upon its grand opening in 1893, the Pfister Hotel was not only opulent and luxurious, but also state of the art. It was one of the first hotels to feature electricity and thermostat controls in each room. Its twenty-foot-high ceilings were adorned with chandeliers and its walls lined with ornate designs and big-scale artwork. (Even today, the establishment claims "the largest Victorian art collection of any hotel in the world.") The Pfister's 1962 renovation added a twenty-three-story tower (the "new wing" that baseball players say is ghost-free) but maintained a historic air. Walk in the lobby today and you step back in the nineteenth century. Even the concierge wears an old-fashioned waistcoat straight out of the 1890s.

For many ballplayers, the old-time feel of the place adds to its eeriness. "When you get into that place, when you see that place, you get scared," says veteran pitcher Jose Santiago, one of many players who switched hotels rather than stay at the Pfister. "Because it has, like, angels on the walls." Reliever Chad Harville says the dark cedar, the heavy curtains, the dim lighting, and the solid doors all contribute to the impression that "This place is full of ghosts."

And, of course, there are the stories players love to tell about the place. Before his first trip in 2004, Harville recalls that "everybody was talking about it. Everybody said, 'Watch out for the ghosts!' You hear the stories before you go."

Journeyman infielder Joe Randa heard that "other guys were having lights turning off, [fire] alarms going on, alarm clocks going on and stuff like that." When Adam Eaton was pitching with the Padres, "guys claimed to have their TV turn on," as well as computers. Pitcher Ricky Bottalico was told that "furniture has been moved around."

Those descriptions will sound familiar to pitcher Dennis Sarfate. When he was first called up to the Brewers in 2006, the team put him up at the Pfister. He settled in, then left for the field. "I had put the Do Not Disturb/No Maid sign on the door," he recalls. "And when I got back to the room, the TV was on and all the pillows were off the bed. And I was like, that's kind of odd, 'cause when I left it wasn't like that."

Sarfate soon heard other tales from players. "I even asked the people at the front desk, 'Is there a part of this hotel that's haunted?' And they said, 'Well what wing are you in?' And I told them where I was and they said, 'No, you're fine.'"

• ◆ •

Felipe Crespo was not feeling so fine when he checked into the Pfister late one night on a road trip with the Giants in 2000. "I was so tired I left the TV on when I went to sleep and I left pretty much every light on. Real early in the morning I heard someone knocking on the door, so I got up. I came out and nobody was there. And I noticed that all the lights and the TV were off. And that really freaked me out." Crespo had to spend the next night at the hotel ("I pretty much drank myself until I slept—a lot of red wine"), but on his next trip to Milwaukee he paid for his own stay at a nearby hotel.

Crespo, too, asked hotel staff about the Pfister's haunted reputation. While management officially denies any ghostly activity, he says workers "have stories of different things. Stuff in the elevators, phony calls for room service and then the room is not occupied, stuff like that."

Such stories make the rounds of clubhouses, dugouts, team buses, and charter planes in no time, and set players up for a wide-eyed stay at the Pfister. Beltre remembers hearing tall tales on the way to the hotel. "They were telling me stories of what happened and what people think. Coming in I really believed it." Gagne (yet another player who requested a hotel change) admits, "I was scared from all the stories I'd heard. I heard the mob used to go to Milwaukee a lot and have meetings and stuff. That's why the hotel is creepy." John Shelby was told that "somebody jumped out of one of the windows." Most versions of that story say it was a lovelorn woman, spurned by a philandering ballplayer.

These rumors influence players from the minute they enter the building. "I always swear I see somebody out of the corner of my eye when I'm turning and walking through hallways and stuff," says pitcher Brad Hennessey, who questions whether or not anything is really there. "You know if you move a camera real fast, you get that blurry image? You never know."

Armando Rios believes that the stories themselves propagate more stories. He was on the same road trip as Crespo and heard his teammate's eerie tales. "After Felipe left, I was asleep and every twenty minutes I'd be up. And I'd feel things, and nothing would happen. Your mind starts playing tricks on you."

San Francisco Giants pitching ace Tim Lincecum's mind is prone to such tricks. "I'm kinda scared of the dark as it is," the two-time Cy Young winner admits. "But when you throw those kinds of stories in there, and a creepy old building . . ."

Lincecum had his own encounter at the Pfister. "My door was shaking at one point in the night, like someone leaned on it and then leaned on it again. I could hear it. And I could see the door pressing." It was 4:00 a.m. Lincecum did not know what was causing the bizarre scene, but he did know one thing: "I'm not answering that door! If it's a ghost or a real person, I'm not answering it!" Instead, he flipped the door latch to keep any marauding spirits at bay. And then he followed the time-honored tradition for expelling unwanted night visitors, known to little kids and professional ballplayers alike.

"I slept with the lights on," he says. "I left one of my lamps on. And one of the lights in the bathroom, just to make sure."

• ◆ •

Matt Treanor feels certain about what he experienced at the Pfister when he was in town with the Florida Marlins in 2006. "I would do any type of test, like a polygraph or anything, to verify my story," the catcher avers.

Treanor had just stopped by pitcher Taylor Tankersley's room around 8 or 9 p.m., down the fifth-floor hallway from his own, to make plans for dinner. Suddenly the two heard an odd tapping noise that seemed to be coming from a door to an adjoining room. "After a few seconds, we both acknowledged we heard it. We opened the door and the tapping stopped. So that was kind of weird." The two looked at the team's rooming list and discovered that the adjacent room was unoccupied.

"We didn't think anything of it really," says Treanor, but minutes later, as he was preparing to head back to his room, "I heard a child scream. A young kid, maybe seven or eight. And I opened the door, looked down the hallway and there was nobody in the hallway at all. And I was like, 'Did you hear that?' We were both kind of tripped out about that."

The next day, Tankersley told Treanor that after the catcher left, the tapping resumed. For about fifteen minutes he looked for its source and couldn't find it. But, he told his friend, "above the TV there was a vent and every time I looked at the vent, the tapping would stop."

Treanor and Tankersley asked a bellboy what kind of ghost stories he heard from guests. "Sometimes you hear children screaming," he told them. "Also, people experience a feeling of cold air rushing across their face while they're lying in bed. And they can't move, they don't know if they're asleep or awake."

"So Tank and I were talking about this stuff in the clubhouse and, not knowing what we were talking about, our strength coach Paul Fournier came in and he's like, 'Man, I had something weird happen to me last night,'" Treanor recalls. "We said, 'What happened?' And he said, 'I was in bed. I felt like I was falling asleep. Next thing I know I felt like I couldn't move and cold air was rushing across my face.'

"It was word for word what the [bellboy] was telling us. It sent chills down our spine."

Treanor has not stayed in the old part of the hotel since. But he has taken an interest in the Pfister, researching its history. When some friends from Chicago visited him there, the group went on a ghost hunt in the early hours of the morning, stationing themselves by the old staircase where original owner Charles Pfister is reputed to be seen. "People see him walking around, going from door to door, making sure people are safe." To the group's disappointment, Treanor reports, "We never saw anything."

Veteran reliever Billy Wagner, however, believes that he may have seen the hotel's namesake. During one visit, he decided to ask for a room in the old section, just for the adventure. "They always said it was haunted. So I went over and I stayed. I was like, 'Hey, I want to see this.'"

Wagner got what he was asking for. "I'm not kidding you—in the night, you would hear the old bellman coming by your room and turn the lights on and stuff. It was unreal."

This was around two or three in the morning. Wagner heard footsteps and the sound of his door opening. "And the lights would flicker on. I got no sleep for three days. None."

•◆•

And so the stories go. Veteran outfielder Ellis Burks once checked into his room, changed his clothes, and as he prepared to leave, discovered the chain was secured on his door. "I didn't put the chain on the door. Then I'm looking back and I figure. I didn't put that latch on the door. I never do that. And it kind of freaked me out."

In 2008, outfielder Carlos Gomez was shocked when his iPod suddenly started playing and vibrating while lying on the table across the room. He turned it off, moved away from it, and the music device started up again. Just out of the shower, Gomez grabbed his clothes and bolted the room.

It seems like every player who has stayed at the Pfister has either logged his own odd experiences, or heard about them from others. Juan Samuel recalls Cecil Fielder waking up in the middle of the night, turning on the light, and "seeing something dark go by." Terry Mulholland tells of catcher Matt Nokes awaking to the image of a ghost on the other side of his room. Reliever Tyler Walker remembers that "my fiancée felt like there was another entity in the room hovering over her, smothering her when she was sleeping."

Despite the stories and room changes and hotel switches, some claim that the ghosts at the Pfister are friendly. Rumor has it that one player specifically requests the same room when he stays at the hotel, because he is visited every time and actually enjoys the experience. Descriptions of Charles Pfister usually depict him as smiling, a portly old gentleman who is merely checking in on his guests.

Even Treanor found he wasn't that rattled by what he experienced. "I slept fine—that was the weird thing about it. It was chilling. And kind of eerie. But it was comforting. I never felt a sense of being scared."

Maybe every player should adopt the attitude of former Red Sox player Butch Hobson. "I like the Pfister," he says. "It's one of those places that was a lot of fun to stay in. It's just a nice old hotel."

Chapter 2

New York's
New Jersey

On Tuesday morning, December 26, 1922, a worker from a company called Daily Brothers was sent to Yankee Stadium—then still under construction—to dig up a graded-over water main for city inspection. Daily Brothers was a subcontractor of White Construction, which was the principal builder of the magnificent new ballpark. Reopening the water main was just the latest in a series of mishaps related to the project: There had been labor strikes, cash shortages, missed deadlines, freezing temperatures that slowed construction, and disagreements about the project among top brass. The building was running behind schedule and everyone was scrambling to get it done in time for the upcoming season. On top of that, there was concern that the huge new park might be a bust—would 58,000 people regularly turn out for a baseball game, especially for a team that had never won a championship, and in a city that hosted two other professional ballclubs?

Perhaps that's why, once the water main inspection was completed, the anonymous worker decided to toss a good-luck item into the pit before it was graded over. Notes on the accounting records don't indicate exactly what was buried in the spot, but its intention was to change the fortune of the team and its owners. And indeed, their fortunes did change. The stadium was completed in time for the 1923 season, Babe

Ruth hit the first home run there in an Opening Day victory, and the Yankees won their first World Series later that year. Over the next eighty-five years, they would win twenty-five more, far exceeding any other team for world championships.

●◆●

Flash forward to a Saturday morning in August 2007. Another subcontractor, this time a mason, walks onto the site of the new Yankee Stadium—still under construction—having decided to bury an item that will affect the fortunes of the team and its owners. The key difference?

"I hate the Yankees. I *really* hate the Yankees. The only thing I hate in life is the Yankees."

His name is Gino Castignoli and, in case you missed it, he hates the Yankees. A Red Sox fan residing in the Bronx, Castignoli is exposed daily to the indignities of a life spent trapped in enemy territory.

So intense is his distaste for all things Yankees that Castignoli had turned down day jobs at the construction site of the new stadium—even though it could be lucrative, even though it was so close to home—simply because he did not want to contribute to the team in any way. And then inspiration struck.

"One day I just had the idea that I would go there and jinx them."

Replacing the House That Ruth Built with the Park That Gino Jinxed quickly delighted the forty-six-year-old, but how to go about it? Castignoli decided he would bury a Red Sox jersey at the new building, planting a little seed of Boston energy deep in the heart of the Evil Empire. After some thought, he decided a David Ortiz shirt was the best choice.

"I came up with Ortiz because [Yankees owner George] Steinbrenner wanted Ortiz, and [general manager Brian] Cashman told him we don't need Ortiz—we have Jason Giambi and Nick Johnson." That was in 2003. Ortiz went on to become one of the most productive hitters in the game and a reliable Yankee-killer in the teams' head-to-head matchups.

Castignoli made no bones about his purpose that day. "I wore the shirt in and one of the guys asked me what I was doing there. He knew I hated the Yankees. And I told him look, I just came to bury this in the concrete. And I really don't care if you throw me off the job after. He laughed and walked me over to where I had to work."

Castignoli had another shirt on underneath the jersey. He approached an area where concrete had just been poured, and in a ceremony that probably lasted less than a minute, he doffed the magical garment, tossed it in the muck, and recited a brief incantation: *The Yankees are done for the next thirty years.*

"And that was it. I wound up working there the rest of the day."

He buried No. 34 against the back wall of the stadium, between home plate and third base. Contrary to later published reports, there was nothing secretive about his actions.

"A lot of people saw me put the shirt in," he says. "There had to be over 40 people there. They all laughed. They all know that I'm a little crazy when it comes to the Red Sox."

But no one said anything until Wednesday night, April 9, 2008, when one of the witnesses happened to mention the would-be hexing to a Yankee-fan friend at a bar. The friend was outraged—drunk, but outraged. He called the *New York Post* and left a series of decreasingly coherent messages, the ultimate point of which was clear: There's something evil brewing at the new stadium. A reporter investigated, and the newspaper issued one of its trademark understated headlines: High 'Jinx' Hits Yankees.

"Friday as I was driving to work, people were calling me up," Gino remembers. "They said you're famous, your shirt's in the paper!" The original article did not name Castignoli, but after he was identified as the perpetrator, he briefly became the most infamous guy in New York. "I had people all over my house. It was a zoo. I couldn't leave through the front door—I was going out the back through the neighbor's yards." The siege consisted not only of reporters, but also angry Yankee fans.

"I had a couple of people drive by the house and leave Yankee stuff on my front steps. I put up a sign by the garbage pail to leave the Yankee paraphernalia there."

The reaction from the team was mixed. It started with bemusement. "It sounds like a tall tale," Yankees PR man Howard Rubenstein said. The Yankees said a review of pouring records indicated the shirt could not have been deposited in the visitor's clubhouse, the spot originally identified as the jersey's crypt. The club suggested the *Post* was being deceived by a belated April Fools' Day prank. When the paper produced photos of the burial ceremony (retrieved from Castignoli's camera phone), team spokesperson Alice McGillion thanked the paper and promised the team would "put an extra layer of concrete over it to make sure it stays buried."

But superstitious fans didn't go for that. Their complaints were so intense they prompted the team to take action. Finding the shirt in the massive new stadium seemed like a needle-in-a-haystack endeavor, but two construction workers came forward to say they remembered Castignoli and could pinpoint the site of his mojo mischief. The Yankees sent in a crew, who spent five hours and an estimated $50,000 jackhammering the jersey out of five feet of concrete to retrieve the bad-luck charm and stop the hex from taking hold. It all happened within thirty-six hours of the story breaking.

Managing partner Hank Steinbrenner was no longer amused. "I hope his coworkers kick the s--- out of him," he was quoted as saying.

Most players claimed not to take the story too seriously. Outfielder Bobby Abreu's attitude is typical. "I think somebody just wanted to be in the news," he says. But infielder Shelley Duncan admits to being a bit unsettled by the whole thing. "I'm a little superstitious, so I was kind of unhappy," he says. "I could see that being a curse."

Outfielder Johnny Damon notes that Castignoli's actions might have actually worked against the Red Sox. "Ortiz was in a nice slump at the time," he says of the Boston slugger, who hit nine home runs and added 180 points to his batting average in the weeks after the exhumation. "So now we're hoping they go bury it again. As soon as they dug it up he started hitting and the Red Sox got hot for a little while."

Pitcher Joba Chamberlain agrees ("They should have left it there because David got real hot after that") but also chides Castignoli for not keeping his ceremony quieter. "If the guy was smart he would have said something after it was all said and done and the whole thing was built." As for the possibility of a curse? "It doesn't bother me as a player."

The jersey itself—badly battered and worn, but still identifiable—was pulled from its tomb in a small PR ceremony and then donated to the Jimmy Fund, the Red Sox–affiliated cancer charity, for auction. The unearthed treasure drew 282 bids from more than nineteen states and four countries. A car dealership owner in Mendon, Massachusetts, prevailed with a bid of $175,100.

There was brief talk of criminal charges or even a civil lawsuit, but in the end, Castignoli avoided any harsh consequences for his prank. In fact, he became a minor hero in Red Sox Nation and received gifts and letters of gratitude for his actions. During his next trip to Boston, bars and restaurants around Fenway treated him to free meals. He also earned points with some New Yorkers. "Half the people I work with are Mets fans and they think I'm the greatest thing in the world," he says.

Castignoli notes that "all my friends are Yankee fans" and says they took it in stride. "They all knew what it was—it was a joke." But, he cautions, "Don't think for one minute that I don't think I set a curse on them, because I do.

"I'm definitely a believer in curses. I took the Curse of the Bambino very seriously." (Castignoli is referring to the alleged hex that befell the Red Sox upon selling Babe Ruth to the Yankees.) He cites odd coincidences in the 2004 ALCS playoff series between the Yankees and Red Sox (New York was up 3-0 in the best of seven series, and then lost four straight), which led to Boston's eventual World Series win that year—their first since 1918—and the end of the dreaded Ruth curse that allegedly afflicted them for eighty-six years.

"Eighty-six runs were scored in that series. The last game that the Yankees won was 19 to 8. If you write it '19/8' it looks like 1918. It's just amazing how it comes up like that."

The fact that the jersey was removed has little impact on the intended curse, insists Castignoli. "The shirt was just an object. It's the spirit, the will of me along with every other Red Sox person when they heard about it—that's still in the ground. There's not a thing they can do to undo that curse."

But is this how curses work? Not according to Dr. Paul Monod, a professor of early modern European history at Middlebury College. "Buried stuff tends to prevent rather than pass on curses," he says. "It was very common for Europeans from the Middle Ages down to the twentieth century to bury things in the walls of houses and other buildings in order to ward off evil spirits." By this logic, he says, "the buried Red Sox shirt would not have the right effect."

It is true, however, that "the ancient Greeks and Romans often buried curses in order to do harm to people," Dr. Monod says. These were not items or trinkets, but actual written-out curses. "They were buried in public places linked to worship of the gods." Sounds like Yankee Stadium. In more modern times, Dr. Monod says, such curses are written and buried anywhere—they don't even have to be placed near the person or group being cursed. Fed up with your boss? Write up a curse and bury it in your backyard.

Ultimately, though, Dr. Monod says that the "rules" around curses are whatever people choose to believe and that their power "is really entirely in the mind of the curser." And, for that matter, in the minds of people who choose to subscribe to it. "If you want to reverse it, just ignore it," Dr. Monod advises. "Or better still, curse him back."

●◆●

Ian Ferris and Gino Castignoli have at least two things in common. As "a frustrated Yankee fan living in the heart of Red Sox Nation" (in his case, Vermont), Ferris knows what it's like to feel outnumbered. And, like Castignoli, Ferris believes in showing a little team spirit by actually invoking team spirits.

On May 31, 2009, Ferris was attending a concert by the jam-rock band Phish, held at Fenway Park. The thirty-year-old had seen the band more than ninety times, but this show was going to be different. He had brought along some official "Yankee Stadium Grass Seed"—the exact strain of Kentucky Bluegrass used at the Bronx stadium and sold by the team as part of its no-stone-left-unturned marketing strategy.

Three weeks earlier, Ferris had attended a game at Yankee Stadium with seven friends, one of whom had purchased the bag of seed as an impulse buy on his way out of the park. In the days that followed, the pair sprinkled some seed around the restaurant where Ferris worked and the golf course where the friend played. It was a small act of rebellion, since both establishments were owned by Red Sox fans.

One day the friends were chatting at the restaurant when Ferris mentioned the upcoming concert. "I don't know who brought it up first, but the idea got knocked around of, 'wouldn't that be crazy if we could get the grass seed on the field there?'"

But how to do that when the field itself would be off-limits to fans and the seed would need to be watered once on the grass? Ferris had the brainstorm to bring a balloon to the show, fill it with water and seed, and then lob it onto the field where it would explode on contact, dispersing and irrigating the seed in one shot.

And voilà—instant home-field advantage for the Yankees the next time they play in Fenway Park.

The plan got modified—Ferris didn't bring a balloon, so a plastic bag stood in—but essentially went off without a hitch. On a set break in the concert, and with some goading from his friends, Ferris filled the bag with seed and water, then made his way down toward the field.

"My concern was getting as close as I could. I was diagonally back from first base, a little bit to the right of the Red Sox dugout, and they had a barrier set up along the base path. If I hopped over the wall, I would have been tackled by four security guards standing right there."

Ferris wasn't sure if throwing from where he stood would do the trick, but ultimately he had no choice. "I just reared back and I threw it in the air. And I was able to see it and see where it landed." The bag did explode and he saw the broken remnants standing askew in the grass. "I just stood there for a second with a big smile on my face," he remembers. "And I just kind of laughed. I turned around and walked upstairs, back to where my friends were sitting, and was like, 'All right. It's done.'"

Ferris knew that "I would have a reason to grin every time I'm sitting in my living room and my roommates have a Boston game on. I could look between the pitcher's mound and first base and know that I made my little mark there." But in those first few seconds after he tossed the seed, another thought crossed Ferris's mind, which made the moment all the sweeter. He thought about Gino Castignoli.

"I was like, 'Ha!' That's a nice little retaliation. They did something to our stadium and I did something to theirs."

Ferris had no intention of publicizing his story, but when he shared it anonymously some days later on an online message board, one reader forwarded it to the *New York Post*. A reporter tracked him down and a new headline was born: YANKEE FAN PUT GREEN MONSTER IN FENWAY. Tipped off by one of Ferris's Red Sox–loving roommates, the *Boston Herald* ran the story the same day.

The reaction was immediate. Ferris heard from indignant Boston fans and chuckling Yankee rooters. The story was picked up nationally and he had requests for radio and TV interviews—which brought more responses from strangers. At one point, a BoSox supporter created a blog entitled "Dear Moron Who Calls Itself Ian Ferris." The news broke just days before a Yankee series at Fenway, and the rhetoric seemed to escalate along with Red Sox nervousness. But when the Sox swept the series, Boston fans seemed to breathe a sigh of relief and the pressure on Ferris eased up.

For the Vermonter, it was a good-natured prank and he rolled with the punches. "The good things and bad things that were said I just found very entertaining and had a lot of fun with." He does take issue with those who deride the effectiveness of what he did.

"I got a lot of 'it's the exact same grass seed' as what is grown at Fenway." Not so, says Ferris. "I forged a bit of a relationship with the guy who owns the grass seed company and he informed me full well that while it's the same strain, it's a different blend specific to Yankee Stadium. So he helped me squash that argument."

Others claimed the mischievous fan ended up cursing himself. When the restaurant Ferris managed closed a short time later, a newspaper ran an update on him. "Ultimately what it says is, 'You mess with Fenway and Fenway messes with you,'" says Ferris. "But actually, it was the best losing-a-job experience I ever had in my life," he claims, noting that he ended up with six kegs of beer at his house and "a lovely party that lasted about two weeks." The person who really suffered from the closing was the owner—a Red Sox fan.

But what about the fact that the Yankees were swept in their next series at Fenway?

When Ferris distributed the seed around his restaurant, he put some in two rose planters that flanked the front door. "And the last day of the restaurant, I was just kind of walking around, and I actually looked in those rose planters. And I probably had looked in there two weeks before we closed and saw nothing. But when I looked in there that last day, both rose planters had a nice, healthy amount of grass growing in them. Which leads me to believe it probably took about a month for that grass to grow. You know what that means? By the time the Yankees played those three games at Fenway Park, that grass wasn't even grown. It wasn't in full bloom yet."

Ferris's conclusion? "It's not over yet." Indeed, when the Yankees played an August series at the park, they won two of three games.

• ◆ •

Although Ian Ferris had been angered by Gino Castignoli's jersey burial, and was pleased to return the favor, he also says that "the fact that he buried the jersey under there didn't bother me as much as knowing that he probably wasn't the only Red Sox fan working on that stadium. So what else did maybe he do or others do that we'll never know about?"

Ian Ferris, meet Mike Reed.

Though his story was never reported, Reed was a much more active curser of the new Yankee Stadium than Castignoli, who only spent one day at the site, after much of the building was complete. "I was pouring the concrete in there," Reed says. "So I was burying stuff from the beginning."

That "stuff" was Red Sox memorabilia. Boston mugs. Miniature batting helmets. And the biggest insult of all: four commemorative 2004 World Series coins.

"I put one coin in each of the major footings that the actual stadium is built on," says Reed. "They'll never be able to get out what I put in—the stadium's built on top of it."

As he deposited the coins, he said out loud, "This one's going to be in your new stadium for sixty, eighty years"—his estimate of the life of the stadium. (By comparison, Castignoli limited his hex to thirty years, "because after thirty years I'll be dead and I really don't care if they win or lose.")

For a lifelong Boston fan raised in northeastern New Jersey, an area only slightly less pinstriped than the Bronx itself, the opportunity to curse Yankee Stadium was simply too irresistible for Reed to pass up. "It wasn't easy growing up a Red Sox fan in Bergen County," he says. "I've been abused by Yankee fans my whole life." In the 1970s, Reed was Yankee manager Billy Martin's paperboy. "He saw me with a Red Sox hat once and asked, 'Why are you a Red Sox fan *here*?' I told him my father landed in Boston when he came over from Ireland and started following baseball there. So growing up, that's what I became."

Reed got the idea to curse the stadium as soon as his company secured the contract to work at the site. It was a simple matter to smuggle Red Sox items into the park in the workbag he brought along each day, and slip them into the concrete as he was pouring it. As with Castignoli, there was no need to be covert. "The laborers around me all knew. They all hated me because they were Yankee fans." They taunted Reed with nasty names, but couldn't argue with his comeback: "I said if you were building Fenway, wouldn't you put something in there?"

Reed doubts that he and Castignoli are the only two to invoke bad luck for the Yankees in their new home. "There were a lot of Mets fans [working at the site], so I'm sure they put stuff in." Reed himself buried a Mets hat around the first base line at a kid's request.

Apart from the surprising fact that it was so easy in post–9/11 New York for anybody to embed stray objects in the foundation of a major public facility, Yankee fans can take some comfort. Pro-Yankee construction workers deposited many good-luck charms at the site. Reed is aware of one colleague who buried Yankee clothing—an outfit for a baby with the trademark interlocking NY logo on it. In Reed's most magnanimous gesture to his many Yankee friends—and "to show that I wasn't a total douche"—he brought one buddy in on a Saturday to inter some of his father's ashes. Dad resides in Section 205, on the Main Level, just beyond right field.

According to Dr. Monod, those are the kinds of items that conform to more traditional spirit summoning. "Baby shoes are supposed to have been common [items to bury for good luck]," says the curse connoisseur, "and other small items associated with the household or children." So the NYY baby outfit scores big. And the cremated remains are definite bonus points. "Ancestral ashes are usually held in high esteem," Monod explains, "so to bury them in a certain place would convey very good karma on it. The burier should of course honor the ashes by returning to them frequently."

• ◆ •

By the end of the two-plus-year construction project, nearly 5,000 workers contributed to the new Yankee Stadium. There's no telling how many of them added their own bits and pieces to the building.

And what has been the result of so many competing amulets? Have Red Sox fans cursed the new stadium or Yankee fans charmed it? Early data in the park's 2009 inaugural season favored a curse: The Yankees lost to the Cleveland Indians on Opening Day, 10-2, and lost their first eight games against Boston, including two games at home. But they had a phenomenal second half in which they swept the Sox in 7 straight home games, ended the season with the best home record in the majors, and—most importantly—won the World Series, clinching in Game Six at the new park. The team's dominance seemed to put to rest any debate about the battle for the soul of Yankee Stadium, at least for now.

But Gino Castignoli believes his curse kicked in even before the new stadium opened. "Think about it," he says. "The shirt was buried in August of 2007—the first year the Yankees didn't make first place [in the AL East] since God-knows-when." In 2008, he notes, they missed the playoffs entirely. "It worked out good."

Yankees veteran Mike Mussina says he isn't worried about a curse; he appreciates this latest salvo in the never-ending battle between Boston and New York. "It made perfect sense for the Yankee–Red Sox rivalry, that something like that would happen. That the story would get out there, that they would do the research to figure out how it happened, where the thing was. And that the Yankees would go through the trouble of digging the thing out. That's just part of Yankees–Red Sox. It's always been that way and it's going to stay that way."

THE CURSE OF YANKEE STADIUM

While mischievous Red Sox fans have tried to hex the new ballpark, players themselves have long spoken of a Curse of Yankee Stadium that favors the home team. As Torii Hunter puts it: "People say when you go in there you just have this chill that you're going to lose. Like the ghosts are telling you you're going to lose and whispering in your ear the whole time you're walking to the clubhouse, to the dugout, on the field. They always whisper in your ear and you have it in your heart that *you're going to lose this game.*"

What Hunter is talking about are the famous "ghosts of Yankee Stadium." As chronicled in *Haunted Baseball,* many players believed that the spirits of greats like Babe Ruth, Lou Gehrig, Joe DiMaggio, and Mickey Mantle resided in the old park and helped the team win in big games. "Yankee Stadium has one of the greatest home field advantages in all of sports," Alex Rodriguez said. "The ghosts of Yankee Stadium are overlooking the guys in the pinstripes." Would the ghosts follow the team across the street to the new park? "We're gonna see," captain Derek Jeter said. "Hopefully that does carry over."

The team went to great pains to honor the past and its departed legends during the end of the old stadium and the start of the new. The final game included a pregame ceremony in which retired play-ers took the field, and the original 1923 lineup was represented by actors in period uniforms. The Yankees won that last game—as they did their final five games in the old park—and celebrated with a sentimental parade around the stadium. Derek Jeter grabbed the mic for some spontaneous and heartfelt comments to the crowd. "There's a lot of tradition, a lot of history, and a lot of memories," in the old stadium, he said, asking fans "to take the memories from this stadium, add them to the new memories that come at the new Yankee Stadium, and continue to pass them on from generation to generation."

The first game in the new park also honored tradition; the bat that Babe Ruth used on Opening Day in 1923—the bat that swatted the first home run out of Yankee Stadium—was laid across home plate prior to the start of the game. The stadium itself restored the facade of the original building (which had changed significantly in a mid-1970s renovation) and maintained the same field dimensions. Archival pictures of great players and historic moments line every area of the new park.

But fans had mixed reactions to the stadium. Monument Park, the Yankees' hallowed shrine to legendary players and moments, has been scuttled out of sight—it's now beyond the centerfield batter's eye, largely out of view from the field. And prices at the $1.3 billion park have caused cynics to dub it the House That Greed Built.

Many Yankee fans were reluctant to trade the field upon which Ruth, Gehrig, and other legends played in exchange for an amenity-filled palace with a martini bar, more than 450 luxury and party suites, over 2,300 square feet of team retail space, and $2,625 home plate seats. (Comparable seats in the old ballpark cost $25 in 1996.) When the new seats failed to fill, embarrassing the team with empty patches visible in each game broadcast, the club slashed many front-row prices by 50 percent, but only for the 2009 season.

True believers worried that all of this might offend the famous Ghosts of Yankee Stadium. At the second-to-last home game in the old park, Babe Ruth's granddaughter, Linda Ruth Tosetti, put a wreath of flowers at his monument and said, "Babe would not like to see his House come down."

Visiting players seemed to notice a difference. Upon his first visit to the new park, Tampa Bay third baseman Evan Longoria told the *New York Daily News,* "You went into old Yankee Stadium and there was just that feeling—almost like the calm before the storm—you knew what was going to happen, you knew it was going to be a battle. When you walked down that hallway, you knew that Ruth and the forefathers of the game had walked down that same tunnel. That was the cool feeling about it." And now? "It feels a lot different. You don't really get to feel the ghosts of the past."

But the World Series victory has gone a long way toward allaying fears that departed Yankee greats are holding a grudge against their old team. The Yankees postseason home games were filled with unusual plays, controversial umpire calls, and bizarre errors, nearly all of which favored the Bronx Bombers—just the kind of thing players have long pointed to as evidence of spectral intervention.

Within minutes of clinching the championship, Yankees president Randy Levine was interviewed on the field, and he summed up the conclusion of many: "I guess the ghosts liked the job we did," he said of the new park, "because they came right over!"

The Yankees' new stadium may or may not be cursed, but the team's spring training facility in Tampa Bay—the former Legends Field, now known as George M. Steinbrenner Field—is said to be haunted. A workaholic accountant died at the park a few years back; since then his ghost has been spotted late at night. In one instance, a maid saw the man at the end of a hallway and addressed him, thinking he was some staffer working late. The figure darted into a nearby room, which was empty when she got to it. Security guards patrolling the field say they look up to see lights on in the dead man's office, when no such lights were on as they passed through the building. One evening, two guards decided to investigate further: one stayed positioned on the field, in view of the illuminated window, while the other made his way up to the room, communicating by walkie-talkie with his colleague. Moments before the second officer reached the door to the office, the guard on the field saw the light suddenly turn off.

Chapter 3
Tiger Tales

What becomes of our baseball cathedrals after the last chords of "Take Me Out to the Ball Game" have faded, the lights have been turned out, and the players and fans have left for good?

For many decades, Tiger Stadium was a place alive with the energy and tradition of Detroit baseball, a park with a history that paralleled the game itself, and a baseball institution with its own distinct character and flavor. But by 2008—nearly ten years after it hosted its final game—even a casual walk past its iron gates revealed a mighty stadium in distress. Litter swept through the inner plaza, occasionally trapped in the weeds that spiked up through the cement. Trees grew out of the upper deck, so tall they could be viewed from the street level, inching above the stadium's walls. Letters that once spelled out T-I-G-E-R S-T-A-D-I-U-M had been pulled from their signpost, leaving shadowy images in their place. The baseball landmark—once home to legends Ty Cobb, Harry Heilmann, and Hank Greenberg—had become a veritable ghost town.

In more ways than one.

Greg Underwood worked for the club as a security guard, often pulling night shifts at the old stadium. One summer night, Underwood was working his shift when he came upon something most unusual.

"I was doing rounds at one o'clock in the morning, walking down a hallway by the Tigers locker room. At the end of the hallway is the groundskeeper's room. And I saw some kind of orb—a ball of light—come out of that room. I was walking toward it and it kept moving toward me—this strange ball of light.

"It looked like a flashlight on the ground but it was moving toward me and that was what was weird about it. Because I figured if it was my flashlight, it would have been moving along with me, in the same direction. This thing was moving *toward* me and it was just really weird."

Underwood was understandably surprised by the sight, but more curious than scared. "I just was mesmerized by it. I knew it was something supernatural, something I never dealt with in my life before.

"I kept on walking, and I kept on watching it—I watched it get closer and closer and closer. Eventually it was right next to my foot. And I saw it—just like a beam of light right next to my foot." Then the orb suddenly moved. "I turned around with the flashlight to see where it went, and it was gone. There was nothing there anymore."

Underwood has no earthly explanation for what he experienced that night. "I still don't have a clue what it was. But it actually ended up being pretty cool. Kind of an interesting thing to witness in life. Obviously it didn't hurt me. Some people may think I'm crazy, some people may not believe me."

His fellow security guards might believe him. Several had their own haunted experiences at Tiger Stadium, ranging from eerie noises to inexplicable sights. One guard claimed multiple ghostly encounters in the stadium. On one occasion, he saw an apparition in the security office late at night. On another, he was sleeping in his chair when a tapping on his shoulder aroused him—and he awoke to discover no one was in the room with him. In his most bizarre report, the guard was watching TV alone in the office one evening when he looked down and saw scratches mysteriously forming on his arm.

Underwood had his own strange experiences in the security office. "When I worked midnights, the phone would ring at two or three o'clock in the morning. I'd answer it and there'd be no one there. This happened numerous times, but only at night—it never happened during the day." Underwood once got a late-night call from a friend who asked if the guard had just called him. "I said no. He said he had just gotten a call and his phone's caller ID showed it came from the office number. But I had never placed a call to him."

In early 2008, security for Tiger Stadium transferred from the Tigers to an independent contractor brought in by the city, which owned the property. And again, guards working night shifts at the facility reported strange noises, odd sights, and eerie experiences. Some said they heard the sound of voices in the tunnels and the roar of a crowd coming from the empty seats.

But these workers were responsible for some late-night shenanigans of their own: several guards were caught by local news crews letting people into the park to ransack the place, hold parties, even play ball games on the field. Occasionally guards would shoot their guns off in the park in the middle of the night, for aimless kicks.

According to Murphy, a worker at a nearby business, stadium guards had been looting Tiger Stadium for years. "Stuff has been coming out of there since they closed the place," he says, admitting that he once bought an entire row of stadium seats—orange with the blue Tigers logo on them—from corrupt security guards. City workers have also been spotted loading seats and other memorabilia into their cars. Police have occasionally responded to break-ins by treasure-seekers. When officers chased one souvenir hunter from the premises, the scavenger dropped a box, which Murphy picked up. "It was full of old programs going back decades, including some World Series programs." He kept a copy of each for himself and put the rest for sale on eBay. But, he laments, "There was so much Tiger Stadium memorabilia available from all the looting going on, you couldn't get a decent price."

●◆●

This is not the legacy anyone envisioned for the great Tiger Stadium.

The famous "Corner" at Michigan Avenue and Trumbull Street was home to Detroit baseball from 1896, when Bennett Park first occupied the site. On April 20, 1912—the same day that Fenway Park opened for business in Boston—Tigers owner Frank Navin unveiled the new Navin Field, with seating for 23,000, reflecting the sport's growing popularity. In the mid-1930s, ownership passed to Walter Briggs, who extended the upper deck across the outfield (the city even moved an adjacent street to accommodate the expansion), giving birth to the rechristened Briggs Stadium with a capacity of 53,000 in 1938. Looking to put his own stamp on the stadium in 1961, new owner John Fetzer spared Detroit the hubris of "Fetzer Field" and instead renamed the ballpark Tiger Stadium.

Throughout the twentieth century, Tiger Stadium was home to some of the game's greatest players and moments. The addition of legend Ty Cobb in 1905 started a new era of competitiveness for Detroit in the American League; with other greats such as Sam Crawford and Hughie Jennings (both eventual Hall of Famers), the Tigers became the first team to win three consecutive pennants (1907–1909) . . . and the first to lose three consecutive World Series, the first two to the Chicago Cubs and the third to the Pittsburgh Pirates.

Cobb was the team's biggest attraction and gained a well-deserved reputation as a fierce competitor. In one of the most stellar careers in baseball history, the Georgia Peach dominated the dead-ball era and is believed to have set ninety records by the time of his retirement in 1928. Several of those benchmarks still stand today, including highest career batting average (.367) and most batting titles (twelve). His .389 average in 1921 helped power the Tigers to what remains the highest team batting average in AL history, .316. His records for most career hits, runs, and stolen bases stood for decades until modern-era players surpassed them.

When the first Hall of Fame ballot was conducted in 1936, Cobb drew the most votes—222 out of a possible 226—outshining other inductees Babe Ruth, Honus Wagner, Walter Johnson, and Christy Mathewson. (Cobb's 98.2 percent of votes cast was a Hall of Fame record for fifty-six years, until Tom Seaver drew 98.8 percent of the vote in 1992.)

Subsequent superstars kept the crowds coming to the Corner. Harry Heilmann won batting titles in 1921, 1923, 1925, and 1927, along the way becoming the first major leaguer to hit home runs in every ballpark in the majors. Charlie Gehringer, Hank Greenberg, and Hal Newhouser powered the team in the 1930s and '40s, leading to the Tigers' first two World Series victories in 1935 and 1945. In the '50s and '60s, Al Kaline, Denny McLain, Norm Cash, and hometown hero Willie Horton called the park home, and helped fuel the team's 1968 World Championship. A decade later, pitcher Mark "The Bird" Fidrych—so nicknamed for his resemblance to *Sesame Street*'s Big Bird—became one of the game's most colorful figures and filled Tiger Stadium with "Bird Watchers" who delighted in his exaggerated delivery and unusual antics: talking to the baseball, wiping away his own cleat marks from the mound, tossing aside balls he claimed "had hits in them," and strutting across the rubber after each out.

The consistent star throughout all those eras was Tiger Stadium itself. The park, which had been named a state of Michigan historic site in 1975 and joined the National Register of Historic Places in 1989, was renowned throughout baseball for its timeless vibe and intimate feel, with seats that were literally right on top of the action. The overhang in right field jutted out above the right fielder. Seats behind the broadcast booth were literally closer to home plate than the shortstop was.

Tom Stanton, who has authored two books about the Tigers, notes that the stadium truly reflected its city. "It was an industrial-feeling kind of place—steel girders and concrete and cement. It felt like a blue-collar place. There were no architectural flourishes about it. It just had this real gritty feel. But on top of that it had a very embracing feel, because it was a double-deck stadium. In most of the spots in the ballpark, you could not see anything outside of the stadium other than the sky. That gave it an intimate feel that you don't get at a lot of places, particularly today. Like you were hugged by the action when you were in there."

Tiger Stadium was one of the best venues in baseball for home runs, especially out-of-the-park shots. Since its 1938 expansion, more than a dozen players launched balls over the rightfield roof, while four select power hitters cleared the higher leftfield roof: Harmon Killebrew, Frank Howard, Cecil Fielder, and Mark McGwire.

Many modern-day players appreciated the park's history. "You think of who stepped in those batter's boxes and who sat in those dugouts, who was on the same pitching mound," says pitcher Eric Milton, who played in the park as a visitor with the Minnesota Twins. When Tim Hudson first came to the park, he arrived early with some teammates to explore the stadium and soak it in. One historical oddity especially impressed him. "In the tunnel right by the clubhouse there's an old urinal. You're standing there right where Babe Ruth probably took a leak, or some of the old greats. It's pretty neat when you look at it like that!"

Pitcher John Smoltz considered the park "tremendous. It was one of the few places left that was enclosed—upper decks and lower decks. So there really wasn't a bad seat, besides behind the poles." CJ Nitkowski loved the history that came from playing on "the same spot as Ty Cobb and all the early-1900s guys," but does admit that many aspects of the building were of an earlier era.

"The amenities were bad. The clubhouse was bad. The dugouts were really small." For the six-foot-five pitcher Jeff Weaver, that was a challenge. "All the ceilings were really low—it was five-foot-eight walking through the tunnels. You had to duck. The dugout was only six feet tall. You couldn't get excited and jump up or you'd smack your head on cement!"

Still, Tiger Stadium consistently ranked in the top five whenever major leaguers were asked to list their favorite ballparks. Tigers hero Alan Trammell, whose twenty years with the club included six All-Star appearances and the 1984 World Series MVP title, sums it up when he says the park had "a great baseball atmosphere, where you felt like playing baseball. It was small, quaint. And it was like no other place in baseball. To me it was just a fun place to play every day."

Like many players, Tram was sad to see it go. Businessman Mark Ilitch had bought the team in 1992 and added modern amenities (a gift shop, new concessions, wait-service for a special seating area, etc.), but the Detroit magnate, who also owns the city's Red Wings hockey franchise as well as other municipal institutions such as the Fox Theater, soon began campaigning for a new venue. The team had not won its division since 1987 and attendance was flagging. In addition, the Tigers' lease limited the money the team could make on potentially profitable sidelines like parking. In 1997, ground was broken on Comerica Park, with Ilitch financing about half of the $350 million price tag and taxpayers footing the balance.

The final game at Tiger Stadium was played on September 27, 1999. Fans arrived hours before the first pitch to revel in the park one last time and witness pregame ceremonies in which the governor and mayor spoke, as well as Ilitch and Al Kaline. The evening was steeped in history, with the starting lineup wearing the uniform numbers of old Tiger greats.

The game itself provided the emotional highs everyone craved. The Tigers defeated the Kansas City Royals 8–2. Prior to the game, Al Kaline had told DH Robert Fick that he would hit a home run and in the bottom of the eighth, with the bases loaded, Fick did just that—a monster blast that hit the top of the rightfield roof before falling back on the field. (Fick was wearing No. 25 in honor of '60s slugger Norm Cash, the only man to have hit four home runs out of Tiger Stadium, over that same rightfield wall.) The grand slam was the final hit in Tiger Stadium, and the 11,111th home run in the park's history.

"It was sort of like it was a well-scripted game," says Ernie Harwell, the legendary Tigers announcer and member of the Baseball Hall of Fame, who considers that game his favorite moment in forty years of broadcasting from the stadium.

Pitcher Jeff Weaver goes further. "It seemed like the ghosts of Tiger Stadium were with us," he says, noting that "there was a lot of talk about the history of the stadium and how special it was.

"You always think about stuff like that. There are reasons why things happen. It sends chills down your spine."

It did for Fick. "My father died the year before and he was my best friend. He died a month after I made it to the big leagues." Fick believes his father was present for his historic grand slam.

"I have a picture of me running around second base and there's a light shining down on my helmet," he says. In addition to the intervening spirit of his departed father, Fick also believes Norm Cash "may have had a part in it." The affable Tiger great died in a boating accident at age fifty-one. As Fick learned more about the hitting star after the game, he permanently changed his number to Cash's 25.

Harwell emceed postgame festivities in which he invoked the park's nonbaseball highlights (the Detroit Lions' thirty-six-year tenure there, a Joe Louis fight, a Nelson Mandela appearance) and introduced a video highlight reel. Then music from *The Natural* played while retired players, unannounced, took their old positions in the field. Mark Fidrych manicured the pitcher's mound one last time, before scooping some of its dirt into a plastic baggie he produced from his back pocket.

Home plate was dug up to be transported to the new ballpark and a special ceremony was held for the Tigers flag. "They had a line of players, past and present, running from the flagpole in centerfield to home plate," catcher Brad Ausmus recalls. "They took the flag down and passed it all the way down. Elden Auker, who was the oldest living Tiger, gave it to me. On Opening Day in the new stadium the following year, Elden and I went out and put the flag up the pole."

The mood was bittersweet but very upbeat, with one exception: When a live feed on the scoreboard showed the construction site of Comerica Park, the crowd booed loudly.

The evening came to an end with a final goodbye from Harwell, which concluded with the promise: "Tonight we say farewell, old friend, Tiger Stadium. We will remember you."

●◆●

Harwell worked hard to make good on his promise. He lent his name and active participation to the Old Tiger Stadium Conservancy, one of at least six organizations that sprouted up to preserve the ballpark and leverage its unique history. Its stated mission: "to preserve, redevelop, and program Tiger Stadium as a public park, youth sports venue, and destination for baseball fans in a practical and economically viable manner to both honor the site's history and create value for the surrounding neighborhood and the city of Detroit."

For the preservationists, saving Tiger Stadium is a deeply personal cause. Peter Comstock Riley, who founded a group called Michigan & Trumbull, grew up in nearby Grosse Pointe and went to his first baseball game at Tiger Stadium in 1976, when he was nine years old. By 1999, he had attended 813 games there. He proudly notes that his son was born on April 28—the "official birthday" of Tiger Stadium's predecessor Bennett Park. Riley worked at the stadium for nearly eleven years in a variety of capacities, but the job didn't matter. "I was working for the Tigers at Tiger Stadium, and that was plenty good enough for me."

In 2006, Riley executive produced *Stranded at the Corner*, a documentary about the suspended state of Tiger Stadium and the battle to save it against a city government resistant to various preservation plans. He rattles off a long series of development options that various groups have proposed, including repurposing the field for minor league baseball, community events, and concerts; building loft apartments around the field, with the lower deck staying intact; housing a Michigan sports hall of fame; and renting the field for high school and college tournaments.

In the nine years after the stadium's closing, these plans and others moved in and out of favor with the city and the Detroit Economic Growth Corporation. Along the way, the city has battled its own demons of political corruption and dwindling number of residents (today's population is literally half of what it was in 1950) further complicating its relationship with the old park. Riley echoes the frustration of many when he opines that Detroit and Mike Ilitch "use Tiger Stadium to make a buck for their own interests while no one is looking out for the best interests of Tiger Stadium."

• ◆ •

"Everybody has a sentimental attachment to it. We like the stadium but we have to be realistic," says Fred Rottach, who has managed Tiger Stadium for the city since the Tigers left. "We need to move on."

It is June 2008 and Rottach is walking through Tiger Stadium one more time. The city has just announced plans to start tearing down the outfield bleachers in a few weeks. There have been similar announcements in the past, which never came to fruition, and there are still no plans to develop the site. But a demolition crew has agreed to do the work in exchange for the scrap. Tiger Stadium will be torn down to resell its steel, plastic, and copper.

The Old Tiger Stadium Conservancy is still working to preserve the first-to-third section of the building, essentially restoring the park to its 1923 Navin Field dimensions, with economic development in the outfield and surrounding areas.

Despite the claims of ghostly activity, the walk through Tiger Stadium is a thoroughly "dispiriting" affair for any baseball fan. The signs of decay visible from outside the classic ballpark are mere harbingers of the disarray inside. The infield is overgrown with weeds. Wires and planks and drywall hang down from ceilings stripped of piping and asbestos. Broken tiles, torn insulation, and battered pieces of furniture crowd forgotten office spaces, while peeling and chipped Tiger logos make the dugouts look even older than they are. One dugout tunnel is filled with fetid water, bits of paper and trash floating on top.

"Last fall the place still looked pretty good," Rottach says. Since then many seats have been removed for sale and hazardous materials torn out in preparation for demolition.

Rottach says the city has done its best to find a taker for the stadium. "We tried for nine years almost to get developers. We advertised nationally. I must have shown that building to a couple hundred developers—people that own Canadian football, world soccer, you name it. They would have required major adjustments to the stadium." The city is still hoping that Wal-Mart might open a supercenter on the spot.

He's confident that once the stadium is razed, commercial developers will be more attracted to the site. But the area around the Corner is terribly depressed. Businesses have fled or failed and numerous empty lots fill Michigan Avenue. Crime in the area is a major problem; in fact, Detroit leads the nation in many violent crime statistics. In a few months, the recession will deepen here, as automakers file for bankruptcy, unemployment skyrockets, and the housing market bottoms out. Still, Rottach believes that residential and commercial development will sprout along the sidelines and outfield of the stadium. "For sure that's going to happen," he says.

He allows that, of the preservation organizations, "The conservancy group is probably the most realistic and practical. The other groups are nice people, well intended, but nobody's got the deep pockets you need to maintain a stadium. Just to keep the place clean and running you're looking at two to three million dollars a year."

Rottach is a baseball fan who attended many games at Tiger Stadium. He knows how important the team has been to the troubled city. "During a lot of times in Detroit when we struggled, the Tigers were all that we had," he says. Perhaps he's thinking of the 1967 race riots, which lasted five days and resulted in forty-three deaths, 467 injuries, 7,200 arrests, and more than 2,000 burned buildings. The riots took place just blocks from Tiger Stadium and the ballpark was considered an off-limits sanctuary that rioters never touched. In fact, black and white fans still came to the stadium in harmony. Willie Horton went to the site of the riots in his Tigers uniform to calm the crowds in the heat of the frenzy. The city's goal, Rottach says, is for the stadium site to be productive. "Whether we take down part of it or the whole thing, we're hoping that the reconstruction of what goes up around this will be a real asset to the community." Personally, he's hoping that the playing area survives. "I want to see the field preserved and set up so we can use it in the future. As long as we're able to utilize it and we pay tribute to all the great players who played there, I think we'll be in good shape."

• ◆ •

Stepping through the scattered debris in the once mighty stadium, it is a struggle to remember that this is the place where Ty Cobb and Hank Greenberg and Kirk Gibson thrilled fans and created legends. The place where Babe Ruth hit what some claim was the longest home run ever, a towering shot that was estimated to travel between 575 and 600 feet before landing on the street outside centerfield. The place where Lou Gehrig, on May 2, 1939, ended his Iron Horse streak at 2,130 games, telling Yankees manager Joe McCarthy he was benching himself "for the good of the team." (Gehrig is said to have then gone down the block to Casey's bar for a drink. The bar still stands today.) It is hard to picture the place alive with fans and players.

But according to John McCormick the place is indeed alive. McCormick is the founder and team leader of Motor City Ghost Hunters. He has come at the authors' invitation to take a walk through the fading cathedral. He has brought along an 8.1-megapixel digital camera, an electromagnetic field (EMF) detector, an air particle tester, and an infrared thermometer—standard ghost-hunter tools for detecting and recording supernatural activity. He uses the EMF meter to establish a baseline for the stadium, and explains how the process works.

"The base reading is 0.1. It picks up electronic magnetic fields. So if there are any apparitions here that are trying to make themselves known, what they'll do is they'll draw as much energy from us or from the building as they possibly can. And the readings will go up."

Sure enough, in the concourse area behind home plate, the EMF meter spikes to a range of 0.4 to 0.6. In the home locker room, it jumps to 0.3 to 0.6. In one of the locker room doorways, it reaches its peak of 0.8.

The pictures McCormick snaps in these areas reveal pale circular images in various spots—orbs, he says, which are a kind of "energy form." This makes sense, he explains, because a place like Tiger Stadium is ripe for ghostly activity. "A lot of entities just refuse to leave because it's a happy occasion in their life and they relive it over and over again."

According to this rationale, departed star players are apt to linger in the ballparks they called home. "They set records, they did unbelievable feats in the park," McCormick says. "And it could be history repeating itself."

That jibes with what fans report. For years, "People would see Ty Cobb running the bases," Tiger enthusiast Greg Giblin says. The stories only increased once the park closed. "People would go by the stadium and thought they heard a crowd yelling, or the crack of a bat. The story was that the old Tigers were playing on the field."

At the Checker Cab Company across Trumbull Street, workers at night swear they hear people walking around the second floor. The space used to house Cobb's office when he was a player-manager for the team. Frank Navin also had an office there. Rumor has it the two men are patrolling their old stomping grounds.

But McCormick also believes that some of the energy forms could be fans who are happy to spend eternity at the Corner. "You've got a lot of folks who experienced some of the best times of their lives in a ballpark. They hold on to their childhoods, they hold onto their memories."

McCormick himself fits that description. Though he is here in professional ghost-hunter mode, he is also a local guy reveling in the opportunity to experience Tiger Stadium one last time. "There are a lot of memories," he says as we move through the vacant concourse that once held concessionaires. "As a kid it seemed like I grew up here." When we walk onto the field, he really feels it. "This is the nostalgia here. This is what it's all about. I get the chills when I walk through here."

He confesses afterward that the competing sensations of paranormal detection and personal sentiment challenge his own reactions. "I'm not one to get goose bumps," he says, "but as we were talking through the tunnels, I got goose bumps. There was something special there. I don't know if it was one of the players walking along with us, or just reliving my own childhood.

"There's such a life to that old park."

•◆•

A couple of weeks later, on July 9, 2008, demolition of the outfield stands begins at Tiger Stadium. After years of back-and-forth with the city, hundreds of thousands of dollars raised, and the dogged efforts of hundreds of preservationists, the moment many had dreaded finally takes place: a bull-dozer rolls into the stadium, crosses the outfield, and starts ripping down the exterior wall and centerfield bleachers of Tiger Stadium.

But all is not yet lost. The city has agreed to preserve the first-to-third section of the park while the Old Tiger Stadium Conservancy continues to raise money to save it. Fund-raisers are held and donations solicited, eventually totaling more than $600,000. The conservancy scores a major coup when Michigan senator Carl Levin secures a $3.8 million earmark to fund preservation of the stadium. More than $18 million in tax credits for the project are identified. The conservancy assumes all security and maintenance costs and puts $300,000 in escrow toward the stadium. All of this represents years of work and agreements between OTSC lawyers and the City of Detroit.

So the conservancy is shocked when, in early June 2009, with no advance warning, the city suddenly announces that it is going to tear down the remainder of the stadium, starting immediately. They cite, among other things, increased demolition costs, which are mainly attributable to recession-lowered steel prices for the scrap metal funding the teardown. The OTSC's attempt to get a restraining order fails. Within days, the remnants of the historic structure are razed.

By mid-July, all that stands at the storied corner of Michigan and Trumbull is a large pile of rubble.

●◆●

Comerica Park is one of those new baseball venues that is part ball field, part amusement park. Its features include a Ferris wheel, a merry-go-round, and a large outdoor food court quite separate from the action of the game.

The Tigers transition to its new home was a bit bumpy at first: The field's wide dimensions discouraged home runs and led to its unflattering nickname, Comerica National Park. (They shortened the fences a few years later.) Attendance the first season was relatively low. Even with the attractions and excitement of a modern new ballpark, the team averaged just 31,280 people per home game, about 76 percent of capacity.

The Tigers themselves have had extreme ups and downs at the park, ranging from their dismal 2003 season (in which their 119 losses set a new major league record) to their 2006 resurgence that took them all the way to the World Series (which they lost to the St. Louis Cardinals). The team's success brought more people to the downtown park and more acceptance of the new venue.

The flashy commercial splendor of Comerica Park seems worlds away from the no-nonsense steel skeleton of Tiger Stadium. But the new ballpark has at least one thing in common with its historic predecessor: rumors of ghostly activity. At one employee entrance, the metal detector occasionally goes off for no apparent reason, as if someone had just walked through it. A security guard died of a massive coronary near the spot and his ghost is rumored to be responsible for the strange occurrences. A construction worker who fell to his death while the park was being built is also said to haunt the place.

In the lobby, a shadowy apparition has been seen by at least three workers, standing next to the security camera. They describe a dark silhouette standing silently in the corner.

Brian Arnold, who works in that lobby, has not seen that apparition, but has had his own encounters. On several occasions, the elevator doors mysteriously open and close on his floor, as if carrying an invisible passenger. He has no doubt who it is.

"I say it's the ghost of Ty Cobb," he declares.

Arnold says workers have also seen the image of Cobb appear in a glass case just to the left of the lobby doors. And he experienced what he can only describe as paranormal activity early one morning while talking to colleagues.

"It was me and two other coworkers standing inside the lobby. There was a garbage can [nearby]. And the top just jumped off. Not fell off—it flew in the air, probably a foot and a half. And we all just looked at each other like, 'Uh-oh!'"

"It had to have been Ty Cobb—the ghost of Ty Cobb," Arnold insists.

According to John McCormick, it makes sense that the spirits of departed players would "follow their team to Comerica Park or wherever the team shall go." That's because "the love of the sport and the bond they share is too great to let go."

"So yes, I believe that our new stadium shall be haunted," says the ghost hunter.

• ◆ •

Meanwhile, the Old Tiger Stadium Conservancy—as well as other groups and individuals—are still working to secure a memorial at the corner of Michigan and Trumbull, and possibly even preserve the field.

For Tom Stanton, some kind of commemoration of a place that was a touchstone for generations of fans is important. The Tigers historian still goes to games at the new park, but his favorite spot was an area behind the rightfield foul territory, behind the stands, where one could look out about a mile across the city and see the light stands of Tiger Stadium.

"To me baseball is so much about tradition—that's really what the sport sells. It's what we have that other sports don't have in the same way. You need these old places that can resonate over the years.

"Any time you lose a place where guys like Cobb and Ruth and Lou Gehrig played, you're losing something that was a critical lifeline to the sport," he says. "I don't think we should give them up easily."

With Tiger Stadium now gone, Alan Trammell, who contributed many magical moments to the park's rich history, speaks for many players and fans alike when he turns his focus not to what has been lost, but to what can never be lost.

"Right now I can close my eyes and visualize some great memories, which will never leave me," Tram says. "Those are always special and they can't take those away."

Chapter 4

Angel in the Clubhouse

For Bubba Harkins, spooky stories have always come with the territory of working for the Los Angeles Angels of Anaheim. For years he heard curse rumors (explored in depth in *Haunted Baseball*) and ghost stories about Angel Stadium— shadows in the corridors and faces on the walls. He never gave them much thought until one gravity-defying incident in the early 1990s.

Harkins joined the organization three decades ago at age fifteen, as a ball boy down the rightfield line. Today he heads a five-man crew that works pregame and postgame in the visiting clubhouse—laundering uniforms and hanging them in lockers, putting out food, brushing dirt off cleats, polishing shoes, running errands, and performing dozens of other small tasks that most baseball fans never think about. He works ungodly hours—a typical shift starts at 9:30 a.m. and ends at 1:30 a.m. If another visiting team is arriving in the middle of the night, he might work until dawn. Harkins routinely finds himself alone in the dark interior of the stadium, in the quietest hours of the night.

He travels eerie passageways that snake deep beneath Angel Stadium. "It's a complex where even during the day when the lights are on, people are like, 'Oh, I ain't going down there.' And I walk around there in the pitch dark and you can't even see your hand in front of your face. And then you know where the light is and flip it on and flip another one on."

The job became creepier late one night in 1992.

"It was after the [visiting] team left," Harkins recalls, "and my assistants and I were doing our work. The radio was sitting on its shelf and we were standing near it and for some reason it caught our eye. It started sliding. It was a big boom box, and it slid for about a foot all the way across [the shelf surface] and fell over in front of my eyes. And I was like, 'Why did it do that?' I don't know if there was heavy bass. It had sat there for five, six, seven years and never did that. And we were like, 'Wow, that was freaky!' And that happened right in front of us. It was like someone just grabbed behind it and just pushed it right in front of us to say, 'Hey, I'm here.'"

Or maybe the ghost just wanted the boom box. One night later that season, Harkins and his crew had finished their jobs and were walking the long corridor toward the parking lot, turning off lights, when Harkins realized he had forgotten his wallet and headed alone back to the clubhouse. As he approached, he heard loud bass and wondered how in the world there could be music in the clubhouse after leaving it empty and shutting off all the lights and electronics. He reopened the door to find a stereo on full blast in the back part of the shower room. The lights were also on. He got close enough to be sure that he wasn't mistaken, then said to himself, "I don't need money tonight." Retreating through the door, he added, "I can drive without my license." When he returned to the clubhouse the following morning the lights and stereo were off.

"There is no way in a minute walking down the hall that can happen," says Harkins. "The light has to be turned off in the very back of the clubhouse and the old speaker that we had in there was on full-bore."

• ◆ •

As unnerving as the experience was, Harkins tries to keep it in perspective. "There are times when you get kind of spooked—three in the morning, alone, walking down the halls and you're flipping on switches. It's only human nature that you're like, 'Wow, it's kind of weird.' But I've always been of the impression that if some supernatural being was in there, I was kind of part of the family, because I've spent so many alone hours underneath the bowels of the stadium. If something bad was gonna happen to me, they would have done it a long time ago.

"I mean, no one has ever said, 'Hey, some guy got killed by a supernatural person or being or whatever.' I've just felt like I'm part of it all, like I've been working here since I was fifteen years old and I'm now forty. I've been walking around there a long time. The visiting clubhouse side probably has its own little dark secret. But for the most part we haven't seen Babe Ruth walking around."

• ◆ •

No Babe Ruth, but perhaps an old roomie of his. Thirteen years prior to playing for the Yankees and bunking with Babe, Jimmie Reese served as bat boy for the Los Angeles Angels of the Pacific Coast League. Nearly eight decades later, Angels bat boy Steve Rivera noted his return.

Reese played sixteen seasons as a solid-hitting second baseman in professional baseball, including four with the Angels. After retiring, Reese went on to manage, coach, or scout for seven different ballclubs. In 1973, at the age of seventy-one, he signed on as a conditioning coach with the Angels, a job he held until his death twenty-two years later. In baseball circles, he was known as the world's best fungo hitter. His accuracy was legendary and it was said he once golfed an eighty-two using a fungo bat and a putter. Among members of the Angels, he was a mentor, friend, and confidante. Nolan Ryan, in his *Pitcher's Bible*, says Reese taught him about nutrition, among other things. As an ultimate sign of admiration, Ryan named his son Reese.

Outfielder Tim Salmon wore the late coach's uniform patch in his back pocket (along with Gene Autry's) throughout the Angels' World Championship 2002 postseason. "I regret not spending more time with [Reese] when I first got called up as a rookie," he says. "From all that I saw, he was a gentleman who touched a lot of people's lives."

Former first baseman Mark Sweeney always wrote No. 50 in his cap in honor of Reese. He got to know him at his first big league camp during the final year of Reese's life and felt strongly even then that Reese was "a man I was supposed to meet in baseball."

"His love of the game kind of molded me," Sweeney says. "Any time I feel like I'm out of touch or something, I just take my hat off and look at it and realize, 'Hey, I'm okay.' In the middle of the game I might do that."

Dave Winfield thought of Reese as one of the game's unsung heroes. The Hall of Famer recalls Reese sharing inspirational stories with him about the Babe.

Joe Maddon, who spent thirty-one years with the Angels before taking the helm of the Tampa Bay Rays, remembers Reese making homemade fungo bats by bringing old, cracked bats to a woodshop. With a band saw, Reese would cut them in half, from the top of the barrel down to the handle. "And that's what he'd utilize for the fungoes. So he would hit it on the round side. When you threw it back, he'd take the flat side and flip it back up to himself."

Maddon recalls Reese's quiet manner and affectionate support. "There was nothing demonstrative in a physical way—no yelling and screaming—nothing punitive. He was just a gentleman," Maddon says. "When I have any kind of lack of confidence I think of him putting his hand on my shoulder, looking me right in the eye, and saying, 'You're the Master. You're going to be a big league coach, you're going to be a big league manager. Just take your time and don't be upset about things, and it's going to happen in the course of time.'" In 2008, Maddon turned his perennially last-place team into World Series contenders and was named American League Manager of the Year.

The Angels organization bestowed two of the finest honors in baseball on Reese: having him throw out the first pitch in the 1989 All-Star Game in Anaheim and retiring his uniform number after his death in 1994 at the age of ninety-two.

The Angels also preserved Reese's locker for four years after his death until the clubhouse was renovated. His framed jersey hangs above the entrance to the training room.

Bat boy Steve Rivera came on board with the Angels after Reese's passing, but having grown up in Southern California he was mindful of Reese's legacy. As he heard more stories about Reese from coworkers and ballplayers, his reverence only grew. Eventually, he says, he made Reese's acquaintance.

Part of Rivera's job is to keep track of which ballplayers are in the clubhouse and keep reporters and the general public out, so he is often taking casual attendance as they work. "I'll be unpacking bags near, say, Garret Anderson's locker, and I'll just feel like, 'Oh, Garret is right there because I can see a player sitting there. Then I turn and nobody is there and I'm like, 'Wow, did he jump up and leave or something?' I'll say, 'Jason, did you see Garret? Did he just take off?' 'Oh, he left, like, an hour ago.' And it will feel like real players are there."

None stronger than Jimmie Reese. On an almost daily basis, he sees the dapper, elderly coach standing near his former locker, leaning on his fungo bat. "He's waiting for the team to go onto the field. A lot of coaches, they'll hang out before batting practice sometimes standing with their hand holding the knob of the bat like a crutch on the ground. They're all just waiting for somebody to go, 'Okay, okay, time to go.' The players start walking out and the coaches follow.'"

"Jimmie Reese lived, breathed, and died baseball," Rivera adds. "Not just baseball, but the Angels. They were his whole being. And I think that if that is really him that I'm seeing there, it's because of how much he gave to the team. That's why that feeling is stronger with him."

Rivera shares ghost stories often and unselfconsciously. "Everybody already thinks I'm an extremist," he says. "I could tell them, 'Oh, I just saw the Incredible Hulk walk down the hallway.' And they won't say, 'Oh, you're crazy. Oh man, Steve.' It's just another Steve story, and they won't believe it's true or untrue. They'll just say, 'Oh, that's Steve.'"

In turn, Rivera separates the wheat from the chaff when he hears ballpark ghost stories from fellow employees. He started with the Angels shortly before the addition of the Big Thunder rock waterfall and geyser in centerfield. The renovations removed the whole upper section in centerfield, and from then on there was considerable echoing in the stadium. Rivera believes that phenomenon alone contributes to most late-night jitters: The sound of an air conditioner, an automatic icemaker, screeches from cats that run loose through the stadium, possums scampering on the floor above, or rats tearing through garbage bags left overnight in the carts have an eerie resonance in the empty ballpark.

Still, he says, the ten-minute walk from the players' parking lot to the clubhouse is downright unnerving. He qualifies it as the scariest walk you can take in any stadium.

"The worst walk of your life," Rivera adds. "The walk of death or something. The green mile. If the lights are off or the lights are on, it doesn't matter. You could be the most courageous person or whatever, but we've had baseball players asking for rides out because they didn't want to walk the hallways."

Rivera knows his imagination can run away down there, given the folklore that the area behind home plate was built over Indian burial grounds, but says that working in a clubhouse requires sharp eyes and ears and some of what he picks up is tangible. Oftentimes when he's heading down the hallway to deliver the Angels lineup card to the visiting club, out of the corner of his eye he'll see somebody packing a trunk, then look and find no person and no trunks. Or he'll be unpacking bags of equipment into lockers and hear magnetized double doors approximately fifty yards down the hallway open and shut as if someone is passing through. "We can hear that even though it's far away," says Rivera. "We can even have music on. Our ears are just so trained, because we have to keep everybody out of the clubhouse. Only media, the players, and we are allowed in there, so when we hear the doors click, we'll normally look down the hallway to see who is coming. But a lot of times I'll see somebody and I'll walk over, and there's nobody there."

The corridor walls are perhaps most frightening to Rivera, and he often has the feeling that there are people buried within. One spot under foul territory behind third base is downright chilling. "It's at a turn where two corridors meet. The wall at that corner pretty much everybody knows because you're like, 'Whoa, something's right there!' It's where we see a face and an image of somebody standing there. That's the wall that I just keep on walking by. Even with a group of people, I do not even look at the wall. In my mind, it's an Indian [buried horizontally] staring straight at me.

"When I drive the golf cart toward the clubhouse, during that whole drive, I'll feel like they're following me or almost like they're chasing me. My hair raises on my arms. The golf cart can't go fast enough."

While many players acknowledge the spookiness of the corridors, Jered Weaver feels more at ease since the team added more lighting. "It's not as bad," he says, "but it used to be [eerie]." Darren Oliver is just grateful that the lights are always on when the players walk through. "It's a long walk to the car, that's all I can say."

"It is something that you would hesitate to walk down by yourself at eight o'clock on an off night," says Tim Mead, who has served in various capacities in the front office for over three decades and is currently vice president of communications. He doubts there are ghosts, but acknowledges the fear factor. "We call it the Catacombs, because as you walk down it—and it's long—right around every corner you can constantly hear noise. I've gone down there to get away.

But, no, I don't carry a Smith & Wesson down there in fear of [former owner] Mr. Autry's ghost or anybody."

• ◆ •

The ballpark interior is frightening enough without gunshots. When Rivera works in the parking lot late at night, he can hear human activity inside the empty park. It typically happens when the crew sits by the curb waiting for the equipment truck to get in, which usually occurs around three in the morning. The stadium's lone night watchman is standing with them. All of a sudden everyone's ears will perk up. "You'll hear people setting up inside the stadium or people walking in there or something. We'll ask the security guard, 'Oh, who is here?' He'll say, 'Oh, it's just me.' We'll be like, Whoa!"

Rivera is even spooked on the diamond. Walking across the field late at night with the lights off, he has the feeling that "somebody is watching you from the stands. From up top or somewhere in the stadium. All around you—not like from any one location. It's just almost like somebody's staring at you from all locations in the stadium."

Could the presence be Gene Autry? The so-called twenty-sixth man wore his love for the Angels on his sleeve and always took interest in his players and staff. He was famous for stopping down in the clubhouse before games and mingling with players and wishing them luck. At one point his wife, Jackie, suggested that after he die he be buried under home plate to counterbalance the negative vibes of a ballpark allegedly built over an Indian burial ground. Jackie remembers the incident in a *USA Today* story: "He didn't think that was such a good idea, especially since the field got torn up occasionally when we staged motorcross events."

"I think the players wanted to think he was there when the team won in '02," Rivera says, "because the latter part of his life, they were really trying hard to win a World Series for him and they never could pull it together. He would have been the happiest person there. Because that team meant a lot to him."

Many players who didn't feel strongly about ghosts somehow thought Autry was there at least in spirit.

Scott Schoeneweis sums it up nicely: "I think he had a presence then. I don't know if you would call it a ghostly presence, but there was a presence there. He was very, very well respected and well liked by the players during his tenure."

Tim Salmon thought it was nice to win with Autry's wife in attendance. "I just thought of it as a nice tribute for Jackie, who was up in the box. Just to finally be there because I know it was one of his passions to get to the World Series. And from the players' standpoint, it was great to be a part of it finally for that family."

Tim Mead felt both Reese and Autry were present. "I will tell you this—and I do believe it with all my heart—in some way, shape or form, those two gentlemen were with us in 2002 in October."

While Mead dismisses ghosts in the tunnels or clubhouse, he's more open to the possibility if the ghosts were the two guardians of the ballclub. "If anybody's seen a ghost down there or any facsimile thereof, they've been good ones and if Jimmie Reese or Gene Autry were down there, then we're blessed."

●◆●

TOUCHED BY AN ANGEL

The Halos added Nick Adenhart to their roster of guardian angels in 2009. The promising 22-year-old starter had been killed with two friends when their car was broadsided by an alleged drunk driver. The tragedy occurred four days into the 2009 season and only hours after Adenhart spun six innings of shutout ball.

The following day, tearful fans deposited flowers, caps, photos and a hand-lettered sign reading "One More Angel in Heaven" in front of the main entrance to Angel Stadium. In the Angels clubhouse Adenhart's dad thanked players and coaches for befriending his son. Friendships with the young pitcher had run deep. Several players on the team had come up through the minors with Adenhart, and many of the veterans took a liking to the focused rookie with a heart of gold. Starter Jered Weaver had offered to board Adenhart for the season in his home in Long Beach. The accident happened two days before Adenhart was scheduled to move in, and Weaver was profoundly affected. "[Adenhart's passing] put a light in everybody's eyes that not everything is promised," Weaver said. "He was just starting his career—he was going to be a big part of our rotation—and to see that happen to a guy who is so talented, who is just a great person. . . ."

Over the season, Weaver would inscribe his close friend's initials on the mound before each of his starts. Weaver was also one of several players who visited Adenhart's tribute mural on the centerfield wall before games. All-Star centerfielder Torii Hunter often tapped his chest and pointed to the mural "just to give him some respect, some love." Players touched Adenhart's uniform jersey, which hung in the team's dugout both at home and on the road. Reliever Jason Bulger wore two medals, blessed by a Catholic priest, in his cap—one to honor Adenhart and one to honor a former college teammate who had been struck by lightning during a game. All of the rituals and remembrance may have inspired the team to play at a higher level.

"There isn't a guy in this locker room who isn't playing for [Adenhart's] memory," Bulger told the *Los Angeles Times*. "I'm not going to lie to you. I've been in some big situations where I've had some success, and I felt Nick was a part of it. I could feel his presence."

"I can go out there feeling like there's no pressure on me," said catcher Bobby Wilson, who was one of Adenhart's best friends. "I've got my best buddy in my heart right now. If I can't do it, I know he's going to help me out."

Jered Weaver told the *Orange County Register* that the young pitcher appeared often in his dreams. "It hasn't been any scary situations," he said. "He just pops in and has one of his funny comments and that's about it. It's nice to be able to wake up to that every once in a while."

In late September of that year, when the Angels clinched the Western Division title, they gathered around Adenhart's jersey in the clubhouse and doused it with champagne. Then they took to the field and posed as a team with the mural for photographs. Mike

Digiovanna of the *Los Angeles Times* wrote "the one player who wasn't there to live [the celebration], to feel it, was the one player who seemed to be everywhere in Angel Stadium."

His colleague Steve Bisheff observed something odder in the final moments of Game Three of the ALDS, in which the Angels swept the Red Sox, their postseason nemesis. In his blog, "Angels Unplugged," he noted that while Angels closer Brian Fuentes was finishing off the Sox in the ninth, the centerfield gate at Fenway suddenly blew open. The umpire called time and Torii Hunter ran over and shut it. "Maybe Adenhart was celebrating with his teammates," Bisheff mused, "not in the clubhouse but on the field."

Although the Angels never made it to the promised land, falling to the Yankees in the ALCS, the team could still boast an inspired 2009 performance, including a three-and-one-half-month stretch in which they went 62–34 and distanced themselves from the rest of the AL West. In recognition of the team's remarkable run under difficult circumstances, the Baseball Writers Association of America named Angels manager Mike Scioscia 2009 American League Manager of the Year. Throughout the season, Scioscia had kept the team focus between the lines and on Adenhart's family, rather than on their own mourning. At the same time, his players felt more than just Adenhart's memory. "[Our run] was almost like tag team—like [Nick and I] were doing it together," says Wilson, who made key late-season contributions behind the plate. "I know he was looking out for me, taking care of me. Bottom line, he's always going to be with me."

Chapter 5
Chasing Babe Ruth

David Ortiz spat on his gloves, tugged on his forearm protector, and leaned into his torquelike crouch for the two-one pitch. From her third base line loge box seats Linda Ruth Tosetti, a loyal Sox fan, prayed: "Grandpa, I'm cold, I'm tired, I want to go home. Please get inside David Ortiz's bat. Please, Grandpa!"

It was the bottom of the twelfth, 1:22 a.m., with the temperature in the low 40s, a raw wind off the Charles. And yet hardly a soul had left Fenway and most were on their feet, some praying as hard as Babe Ruth's granddaughter. Some held signs reading WE STILL BELIEVE, MAKE HISTORY OR BE HISTORY, IT AIN'T OVER YET, and the new team slogan REVERSE THE CURSE. The Red Sox were down three games in the ALCS, and another loss to the Yankees would bring a humiliating end to the team's most promising season in eighteen years.

Yankees reliever Paul Quantrill delivered an inside sinking fastball. Ortiz, who had been sitting on the pitch, unloaded, and with one swing restored hope to his team and answered Linda's prayers. As Ortiz rounded first base with finger pointed skyward, Linda's husband, Andy, crossed his index fingers in the direction of his wife as if to ward off a vampire.

After all, it wasn't the first time Linda had invoked Babe Ruth, and it would not be the last in the historic 2004 postseason. She had summoned her grandfather in the tenth inning of Game Three of the ALDS moments before David Ortiz's series-clinching walkoff.

Then there was Game Five of the ALCS, another epic battle that extended deep into extra innings. Andy dared his wife to try again as Ortiz strode to the plate in the fourteenth inning. Linda looked to the heavens one more time and again the result was magic as Ortiz plunked a walkoff single in front of Bernie Williams.

By no means would Linda take credit away from Ortiz. "I'm not saying I won that championship for Boston," Linda says. "I would never say that. They worked hard and won. It's just really funny when I ask something from Babe and that something happens. I call them Ruthian moments— Grandpa moments."

The urge to connect with Babe Ruth has led many to believe his spirit continues to work magic. One of the most wondrous athletes of the twentieth century, the Great Bambino rose to prominence as a pitcher with the Red Sox and superstardom with his brawn in the Bronx. His majestic home runs and enormous personality made him the ultimate American icon at a time when America needed renewal, on the heels of World War I, the 1918 flu pandemic, and the Black Sox gambling scandal. He became a celebrity of such stature that sixty years after his passing, he remains topical and larger than life. Many of the most intriguing moments of his biography are debated and reinterpreted. It's difficult to separate the man from the compelling legend. And for this reason more than any other, his memory persists long after his death.

Baltimore-based writer Charlie Vascellaro believes the Great Bambino "barnstormed" with him across America. During the

2001 and 2002 baseball seasons, Vascellaro was docent for a traveling exhibit from the Babe Ruth Birthplace Museum. He drove from ballpark to ballpark, curating on stadium concourses an interactive display featuring photographs, narrative, and cases holding precious Ruthian artifacts, including the Babe's 1927 Yankees uniform and bat, the catcher's mitt that he wore in his youth at St. Mary's Industrial School for Boys, the last contract the Yankees offered him, and a life-size cardboard cutout of the slugger himself.

The exhibit served as a real-life example of the Babe's enduring appeal. No matter where Vascellaro traveled it never ceased to amaze him how familiar baseball fans are with Ruth—a player who has been dead for several generations. Even toddlers would point and say, "Look, Babe Ruth!" Their parents would duck into the twelve-foot-by-twelve-foot exhibit and in many instances become so engrossed that they would seemingly forget they were at a game.

For Charlie, the outpouring of adoration for and interest in Babe sparked magic: Keeping Ruth's memory alive also kept his soul alive.

In March 2002, Vascellaro brought the exhibit to Tempe Diablo Stadium, spring-training home to the Los Angeles Angels of Anaheim. In the entrance lobby near Vascellaro's display was a bronze bust of longtime team owner and celebrated film star Gene Autry, who was to Hollywood Westerns what Ruth was to baseball. For fun, Vascellaro posed the cutout of Ruth next to the Singing Cowboy and snapped a photo. Later, when he saw the picture, he noticed an orb covering Babe's head. The glowing white globe gave an eerie luminescence and a lifelike quality to his face.

Over the course of the season, and looking back through hundreds of photos from the prior season, Vascellaro would discover more photos with orbs in oddly appropriate places and concluded that the orbs were indeed Babe Ruth, showing appreciation for the attention the exhibit bestowed on him. One snapshot from Milwaukee's Miller Park showed an orb illuminating a memorial plaque for three workers who had died in a crane accident during construction of the ballpark. A beam resembling a spotlight seemed to be coming from the upper corner of the photo. Vascellaro concluded, "That's the Babe's ghost shining recognition on these construction guys. He's saying, 'Look at these guys who died building this ballpark.'"

Vascellaro thought that Ruth also may have been stirred by a story about the legendary Willie Stargell. Outside of PNC Park in Pittsburgh, by the statue of Stargell, Vascellaro was mentioning to a colleague from the museum the irony of Stargell passing away on the same day the ballpark opened and his statue was unveiled. Vascellaro thought it was a mystical occurrence that Pops held on for that moment. Vascellaro was a longtime fan of Stargell and still keeps his baseball card on his mantel. He warmly recalls Stargell's generous spirit and his gentle, expressive countenance—qualities that Ruth shared. So it was meaningful to Vascellaro that an orb showed on Stargell's face in a photo taken that afternoon. In Vascellaro's mind, it was one Hall of Famer's nod to another.

On the way to Portland, Maine, Vascellaro stopped in the town of Sudbury, Massachusetts, where Ruth wintered for the better part of twelve off-seasons. An attempt to dredge from a local pond a piano that Babe and his first wife, Helen, had used was making national headlines that week. Town historians believed that in 1918 Ruth had slid the piano down an embankment at the edge of his property, onto frozen Willis Pond, and played for neighbors and area children.

Vascellaro met with Eloise Newell and Kevin Kennedy from the Restoration Project, a nonprofit vocational reha- bilitation program that teaches students with cognitive impairment skills in refurbishing antique furniture. Both had spearheaded the efforts to raise the sunken piano. In fact, Kennedy would later say the idea came to him as from an Iowa cornfield. He had been coaching first base for his son's little league team on a field near the pond, and in the middle of the game he suddenly had a vision. He thought of Babe Ruth's piano on the murky pond bottom and then of students at Restoration Project working to restore it. It would raise awareness and funds for the group. He imagined introducing the piano at Fenway Park to end the Curse of the Bambino. What made the vision so prophetic, says Ken- nedy, is that up until that moment, he wasn't even aware that there was a sunken piano legend in Sudbury. The vision had come to him almost as if from Babe Ruth or some other mystical entity. And yet it was so real and compelling that he set to work right away researching the history of Ruth in Sudbury. He learned from the historical society, old timers, and historical records that Ruth had indeed lived along the shores of the pond in a cabin called "Ihatetoquitit" and had indeed stranded a piano on the ice. As the evidence grew more compelling, he received help from more townspeople and ultimately from a professional diving crew that became interested in the story. And so began several failed attempts to uncover a new Babe Ruth artifact.

Vascellaro was flattered that in the midst of the search and the media coverage, Kennedy and Newell took time from their schedules to show him some of the town's Ruthian landmarks and the location where the search effort was taking place. Back at Restoration Project, he took parting photographs of the building. Later, when Vascellaro looked at the photos, he discovered a massive orb hovering just above the front door.

As a camera hobbyist, Vascellaro was struck by these splashes of light that mysteriously danced around in about a dozen photographs taken using two different cameras and several lenses. "The occurrence [in Sudbury] was kind of appropriate," Vascellaro says. "There was something going on that day spiritually and there was a spiritual connection to the [building], where they were trying to pull the piano, where they were spending a lot of time thinking about Babe Ruth. Babe's ghost appears because it is going where energy is directed. I think [Babe's ghost] is even created by belief itself. The act of believing drew Babe out of the cosmos where his spiritual matter or energy might have been lying and redirected it and brought it to us."

The first book Vascellaro ever bought, *The Babe Ruth Story*, Ruth's autobiography as told to Bob Considine, was on sale for fifty cents at his primary school cafeteria, and Vascellaro hurried home after school and read it cover to cover. "The Babe was eloquent for a big lug," Vascellaro recalls. "And when you read that book you really heard his voice in every sentence—it sounded like he was talking in your ear. It really fascinated me as a kid." Thirty-five years later, Vascellaro credits his ever-deepening, lifelong interest in Ruth for shaping his own career. Early on as a journalist, Vascellaro was assigned by *Cigar Lovers* magazine to write an article about the popular annual Babe Ruth Birthday Bash at the Havana Club in Baltimore. At the event he met the owner of three minor league affiliates of the Baltimore

Orioles, and their friendship landed Vascellaro a job as a publicist, which, in turn, ultimately landed Vascellaro his dream assignment at the Babe Ruth Birthplace Museum.

"Here I came out to Baltimore from Arizona to write a story about Babe Ruth," says Vascellaro, "and I ended up moving there. So I figured there was some pull on me from [Babe]. I think he's just recognizing my own adoration for him. I think he has felt it over the years. 'Boy, this kid. I don't know why he loves me so much, but I'm going to love him back a little bit.' "

Of all the Babe Ruth haunts that Vascellaro visited during his barnstorming journey, Babe's grave site at Gates of Heaven cemetery in upstate New York affected him most personally. Vascellaro had stopped by on the way into New York City and left a Cuban cigar at the headstone and a thank you note for all the good times that he'd been having in Ruth's name on the road. He took a belt of Maker's Mark bourbon whiskey, and poured one into the ground for Babe. He then took three photos of the site. The images showed what appeared to be orbs darting around the gravestone and one shining from the trees. "Now I think that also might have been the ideal place for Babe to be at that moment," Vascellaro says. "His spirit moved around in different places and was following our paths too. And then we met up at his permanent resting place. It's like he never died."

• ◆ •

The day after Ruth's passing, his body lied in state at home plate at Yankee Stadium and an estimated 20,000 fans streamed through the House that Ruth Built to pay final respects. Now, six decades later, Americans still pay homage. Thousands have made the pilgrimage to Babe Ruth's grave site and left balls, bats, caps, flowers, rosary beads, prayers, and Yankees T-shirts. Tens of thousands more visit Monument Park at Yankee Stadium every year. A smaller set of Babe Ruth fans travel the country visiting Ruthian sites and staying at inns where Ruth slept.

"Usually it's people in their sixties or seventies following the Babe Ruth Trail," says Tricia Anton, who owns Anton's on the Lake inn in Greenwood Lake, New York, a hotel that Ruth frequented in the late 1930s. "It's like they're searching for Elvis—they're interested in just having a connection."

Ruth vacationed at the inn and kept a boat on the property. He frequently came down to the lobby in his pajamas and joined fellow guests in gambling on the horse races that were broadcast over the lobby radio. Legend has it that owner Theopold Greck kicked Ruth out of the inn after learning that the ballplayer was getting race results by phone from a friend at the track prior to their time-delayed broadcast.

Some visitors request Babe's old room or have their photo taken by his door. And that's where Tricia and guests sense a presence. "The hair on my arms stands up when I think about it," Tricia says. "There's a creepy, eerie feeling that you sometimes have. I'm not saying that it's Babe Ruth. It could be anybody or nobody."

Retired airline pilot Sven Bertelson reports a more definite presence at his Mediterranean Revival home in Gulfport, Florida, which the locals affectionately refer to as the "Babe Ruth House." He describes a six-foot-tall shadow that moves hurriedly past as one enters the home's east bathroom. "I never see it [directly]," he says. "It's something like an aura or silhouette and then it disappears." The bathroom was adjacent to the room where Ruth slept, which still has inlaid furniture from the 1920s. But what convinces Bertelson that he's encountering the Babe is the imposing size of the apparition and the authoritative manner in which it moves. "It fits his persona," he says. "Who else could it be?"

For many years, Bertelson wasn't convinced that the Babe had stayed there. There was no archival evidence, just rumor. But when he and his wife, Kathleen, opened their home to public showing for an annual Pink Flamingo Home Tour, local author and psychic Deborah Frethem, who offers ghost tours of Gulfport, stepped into the room and then walked out in a hurry. She approached Kathleen and confirmed what Sven had long suspected: that there was a male presence in their bathroom. The couple got more flesh-and-blood confirmation one afternoon when Linda Ruth Tosetti pulled up and asked if she could tour the home. She shared that the house was once owned by the New York Yankees and her grandfather would occasionally room there.

The Babe Ruth Trail inevitably leads to the bedroom. One of Babe's legends that has grown over the years is his late-night stamina. The rumor was that Babe slept with six women one night in Chicago, seven in a house of ill repute (known among his teammates as the House of Good Sheppard) in St. Louis, and perhaps a dozen over a two-night span in Philadelphia. Former roommate Jimmie Reese (who stars as a ghost of his own in Chapter 4), often said that he roomed only with Ruth's luggage.

Denise LaValle wonders if the Babe rediscovered his scoring touch during the late 2004 baseball season. Around two in the morning in her Marlborough, Massachusetts, home, she rose from bed to use the bathroom and heard loud thumping on the stairwell, a man's heavy footsteps. She had heard from longtime neighbors that the home was a former bordello and that Ruth had been one of the best customers.

From time to time she had also heard phantom women's giggling on the stairwell and smelled the waft of cheap perfume in her bedroom. "But this was really loud. I think it's the first time I panicked knowing, 'Oh my God, it's actually coming up to the top of the stairs.' I didn't want to wake my husband, because he's a skeptic and probably wouldn't believe me. So I froze for a moment and then ran in the bathroom and locked the door."

The following morning she shared the incident with her husband Joseph, who had somehow slept through the commotion, and concluded that the home had been revisited by Babe. "I said, 'Joseph, who else could it be?' The Red Sox were on the verge of winning the World Series. The whole Reverse the Curse thing and the years of waiting for the Red Sox to win brought him back to life. I think he came back and reversed the curse."

If Babe indeed returned to his old haunt, he probably felt welcomed. On the wall in the keeping room hang two side-by-side photos of Babe—one in Sox uniform, one pinstripes, reflecting dual allegiances of husband and wife: Denise is a lifelong Sox fan and Joseph grew up in the Bronx and roots for the Bombers. On display upstairs is a photocopy of the contract that sold Ruth from the Red Sox to the Yankees. Directly across the street are the remnants of Old Concord Road, now a conservation trail, which leads almost directly to Babe Ruth's house.

In 1922 Ruth purchased Sylvester Perry Farm, eventually renaming it Home Place Farm, on Dutton Road in Sudbury. Babe, Helen, and his daughter Dorothy lived there and raised hens, turkeys, pigs, and one cow. In her book, *My Dad, the*

Babe, Dorothy explains that Helen thought it would be good for Babe to get away from all the distractions of living in New York. But it was the Prohibition era and the neighboring towns of Marlborough, Sudbury, and Maynard had more than their share of speakeasies where Babe could imbibe. Ruth painted the town of Marlborough with the actor Warner Oland, best remembered for playing the role of Charlie Chan in the movies. They visited a local watering hole called Pastimes. The brothel on Concord Road may have been where Babe went for a nightcap.

The former owner of the LaValle home, James Agoritsas, never encountered ghosts there. He says half-jokingly that he may have cleansed them when he stripped the fire-engine-red paint off the walls and stair treads. Still he was fascinated to learn from neighbors about the home's racy past and Ruthian ties. "Having been born in Marlborough, I would hear those stories briefly, but you never heard them as detailed as when I bought the property," he says. "And then people went out of their way to let me know what was going on in that house. I did go out of my way to confirm what I was told. I got the confirmation from people who were active in the community in the '20s and '30s. These people that would tell you these stories, they're all gone. But they just took delight in the fact that, 'Oh yeah, I used to see Babe Ruth all the time when he was in town.' When you asked where, it wasn't at church. From the stories I heard, you never knew when he was coming. He would just come in and he would leave quickly. It wasn't a situation where he spent a lot of time."

Agoritsas is just as fascinated by Babe's persona. "It was amazing. He was such a fantastic player, and yet he was famous for burning the candle at both ends. His drinking escapades were legendary. I mean how could anybody drink and consume as much as he did and still perform well in baseball?"

• ◆ •

"[Babe] spent some quality time in Marlborough at various watering holes," says William Downey, whose father remembered the Babe. "He may have been around the LaValle house, which was supposedly back then a house of ill repute. I have nothing to substantiate that—just what's been passed down to me by people in this town."

Gary Brown from the Marlborough Historical Commission says it's difficult to confirm if the LaValle home was indeed an adult funhouse. "There are no written records," he says, "and the only source of history is oral history, mostly from locals who have passed on." Lee Swanson, curator at the Sudbury Historical Society, agrees and says it's challenging even to confirm the exact years that Ruth lived at different residences in Sudbury. Local real estate and tax documents concerning Ruth are mostly stolen or missing, and those that do exist often have the signature cut out.

So Swanson has tried to document Ruth's extracurricular activities through oral histories. "Certainly there were many tales that I heard for years of Babe Ruth walking across Willis Lake in the winter and going to [nearby] Maynard, visiting various places," Swanson says. "There were a couple of houses of ill repute or speakeasies that he frequented. Another [bordello] on Hudson Road in Sudbury near Willis Lake—an antique house that the owners say Babe spent a lot of time at. But I can't support that."

And of course Denise LaValle can't support that the Babe still frequents her home, but she swears on it. "I think he came back and reversed the curse," she says. "Why would he return to a bordello? Sometimes it's just the comfort of a place that they've known and felt good being there. And if my house really was what my neighbors said it was, obviously he felt really good coming here and having a great time. And maybe it was just the comfort—he wasn't far from home and it was something that was familiar to him."

• ◆ •

Many paranormal researchers contend that people leave figurative footprints in places and that the essence of someone like Ruth, who had so much charisma that when he walked into a room heads would turn, may have been recorded in places he frequented. Orlando parapsychologist Emilio San Martin, who has investigated several of the sites along the Gulf Coast of Florida that Babe Ruth visited, frames it in terms of electromagnetic energy that he says doesn't dissipate when we die, but simply transitions to another form. He adds that in certain cases the energy may leave an imprint of a past event repeating itself over and over again. He gives the example of a scratch on a vinyl record where a song keeps skipping the same line repeatedly.

"The more vibrant the personality, the more likely that the energy that remains afterwards is going to be strong," says San Martin. "And with Babe Ruth, you have a situation where he is a very magnanimous personality. Very high profile, very high energy personality who traveled to a great many places and lived his life fullest in the majority of those places. As many places as he visited, he is likely to have left his energy's signature or imprint and that's why he's seen so often."

Jeff Belanger, bestselling author and founder of Ghost village.com, offers a different slant. While acknowledging that traces of Ruth may linger, he says that oftentimes reports of Babe's ghost haunting places would fall under Most Famous Phenomenon, the idea that some ghost stories are born out of society's infatuation with celebrity. The fact that a well-known personality had once passed through the site leads to the conclusion that his spirit now haunts the place. Belanger speculates that people reach for the well known and perhaps even yearn for it, because it's less scary. And for a handful of compelling historical figures, people yearn to connect. "Babe Ruth has got to be the most famous baseball player of all time," Belanger says. "If one can't meet him in life, maybe they could meet him in death."

•◆•

The Babe left his most enduring signature in old Yankee Stadium. His spirit was widely believed to have inspired baseball's most storied franchise long after his passing, and the chapter "The Ghosts of Yankee Stadium" in *Haunted Baseball* captures firsthand stories and insight from dozens of current and former major leaguers.

His ghost was also suspect at Fenway during the Curse Years and thought by stadium workers to prowl the park late at night. Urban legend has it that Ruth's spirit roams in neighboring Kenmore Square. Boston University students living in Myles Standish Hall have for years heard rumors that the ghost of the Bambino holds keys to the dorm. The university purchased the boat-shaped, nine-story building in 1949; prior to then, the Myles Standish Hotel had been one of the most fashionable residential hotels in Boston. While most of his Yankee teammates stayed at the Kenmore Hotel when the team played the Sox, Babe roomed in corner suite 818 of the Myles Standish, a large, multiroom triangular suite that looked over the Charles River and downtown Boston. During Prohibition, Babe may have also liked the two speakeasies hidden in the hotel basement.

The Myles Standish was built in the 1920s to commemorate the tercentennial of the landing of the Pilgrims in Massachusetts, and still has original trim and moldings, ornate oak woodworking in the halls, and preserved wall murals and paintings, which make it easier to envision ghosts having a run of the student residence. Former building director Paul Hughes says, "I never even heard specific stories. I think they have just grown over the years and kind of have been passed down to folks." In recent years, residents of suite 818 have been very aware of the Babe imprint, particularly during the 2003 postseason when banter about the Curse of the Bambino reached fever pitch. The Sox were squaring off against the Yankees and five coeds were hoping that their cohabitation in the Babe's old home provided them with special powers needed to reverse the curse. "I'm praying that if I'm here and root hard enough and bring enough good Sox karma to the room that maybe this will be the year," sophomore Lisa Kelly told the *New York Daily News*. "I feel like some of it is on my shoulders."

●◆●

Actor Stephen Lang may have felt Ruth's burden behind his shoulder. Shortly after the premiere of the Emmy-winning TV movie *Babe Ruth*, the acclaimed actor, who played the title role, approached Linda Ruth Tosetti and shared a few of his more mystical experiences. According to Linda, Lang was originally unsure if he wanted to make the film. He was on a wilderness retreat and as he hiked through forest, deep in thought about the role, he suddenly tripped. As he recovered, he saw a broken bat under his feet seemingly miles away from any baseball diamond. Weeks later Lang was researching at the Babe Ruth Birthplace and Museum. Lang, who is known for thoroughly immersing himself in his characters, was alone browsing through photographs and reading exhibit cards when all of a sudden he smelled cigar smoke. He later shared with the museum archivist that he was convinced that Babe Ruth was looking over his shoulder. "I know he really felt that Babe was directing him," Linda says. "That story I will go to the grave on. He put his arm around me and he said, 'I visit your grandfather's grave site. It's not like I keep talking to him, but I'm feeling him and I just meditate and he talks to me just like this.' And he just went *ssshhh* in my ear."

● ◆ ●

Babe's birthplace is a must-see on the Babe Ruth Trail, but his true home was St. Mary's Industrial School for Boys, and he never forgot it. Not surprisingly, on the grounds of the institution that raised and nurtured him, now the campus of Cardinal Gibbons School, the late slugger's ghost reportedly has sat on the wall overlooking his ball field. And a hair-raising, late night encounter with Ruth was used as a motivational tool by two generations of basketball coaches.

St. Mary's was a city-sponsored reformatory school, an orphanage and vocational school all rolled into one. Babe was sent there by his father after the seven-year-old had been caught stealing, smoking tobacco, and skipping school. Ruth was then under the care and discipline of the Xaverian Brothers. He would live year-round at the school off-and-on for twelve years and early on latched onto Brother Matthias, who took an interest in him.

At six-foot-six and 250 pounds, Matthias commanded respect among students and could crush towering fly balls during baseball practice. Matthias saw early on the ball-player potential in Ruth, and introduced him to all nine field positions. He taught Ruth the nuances of being a ball-player, and Ruth emulated Matthias's pigeon-toed style of running the bases and his powerful swing. Ruth would later recall in his autobiography that Matthias singled him out. "He concentrated on me probably because I needed it. He studied what few gifts I had and drew those out of me and amplified them. He always built me up."

More important, his mentor taught him right from wrong and how to read and write, and looked after him like a father. In Wayne Stewart's *Babe: A Biography*, Babe's second daughter, Julia Ruth Stevens, told the author, "Daddy had a God-given gift, he really did, and Brother Matthias encouraged it and helped bring it along—he said himself he would have wound up in jail if he hadn't been at St. Mary's because he started off on the wrong tracks. Who knows what might have happened."

"I always had heard that Babe loved this place just because he appreciated so much what they did for him," says Michael Hoos, director of admissions at Cardinal Gibbons School. Hoos is the school's unofficial Ruth historian, and during his four decades at the school he has spoken to former St. Mary's students and neighbors who remembered the Babe's frequent return visits to see the children and the brothers. The slugger would bring coins and candy and hit fungo. After fire ravaged most of the campus in 1919, Ruth went on a national fund-raising tour with the St. Mary's band and raised over $100,000 to rebuild the school's main building.

"We take great pride in the fact that Babe Ruth was here," Hoos says. "We call Cardinal Gibbons the House That Built Ruth and have a sign that says that as you walk in the front door. We have Babe Ruth stuff up all over the place—especially on the first floor here, where visitors come and walk in."

"We have a mosaic tile mural of Ruth in the gym and the baseball field is called Babe Ruth Field," adds Don DelCiello, a former school principal who first started teaching at the school in 1966. "Our kids are playing on the same field as he did. We always tell them when we take the field, 'We're on hallowed ground.'"

•◆•

Legend has it that the Babe's ghost drops in on occasion. Students reportedly have seen him floating across the field or sitting on the stone wall overlooking leftfield. When Linda Ruth Tosetti first heard the rumors, her gut feeling was that it was true. She had known of her grandfather's love for the school. And she knew of Babe's fondness for the wall. "That's where he would watch games," Linda says. "Even later on when he returned to visit the school he would sit on that wall. So that wall is part of him."

If anyone understood Ruth's devotion to his alma mater it would have been Cardinal Gibbons' late basketball coach Bob Flynn. In 1999, he left his head coaching position at St. Mary's College of Maryland to coach at Gibbons, his high school alma mater. He redesigned the gym floor, organized a student cheering club, and created a high school version of March Madness. At every home game he left an empty chair on the bench dedicated to his mentor, departed former Cardinal Gibbons basketball coach Ray Mullis. Flynn also draped a red towel over his shoulder during games as Mullins had done during his thirty-one years of coaching. (Coach Flynn even named his family dog Rebound, like his former coach had.)

Flynn and Mullis shared more than tradition. Both were detail-oriented and their teams were always prepared. Both were great motivators, teachers, and ambassadors for the game. They strove to make their players better people and athletes than when they arrived. Both also had tremendous coaching success and commanded deep respect in Maryland basketball circles. Flynn coached the East squad at the McDonalds All-American High School Classic in 2004; Mullis had coached the East thirteen years earlier. Mullis had also told his teams a Babe Ruth ghost story, and Flynn continued the tradition. "[Mullis] was locking up and he had to go downstairs because some lights were still on down there," Flynn recalled. "And he went down and he heard balls bounce and he quickly ran upstairs and there was no one there. The outside doors were locked and the gym lights were off. And there was no one there. But he heard either a basketball game or the ball bouncing.

"I remember he would often warn the kids, 'If you're gonna go down there, you might encounter the ghost of Babe Ruth,'" Flynn continued. "It was another way of reminding us that Babe made a mark on sports history. And it all started here at Cardinal Gibbons."

• ◆ •

The metropolitan areas of New York City, Baltimore, and Boston hold many Babe Ruth memories. But the greatest concentration of stops on the Babe Ruth Trail are on Florida's Suncoast. Ruth enjoyed twelve spring trainings in the Tampa

Bay region, then purchased a winter beachfront home on Treasure Island. In Sarasota, he stayed in a lavish apartment right across from the golf course. The Villa Serena opened for business during the winter season of 1926–27. It was intended to accommodate wealthy snowbirds. The Roof Top Bungalow (as it was then called) where Babe Ruth stayed covered the entire third floor and was larger than four standard one-bedroom apartments combined. It featured a covered open balcony about 100 feet long with doors directly accessing various rooms from the outside, and two outdoor porches for sunbathing. The interior of that apartment is the same now as it was then, with a large sitting room and fireplace and Venetian-style arches and columns leading into a large formal dining room. Adjacent to the dining room was a screened "breakfast porch" and French doors opening into a very large screened lounge. At the opposite end of the bungalow were the private sleeping accommodations, which included two standard bedrooms with a hall bathroom, one master bedroom (used by Ruth) with a private bathroom and walk-in shower, and doors leading to a very large screened sleeping porch large enough to accommodate four more beds.

Before Babe stayed in the Roof Top Bungalow, legendary golfer Bobby Jones occupied it in 1927. At that time, Jones was employed as a golf pro by the Whitfield Country Club, which is situated immediately across the street from the Villa Serena. It is not surprising that Ruth came to Sarasota to golf at the club since it was a Donald Ross–designed course and considered one of the finest in the United States at the time. According to legend Babe loved dining and drinking, often to excess, at the clubhouse after a round of golf. He would then walk across the street to the Villa Serena in the company of one or two attractive females.

Several former tenants of the Roof Top Bungalow over the past ten years have told the Villa's current owner Christopher Brown that it is indeed haunted. One claimed she often heard strange noises and was periodically unable to sleep in the master bedroom where Ruth slept. Another tenant who lived in that apartment claimed furniture and personal items had been moved about from time to time. "Last year I was contacted by the daughter of a prior owner of Villa Serena," Brown says, "who insisted the entire third floor Roof Top Bungalow was haunted when they lived there during the 1970s. She described hearing loud whistling sounds when she was all alone in the apartment that so terrified her she would run to the balcony and down the interior three-story staircase and wait outside until her parents returned home!"

Travel writer and paranormal author Kim Cool has profiled plenty of alleged hauntings in buildings associated with Ruth. Considering that all the major older hotels in the city were visited by Ruth, the correlation is not surprising. "He's such a legend that everyone wants to say that he slept here, ate here, read a book here," Cool says. She toured the former Tampa Bay Hotel with spiritual medium Rosemary Altea and records in her popular 2007 book *Ghost Stories of Tampa Bay* that the ghost of Henry Plant, railroad magnate and builder of the Moorish-influenced hotel, followed them on the tour, "quietly checking out the building we were in." During spring training in 1919—twenty years after Plant's passing—Babe and his Red Sox teammates stayed at the hotel, which was adjacent to their training grounds, Plant Field. In an exhibition game versus the New York Giants, Ruth connected with a fastball down the middle and, according to media reports, the ball kept rising and landed beyond the railing of a racetrack encompassing the field, more than 550 feet away. Giants manager John McGraw commented that it was the longest ball that he had ever seen hit. A bronze plaque on the University of Tampa campus now marks the spot where the ball fell.

McKay Hall, a two-story coed dormitory, now rests on the former ball field. Student residents have reported apparitions in the upstairs windows and marbles rolling across their dorm room floors. Or might the latter be the Babe's home run landing on the track?

Across the street, the former Tampa Bay Hotel houses classrooms, administrative offices, and the Henry B. Plant Museum. Rumors of otherworldly activity in the building run rampant. The most commonly reported activities include doors opening and closing by themselves, a feeling of being watched, the sound of objects being dropped, mail and paperwork getting shifted around in the mail room, and the apparition of Henry Plant sipping tea. "It's funny how old buildings get the reputation for being haunted," museum education director Gianna Russo says. "I have certainly heard stories from some of the students about unexplained phenomena, but none of us working have experienced anything or heard anything other than hearsay of students."

Some faculty and campus employees have a different perspective. Brandy Stark, an adjunct professor of world religion at the University of Tampa, was climbing the staircase to the second floor of Plant Hall, the former Tampa Bay Hotel, when she passed through what she describes as "a dense burst of cold air." She turned and put her hand behind her to find the cold spot, but it was gone. "What's so remarkable is the main lobby is not air-conditioned," she says. "They open the front and the back doors and have huge fans that blow through. But by the time you hit the stairwell, there's no breeze and it's literally just dead. So I probably walked through Henry Plant—oh, I guess he's forgiven me."

●◆●

Plant may have preferred the elevator at another old Ruthian haunt, the Belleview Biltmore Hotel in Bellaire. One of the sales representatives had to be treated by paramedics after she was confronted by an apparition during the ride down from the second floor to the lobby. As the elevator descended, she turned and saw a dapper man there and he tipped his hat to her. She started hyperventilating and had a heart attack.

Adding to his roster of hotels, in order to lure tourists on his passenger train line, Plant built a majestic green-roofed Victorian-style framed resort with Swiss-style gables on a wooded, sandy bluff. Completed in 1897, the White Queen of the Gulf, as the hotel is known, quickly became a luxurious destination for the idle rich, dignitaries, and heads of state. Ruth stayed at the hotel mainly because of its proximity to the Casino, an exclusive gambling resort that was a gathering place for the likes of Ring Lardner, Thomas Edison, Henry Ford, and the Vanderbilts. The exclusive club required evening dress of its patrons, attracted Radio City orchestras, and boasted a spacious ballroom, sunken bar, and club rooms with arched corridors and checkerboard tile floors. Ruth also loved golfing on the Belleview Biltmore's scenic, championship-style course and would routinely drive up from St. Petersburg on Sundays to play a few rounds. As early as 1920, he would tee up with the legends and stay competitive. He could often be found on the links in the off-season and before practice in spring training. It was said he was world-class on the fairways, though below par on the greens. One year Ruth even finished in second place in an amateur tournament on the Belleview course.

So it comes as no surprise that the ghostly legends of the resort concerning Babe mostly have to do with golf. Several of the faded photos lining the walls of the hallway off the main lobby of the Belleview Biltmore show Ruth with his fairway buddies, including golf legend Gene Sarazen. And one of the more endearing local stories about the remarkable affection Babe had for kids took place on the resort's golf course. A five-year-old girl named Ardith Rutland and her older brother were on the edge of the fairway selling orange juice and peanut butter cookies. Babe was a frequent customer. One time he asked Ardith if she recognized him. The little girl had never heard of him, although she had heard of the Baby Ruth candy bar, which had no direct affiliation with Babe and was ostensibly named after Grover Cleveland's daughter. The next time Ruth golfed, he had a Baby Ruth bar in his pocket for her. She pouted when he handed it to her and said her uncle usually brought her two. The next day Ruth returned with a whole carton.

The most commonly reported ghost in the Belleview Biltmore is Maisey Plant, Henry B. Plant's daughter-in-law, thought to be searching for her lost $1.2 million Cartier double-strand pearl necklace. Guests and staff have reported seeing her roaming the hallways in a hoop skirt gown that appears gold or auburn in color. "I've caught a very passing glimpse myself," says Emilio San Martin, who gives ghost tours of the hotel. "I heard the rustle of the dress, then she walked by me. And that's generally how people will see her. People, especially couples, will see her walking down the hall in a very fancy dress walking toward them or by them and actually say hello to her and she'll disappear before their eyes."

Another rumored damsel in eternal distress is a newly-wed who waits for her husband, who died on the first night of their honeymoon. After hearing the news from hotel staff that her husband had been involved in a fatal car crash, she retired privately to her fourth-floor bridal suite and was found dead the next morning in the bushes underneath her terrace. "She tends to stay more on the exterior of the property," San Martin says. "In the shrubs near where she jumped and also around a beautiful oak tree to the left of the main entrance."

Unlike some other hotels where employees are discouraged from sharing their ghost stories, the Belleview Biltmore staff are eager to talk about bizarre and unusual occurrences at the hotel: old ballroom dance music playing in unoccupied Room 4301, doors opening and shutting in the main corridors, ceiling fans that spin when they're turned off, and apparitions of children running the first-floor halls.

The encounters with Babe are more subtle. Paranormal investigator and Tampa Bay area DJ Tim Huck mentions that hotel guests have reported seeing Ruth's ghost near the golf course. In 2007 Huck also photographed an orb that one could argue was Babe. He was involved in the making of a television commercial for the Toronto Blue Jays and snapped a photo afterward of slugger Lyle Over-bay standing alongside Huck's DJ partner. An orb was hovering between them.

Hotel staff members have their own favorite Babe story. Several report seeing two indentations in one of the sofas and hearing two gentlemen discussing golf. Few would argue beyond a shadow of doubt that it was Babe schmoozing, but few would rule it out.

• ◆ •

Many of the stops along the Babe Ruth Trail that don't have Ruthian ghost stories still have reports of hauntings, particularly in St. Petersburg, where Babe's presence drew thousands and helped put a small, sleepy town on the map. The locals appreciated his kindness toward children and his tireless altruism, which ranged from spearheading a campaign to raise money for the surviving children of a young couple who died in a car accident to helping raise funds for the Crippled Children's Hospital.

"The town was just infatuated with him, and he was infatuated with the town," says Will Michaels, president of the St. Petersburg Preservation Society. "Through his actions and the amount of time that he spent here, he clearly connected with St. Petersburg [and it wasn't just for baseball]."

Ruth kept a penthouse apartment downtown in the late 1920s and '30s, but also stayed in every major St. Petersburg hotel, and perhaps because most of the original buildings still stand—in the form of schools, shopping centers, apartments, and modern hotels—and hold history, they're now steeped in ghost stories. The Don Cesar, where Ruth bunked in 1926, has more than its share of supernatural lore. Guests sometimes report seeing moving shadows in the rooms. Gift shop workers at TR General Store, one of several specialty gift shops on the garden level, share stories of books slamming shut and purses flying across the store. In the hotel kitchen, workers describe hearing objects dropping and breaking and feeling that someone else is in the room. And then, of course, there are the apparitions seen both in the hotel lobby and along St. Pete Beach.

The Jungle Hotel and Country Club was part of a larger development called Jungle Prado that was built over a former Native American village on the eastern shore of Boca Ciega Bay. The entire complex entertained Babe day and night. Ruth golfed at the country club in the mornings before baseball practice and at night frequented the Gangplank, a popular Prohibition-era speakeasy, where they served what the establishment called "mini-tea," hard liquor in a tea cup. The building is still preserved and holds some interesting decorative work that's in the shape of small boats. In his fine history, *St. Petersburg and the Florida Dream: 1888–1950*, author Ray Arsenault described the Jungle as "lavishly punctuated with inlaid tile and Spanish-style patios and surrounded by tropical gardens and a meticulously manicured golf course."

The ghost stories from Jungle Prado are thought to be connected to the ancient Tocobaga Indian burial mounds that Jungle Prado builders leveled in the mid-1920s. According to author Tim Reeser in his book, *Ghost Stories of St. Petersburg, Florida*, "One developer claimed there were so many Indian mounds in the Park Street area between Bay Pines Veterans Medial Center and the Admiral Farragut Academy, that they considered turning the entire complex into a macabre tourist attraction." Reeser goes on to describe "restless spirits" scattered throughout the compound and the apparition of a "Gray Lady" in the building that formerly housed the Gangplank.

Reeser also writes that pitcher Scott Williamson's frightening ghost encounter at the Vinoy Hotel (covered in depth in *Haunted Baseball*) could have been a Ruthian omen. The incident, Reeser explains, occurred in 2003, the year the Sox lost their lead and then the series in Game Seven of the ALCS. Reeser lays out more evidence:

> St. Petersburg hosted the New York Yankees for spring training from 1925 to 1961. The Vinoy Hotel opened for business the same year the Yankees first came to town for spring training in 1925. Babe Ruth and the rest of his Yankee teammates spent many nights in the Vinoy Hotel while training in St. Petersburg. For many decades, St. Petersburg's baseball affiliation made it a "Yankee town." Is it any wonder that an eighty-five-year-old "Yankee curse" might manifest in the very hotel, perhaps the very room, in which Babe Ruth might have stayed?

In her own volume of regional ghost stories, author Deborah Frethem writes that the former Rolyat Hotel, now Stetson University Law School, is thought to hold the spirit of a woman dressed in a flapper outfit: no Babe, but representative of the Jazz Age and the spirit of his times. Ruth signed one of the biggest Yankee contracts of his career ($75,000 with 25 percent net receipts for Yankee exhibition games) in the hotel foyer. And then as the media watched, Babe and his second wife, Claire, threw coins in the patio wishing well for good luck.

•◆•

Babe Ruth historian Tim Reid heard that Babe Ruth's ghost haunts the halls of the former Sunset Hotel, which is now the Parkview. (The building, in its prior incarnation as the Crystal Bay Resort, had also been fodder for ghost hunters hot on the trail of Al Capone's spirit.) Situated on the west side of town overlooking Sunset Park, the hotel guest list included the Babe, Marilyn Monroe, the Three Stooges, and even Robert Kennedy. Babe would also put up guests at the hotel possibly including Juanita Jennings, Babe's former mistress and Linda's maternal grandmother.

Reid has dedicated years to preserving the memory of Babe Ruth in St. Petersburg. He has also spearheaded a grassroots effort to commemorate the King of Swat in the Sunshine City by building a memorial downtown or renaming a boulevard, ball field, or park in Ruth's honor.

"One place where his spirit is stronger than any other I know is Crescent Lake," he says. He's referring to Huggins Stengel Field, a former spring training grounds for the New York Yankees. Babe practiced there from 1925 to 1934, and those who take care of the field and work in the former clubhouse claim that it's haunted.

Reid shares his own story of a recent visit to the ball field with an entourage that included Babe Ruth's granddaughter, her husband, Andy, and Bill Jenkinson, the leading historian on Babe Ruth's playing career and author of *The Year Babe Ruth Hit 104 Home Runs*. Jenkinson has traveled the country surveying and measuring all the home runs Ruth has hit. Reid had been researching a batting practice session on March 6, 1928, when Ruth hit six home runs into Crescent Lake, which was 590 feet from home plate—perhaps the most powerful display of hitting in baseball history. He had been searching for years for firsthand or secondhand accounts of that particular day without success. Still, he was thrilled to show Linda the ball field and informally survey the distance from home plate to the lake. (A more formal survey was conducted months later.) A high school game was in progress as they walked off the distance between the rightfield fence and the lake. They stood at the edge of the lake for twenty minutes talking when a seventy-year-old gentleman approached them.

"Out of nowhere—doesn't know who we are and cannot possibly hear what we're talking about," Reid recalls. "And he says, 'You're probably here to see where Babe hit the longest home run ever. Let me tell you about that.' And we were all looking at each other stunned, because I had actually been digging for years."

The gentleman proceeded to tell them with tremendous specificity that ten years earlier he had played in a senior league alongside a former Philadelphia Athletics first baseman who remembered a ball Ruth hit into the lake in 1929. As Ruth rounded first base, he looked at him and said, "How do you like that, kid?" Several on the field that day claim that it was the longest of all the balls that Ruth hit over the years into Crescent Lake. The gentleman then passed along his name and number to Bill Jenkinson and walked off. Reid and Jenkinson now refer to him as Mystery Man because they have never been able to locate him since. But in Reid's mind there may have been even more to the story. "I believe that Ruth actually sent this man as a messenger. Almost as if to tell us, with Bill Jenkinson and Linda there, 'I want this one recorded too.'"

The entourage then headed back toward their cars. As they were passing the former Yankees clubhouse that Babe once used, Reid turned to Linda and said, "I believe that your grandfather is at this field right now." And at that exact moment, a sliced foul ball came screaming toward Linda. She ducked and it barely missed her head.

"The day was already eerie and that was almost like the exclamation point on an already emphatically strong point," Reid says. "Just amazing—the whole visit there. And we all sensed independently that we were actually being guided on our visit. We never saw an apparition of Babe Ruth or anything like that. And almost nobody there knew anything about the reports of ghosts at Crescent Lake. But we all independently felt that Babe's spirit was there and was guiding us."

• ◆ •

Linda Ruth Tosetti needed no convincing. She was born seven years after her grandfather's passing, but often feels like he's standing just over her shoulder calling her shots and filling her life with purpose. It was an intuitive feeling that first came over her in 1994 during the drive up to Cooperstown for Hall of Fame Weekend.

The trip was her first since her mother Dorothy Ruth Pirone's passing and the prospect of filling her mom's shoes worried her deeply. At past inductions, Linda had shyly tagged along as her mother mingled with Hall of Famers and their families, autographed for museumgoers in the Babe Ruth Gallery, ducked into Main Street shops to say hello, and posed for photographs with whomever asked. All throughout, she would instruct Linda to pay attention to how to conduct oneself. Once Linda quipped, "You're the daughter. They don't want to know me." And her mother looked at her and said, "I'm telling you. Some day you're gonna see."

"My mother must have known that out of the six grandchildren I'd be doing this," Linda continued. "She knew before I knew. She didn't say, like, 'You're gonna do it.'

It wasn't that kind of thing. It was very subtle, how she started talking about her dad. And just kind of pay attention to what she was doing. So I learned by watching her."

In the final days before her passing, Dorothy asked Linda to continue representing Babe at Hall of Fame Weekends. Years later Linda would realize that her mother saw in her an uncanny resemblance to her grandfather.

In her one prior public appearance since her mother's death, Linda had suffered an anxiety attack. She was midway through a speech at a youth baseball league event when she froze in panic. She looked at her notes for guidance, but in her state of nervousness she could not even make out the words. Now she was facing Hall of Fame weekend, an event with far more protocol, and as the only grandchild of a Hall of Famer formally invited to the event, she felt undeserving. Throughout the nearly five-hour drive from her Connecticut home to Cooperstown, her palms sweated and she had difficulty breathing. Her symptoms only worsened the closer they got to Cooperstown. Then all of a sudden, about one mile out of town she felt a "warm energy" pass through her starting at her head and moving in a wave down to her toes. "It was like a physical lever—like a line going right down my body. It was almost like my mom put her hand on my head and said, 'Okay, take it easy, you're going to be fine.' If anybody has ever been hugged by their mother when they're really upset, that's the feeling that I had. It wasn't gradual, but profound within seconds. I turned to my husband and said, 'It's okay, Andy. I can do this.' And he looked at me like I had four heads."

From then on, she has had mystical moments sometimes involving her mother, but more often Babe. She feels her grandfather calling, even though she didn't know him. She has had spiritualists tell her that his spirit is not far off. Babe was a force that came through. He did things that were never done before. At a very young age, he was famous. And wherever he went, crowds showed up. He had great power over human beings. And everything about him was gigantic. Linda believes that people like that don't just go away.

She often invokes her grandfather and trusts he'll answer the call—helping her to hail a cab in Times Square, turning over a hopelessly stalled car engine during a parade in his honor, or bringing a halt to an extra-inning game. Linda now feels his presence before she gives talks. Before she walks up to the podium, she says, "Okay, Babe, if there's something you want to be done, it better come out of my mouth." Then she is often surprised by her own ability to speak. "The words come flying out of my mouth that I didn't even plan to say," she says, "almost as if they're coming through me. I believe I have no control. I may be part of it, but I'm not doing it. Somebody else is in control of what I'm doing."

After her return to Cooperstown, Linda became more involved in preserving Babe's legacy and using his name toward goodwill endeavors that Babe would have supported, such as children's hospitals and youth baseball. Over time she became a quasi-historian, talking on a daily basis with researchers who would often supply her with articles and share their latest findings. The more she learned about the man, the more her curiosity grew. And she rapidly concluded that Babe was assisting her and other Ruthian researchers. "If I had a question about Babe, it was provided no matter how obscure it was," she says.

As she found out more about Babe's boundless humanitarian efforts, she wondered if he ever felt he was being taken advantage of because of his stature. She was also learning about his extensive off-season barnstorming with Negro Leaguers and wondered about her grandfather's attitudes toward race, playing in an era of segregated ball. She was in Cooperstown at the time for the induction ceremony of Mike Schmidt and Richie Ashburn. The town had closed down Main Street. And legendary Negro Leaguer, Ted "Double Duty" Radcliffe, who had played from the 1920s through the 1950s, was on the sidewalk signing copies of his book. Linda went over and introduced herself. Double Duty immediately pulled up a chair for her and before she could ask him what he knew about her grandfather, he said, "Your grandfather was a good man. He was aware people were using him, but he helped them anyway because he wanted to give a fair chance to everyone. That's a fine tribute to a man."

He then launched into memories of Babe's barnstorming against Negro League teams, which was more extensive than Linda knew. He said Babe would go into small towns that were hostile toward African Americans and would break bread with Negro League players—they were his friends. "He was a great crusader of Negro Leagues," he told Linda. "He believed that we should always be in the major leagues."

Linda recalls, "The mystical thing about all this—I never uttered a word other than 'Hello, Double Duty. Nice to meet you.' He was like a machine gun telling me what I had been dying to find out. Now you could say the information is out there and sooner or later I would have found it. But not delivered that way. And it's not just one isolated example—it happens so many times that we just sort of rely on it."

She once wrote to well-known television psychic medium John Edward hoping that he would "fill me in with an answer," but she never heard back. She also visited spiritual readers. One told her, "Yes, your grandfather is helping you, but not to the extent that you think he is. A lot of it is coming from you. You seem to know what people want to know."

A second spiritualist told her that she had three people with her from the spiritual world who are there for her when she needs them. And other spiritually sensitive acquaintances told her the same. One came up to her and said, "Do you realize how many people you have around you? Do you sleep at night? You have a horde of spirits around you. Wherever you go, you have this group."

Linda didn't trust one other medium. "She wanted me to do a public ceremony to break the so-called curse, and I thought this woman was looney-tooney. I didn't feel comfortable doing it." When she came home, she discovered two sturdy statues in her yard had toppled: a hundred-year-old donkey that was her maternal grandmother's and a life-size sitting angel that was her mother's. Both were nearly impossible to tip over and seemed almost to have been thrown. She spoke with her neighbor who had been sitting at her window overlooking Linda's garden until five minutes prior, and she reported the statuettes had been upright that whole time. Linda concluded it was a message from her grandmother and her mother telling her not to do the ceremony. They didn't want to validate the curse.

"Babe didn't throw a curse," Linda explains. "They were burning him in effigy, for pete's sake. Babe simply said, 'They're not gonna win another World Series without me.' And he was right. But he didn't will it, he just mentioned it. They were dead in the water. He was stating a fact."

Linda also suspects late family members have dropped by her home. It started when she was in her front yard saying goodnight to somebody and turned to see a silhouette floating past the bay window in her living room. Her husband was at work and no one else was home. It was about the height of her father and her grandmother. Since then, she and her husband have occasionally seen apparitions of similar build. She also hears heavy footsteps in the attic. One night she pulled the stairs down and went up to check, but saw nothing. "Whatever this thing is, I think it comes in visitation and leaves," Linda says. "And it's gotta be either my grandmother or my father—I think they're checking in on what's going on and leaving."

Linda has never seen her grandfather, although she sometimes feels he's viscerally with her. She says when she travels the Babe Ruth Trail and visits locations where he spent time, she can almost feel his presence. Whenever she stepped into old Yankee Stadium, she felt goose bumps. She also got a strong "feeling of him" at the Flori de Leon and at Admiral Farragut Academy, which occupies the former Jungle Hotel and Club. "I read that when you touch a piece of wood, it records you touching it. It's not so much Babe's ghost; it's the essence that he left behind."

Ruth also appears in her dreams. Oftentimes he's sad about the state of baseball—particularly steroids. And in the earliest dream that Linda can remember, he was concerned about his family's actions. Linda recalls several family members raising a fuss over the mysterious disappearance of several of Babe's World Series rings. Linda recalls going to bed during the height of the drama, and having a dream about her grandfather sitting on the end of a big leather chair in the parlor. Over his shoulder was a lighted door. Arguing could be heard from the kitchen. Linda was sitting on an ottoman looking at him. And Ruth was looking down with his rings in his hands and he said, "I can't believe all the fuss over these rings. And you know they really don't mean anything. This is all they want to know about?"

Linda said, "No, I don't want to know about the rings. I want to know about you! Talk to me!! Talk to me! I always wanted to meet you. Talk to me, I don't care about the rings."

And Ruth was saying, "Do you know, these rings—they're just rings. They're just rings—what's the big deal?"

Ruth said, "Do you want to know where they are?" Then Linda woke up.

"It might have been a [processing]-the-day dream," Linda says, "but it's still so vivid. I remember every bit of that dream like it was yesterday. Who knows where the psyche ends and reality begins? Perhaps Babe was telling us you had to look further than the rings. Or was Babe actually sad that that's all the family cared about? Who knows?"

The following morning Linda told her mom, and they discussed it and decided, "It really doesn't matter about the rings, because over time you realize things are just things. It's what's behind them that matters most, anyway."

Linda's keepsakes are the artifacts that fans leave at Ruth's gravesite. She keeps an alcove in her house to display some of the memorable and touching items—poetry for Babe, a small box that says ANGELS GATHER HERE, rosary beads, and countless other sentimental gestures to a ballplayer who had passed away before most of his gravesite visitors were born. On the back of each item, she writes, "For future generations. This was left on Babe's grave on this date . . ." Her all-time favorite is a Ziploc bag containing a plastic key and a note in kid's scrawl: "Babe, here's a key to the new Yankee Stadium so you can get in."

Linda preferred his old home. Beyond her mourning the loss of the most precious Babe Ruth landmark of all, she was disappointed by the manner in which the Yankees officially unveiled their plans to build the new ballpark. She recalls that during the announcement ceremony, which took place on the fifty-eighth anniversary of Babe's death, the team announced that the new stadium would no longer be the House that Ruth Built, but rather the House that George Steinbrenner Built. Adding insult to injury, the new ballpark would be built *over* the former Babe Ruth Field, a patch of diamonds adjacent to the stadium once dedicated in her granddad's honor.

Ironically, Ruth's monument was moved from the old stadium to the new on the seventy-fourth anniversary of the day the Yankees released him. And Linda found it fitting that the 5,500-pound granite slab proved a force to be reckoned with. While the other monuments came out easily, it took a construction crew ninety minutes to wrench Ruth's from the ground. "I think Babe was sitting on it saying 'No!'" Linda quips. "Of all the monuments, Babe's was the last one [to be removed]. After ripping out the other ones, don't you think they would have had it down pat how to do it? My grandfather's wouldn't come, his wouldn't come."

Linda visits Babe's grave twice per year, but it took eighteen years from Dorothy Ruth Pirone's passing before she visited her mom's gravesite at Ferncliff Cemetery, just fifteen minutes to the north. It was too painful for her to see her mother's name on the stone. And not just because of the finality. Linda's father had died five weeks before her mom, and at her mom's burial, Linda looked over at her dad's stone and at that moment something cold ran through her chest. It literally felt like something walked through her. It was an unpleasant feeling that she didn't want to experience again, so she stayed away.

Linda says she has never had a similar experience. Her relationship with her grandfather, her mother, and her father has been positive and one might say entertaining. She often likes to say she's on the "Babe Ruth roller coaster."

"Babe is a very positive name," she says. "When you say his name, people smile from ear to ear. So it's a fun thing to work with, because it's always happy. It's never unhappy. So we all have fun on it. We all have fun on this Ruthian ride, as we call it. The Ruthian ride with the Ruthian moments.

"The effect I have on people is in the spirit of Babe," she adds. "It was something that was handed to me from Babe to my mom to me. I do signings. People would walk away snapping their fingers. And I would wonder what the heck they were walking away with. Then I found out they're walking away with a piece of the man or the closest they can get to the man. Do I believe I'm Babe Ruth? Most certainly not. Am I filling his shoes? Well, I probably couldn't fill a toe. But for that moment they are getting whatever they need. I'm not consciously giving it. There's just something very mystical about all this. And I think Babe's force was so great that it hasn't gone anywhere."

Chapter 6
The Great One Lives

The Pirate City baseball complex has been the spring training home for the Pirates for almost four decades. Even without the ghost stories, the presence and contributions of Roberto Clemente at camps here represent an important chapter in baseball history.

When the Pittsburgh Pirates moved their Florida spring training camp from Ft. Myers to Bradenton in 1969, the team implemented a rule requiring minor leaguers and major leaguers with less than two years of experience to stay in Galbreath Hall, a motel-like dormitory in Pirate City. The rule did not apply to Roberto Clemente, who already had twelve phenomenal seasons in the big leagues. Like his veteran teammates, he could have easily chosen to spend his leisure time in a beachside resort on the Gulf of Mexico.

But the Great One was the consummate team player who cared deeply about the well-being of the younger ballplayers in the organization. He wanted to be there to help them adjust to life in professional baseball. So for four spring trainings, up until his death on New Year's Eve in 1972, he stayed in Room 232, a corner suite on the second floor overlooking the batting cages.

Conversations would often run late into the night in Room 232. Clemente, the maestro, would lean back in bed with arms folded behind his neck and offer baseball wisdom for the young players. He would instruct rookies to meet him at the batting cages after supper. He'd take time with them, showing them hitting approaches. The Pirates had a considerable number of Latin-American players in their minor-league system, many of whom hardly spoke English and had never traveled. The Puerto Rican Clemente routinely gathered them in a room and talked with them, telling them things like how to act in public, how to order from an American menu, and what to order. "It was like they were in school and he was their teacher," says Tony Bartirome, who played alongside Clemente and later served as his trainer. "Not only did he make it easier for them to react in baseball in the United States, he made a difference in many of their playing careers."

"A lot of the big-name players are approachable," wrote former Pirates ace and current TV analyst in *Sport* magazine Steve Blass, "but where Robby was different was that he would come to you."

"He looked out for us," says veteran minor league coach Woody Huyke, who was in the minor leagues when he first came to know Clemente at Pirate City. "He would try to help you out and you could always go to him if you had a problem."

Much to Huyke's displeasure, Clemente once asked the Pirates front office to change Huyke's assignment after spring training so that he could play under Don Hough, at the time the Triple-A Columbus manager thought of as a disciplinarian. "I was afraid of Don Hough," Huyke says. "But that was one of the best things that happened to me. Clemente was the one who got me here. God knows that's the way he was."

●◆●

When word spread that Clemente had died in a plane crash off the coast of Puerto Rico, there was some measure of disbelief among those who knew him. How could somebody with such a robust spirit and remarkable physical prowess perish? In Puerto Rico, droves of people waited for days along Piñones Beach, which happened to be Clemente's favorite beach in Puerto Rico, dimly hoping he would emerge from the sea. There were reported sightings of Clemente in La Perla, a residential neighborhood in the heart of San Juan.

To this day, Puerto Ricans continue to evoke Clemente's spirit. When the Puerto Rican national team plays at home or abroad, fans carry signs reading, ROBERTO LIVES.

For years Puerto Rican stars such as Carlos Delgado, Rubén Sierra, and Candy Maldonado have worn Clemente's uniform No. 21 in his honor. Delgado says that Puerto Rican children still love to don the number. "All the times we play baseball in Puerto Rico, there's always the connection to Roberto Clemente. His presence never goes away."

Carlos Beltran adds, "If you come from Puerto Rico, you have been living from the achievements of Roberto Clemente, not only in the game of baseball, but outside the field—the person that he was, everything he did for the community."

•◆•

In the first few camps following Clemente's death, no one stayed in Room 232. A plaque was placed on the door with an inscription that read:

I WANT TO BE REMEMBERED AS A BALLPLAYER WHO GAVE ALL HE HAD TO GIVE.

—ROBERTO CLEMENTE 1934–1972

When the room was finally reopened in the late 1970s, dozens of players stayed there during spring training or in rookie league practices, and slept under an autographed painting of Clemente. The talents of Clemente may have rubbed off on some, including outfielders Barry Bonds, Bobby Bonilla, and Tony Armas. For others, assignment to Room 232—or for that matter, that side of the building—meant only worries.

Pitcher Bronson Arroyo reluctantly stayed in the Roberto Clemente room with a roommate for two spring trainings and often felt uneasy about it. "When you're alone in there and taking a nap in the afternoon," he says, "you know there's just the picture on the wall of [Clemente] sitting there, it gets a little creepy."

Arroyo had heard unsettling stories of apparitions and strange noises in the room. "I know for a fact that there were guys who didn't want to be in that room anymore because weird stuff was happening. The room had these two doors that you swing open to go in the bathroom, kind of like the old Western movies, and I vaguely remember one guy saying something about those doors moving with nobody in there and stuff like that."

Middle reliever Jeff Bennett, who came up with the Pirates, was looking in the mirror one evening when he thought he saw a woman walking across his room. "There's no doubt I saw her," he says. "There are several people who have seen things like that there."

Shortstop Brice Pelfrey tells a similar story of brushing his teeth in his quarters, which shared a wall with the Clemente room, and glancing up to see a woman standing there. "It was weird because there are no women at Pirate City. [I see] a long, dark-haired, dark-skinned woman. And I look back and nobody is there. I go look out the door and nobody is there.

"I brushed it off. And the hitting coach came and asked me about it. He goes, 'Yeah, we've had people say stuff like that all the time.'"

Lefty specialist Mike Bumatay recalls his rookie league roommate, third baseman Eric Stanton, "waking up in the middle of the night and saying, 'Mike, did you see that? Some lady was standing there.' I said, 'I didn't see nothing.' It kind of freaked me out."

Over the years, plenty of players have dismissed the stories.

"I stayed in that room for like a month and a half and I had no problem," Chicago Cubs slugger Aramis Ramírez says. "People speculate way too much."

Maybe the ghost stories originated as a way for players to entertain themselves in the remote and somewhat staid Pirates complex. Barry Bonds remembers the Spartan life there, with four players sharing quarters and no TV sets in the rooms. "It was a very boring place. There was nothing around there. And we had an eleven o'clock curfew. I used to sneak out. I never got busted—I got told on a few times, but I never got busted." The superstar would tiptoe back around 4 a.m. "If you come back too early, you'd get caught," he remembers.

•◆•

Yet, for every ballplayer that stayed in the room and downplayed the rumors, there are dozens more who transferred out. Pat Hagerty, equipment manager at Pirate City since 1984, says that when players check into camp and are assigned Room 232, they ask for a room change. "Nobody will stay in that room. None of the Latin kids, for sure. Because they are scared of ghosts—honestly."

"I remember when I got traded over from Toronto," says shortstop/second baseman Abraham Núñez, "one of the first things the guys told me was, 'Listen, if they put you in Clemente's room, don't take it because everybody says there are ghosts.'"

Kevin Haverbusch, considered a prospect before a 2000 shoulder injury, says, "I asked not to stay there. I've had enough bad luck."

Longtime Pirates minor league coach Ramon Sambo says that Latin players do like to photograph the room, unable to resist the lure of the Clemente mystique. But bunking there is another matter. Huyke, who managed the Gulf Coast League Bradenton Pirates for twenty-nine years, says their skittishness has to be respected. He has transferred ballplayers out of Room 232 from time to time. "If the player thinks it has something to do with [ghosts], I will do it. Because we don't want them to be conscious of stuff like that."

Huyke remembers Pirate City as being very different when he first started coaching. Back then, there were far fewer trainers and coaches and Huyke had a broader range of duties. Players in the earlier years were more mischievous and disrespectful (though he also believes his advancing years earn him more respect today). On the other hand, players, particularly Clemente, signed more autographs and mingled more freely with the people. "The public was part of the baseball family," Huyke says. "Now it's not that way. The Pirates cherish their privacy more than they used to."

He prefers having dormitories at Pirate City, because he can keep track of players more easily. "You're closer to them," he adds, "especially when you live with them. When I got my house, I missed being here."

Huyke recently learned that Galbreath Hall will be replaced, after Bradenton's health department showed up and found six different fungi in air samples. Huyke lived in the building for thirteen years and remembers that the humidity would do a number on his clothing, even with the air conditioner running. If he left his shoes in the closet and didn't touch them for a week, the soles would be full of yellow mold, like forgotten cheese. The maintenance man, Henry Ponzera, used to shout at the Hispanic players, who preferred sleeping without air conditioners, having grown up without them. "Don't you turn those things off! You have to keep them on because of the mildew! The mildew!"

Huyke learned this firsthand. In 2004, the electricity went out in his apartment, so he spent the night in Pirate City. "I got up [the next morning] and I couldn't talk. I lost my voice. I could smell the fungus right by my air conditioner. God knows how many people got sick there."

During spring training in 2005, as many as a dozen ballplayers and organization personnel fell ill while staying in the building. Pitcher Ron Chiavacci was bed-ridden for thirteen days and developed walking pneumonia.

So, for Huyke, the replacement of Galbreath Hall was a blessing. He admits he never set foot in Room 232 after Clemente's death: not because he fears a brush with the paranormal, but because there are too many memories. Until a few years ago, Huyke lived in a separate building at Pirate City, where nothing otherworldly happened. But he doesn't doubt that "strange things" occurred at Galbreath Hall. His players in rookie ball would tell him, "Woody, someone is walking at night. I know it. I heard it. I hear the steps." When the stories first started circulating, the alleged phantom could have been Bonds or other truant players sneaking back, but over time Huyke grew more vigilant about enforcing his curfew.

"One time [the ghost] was a Canadian guy, Doug Frobel," Huyke says. "He played in the big leagues with the Pirates a little bit. He was a park attendant in Ottawa. And he used to get up very, very early—like four or five in the morning. That's the hours he worked. So he was used to it. So the ground crew used to get here at six in the morning. And he would stand over here and have coffee, but sometimes he would walk around the building a few times because he was bored. And people heard that and thought it was somebody haunting them."

Pat Hagerty wonders if the whole grounds are haunted. "It is pretty eerie here at night," he says. "It feels just like somebody is watching you. Even in the clubhouse. This place is built on a dump, too. So Lord knows what is in there."

In all his years at Pirate City, Huyke has never encountered a ghost firsthand, although he claims to have once woken to hear a ghost calling his name in his home in Bradenton.

Asked if he would enjoy a visitation from his old friend and mentor, Huyke beams. "See, that wouldn't bother me. I would be happy if Clemente shows up in my room."

Chapter 7
Enshrined Ghosts

When most Americans hear the words *ghosts of Cooperstown,* they think figuratively of the enshrined legends and their contributions to the game. But when folks from Cooperstown hear the expression, they think of unidentified wailing inside the village's oldest building, phantom whistling and singing in a home built by famed American novelist James Fenimore Cooper, the watchful eyes of a portrait in one of the town's most stately mansions, an apparition said to appear at the stroke of midnight in the Church Street Cemetery. And, of course, things that go bump in the night in the Baseball Hall of Fame.

The mere suggestion that the mecca of baseball might harbor ghosts conjures up images of the illustrious plaques along the oak walls in the Hall of Fame Gallery coming to life at night and interacting with one another—perhaps heading upstairs to the exhibits to slip on their gloves and uniforms. The greatest legends of the game celebrating their immortality in America's greatest sports shrine.

The Hall was founded in 1936 by philanthropist and Cooperstown native Stephen C. Clark as a repository for many of baseball's historical treasures and as a place where Americans could come to learn about baseball's past. Although the museum has expanded to comfortably accommodate the more than 350,000 fans that make the pilgrimage each year, only a small fraction of the 35,000 artifacts and 2.6 million archival documents and recordings are kept on display in the building's exhibition halls and galleries. (The remaining items are kept in storage and are accessible only by staff and researchers.) With reminders of history at every turn, it's small wonder that ghost stories abound at the Hall, particularly among those who frequent the building after hours.

Bruce Markusen, who runs Cooperstown Candlelight Ghost Tours and is writing a book on Cooperstown hauntings, is well versed on the stories of the Hall. During his ten-year tenure with the Hall as manager of programs, Markusen heard stories from overnight security guards of unusual happenings: motion detectors sounding without apparent cause, elevator doors opening without passengers, flashes of light, disembodied footsteps, and unidentifiable voices. Markusen was also keenly aware of the change of atmosphere in the building after the museum closed and the tourists departed. Like many of his coworkers in the Hall, he would often work late into the night. Most of the lights were off, except in a few offices. Occasionally, bats of the "winged variety" could be seen flying through the rooms. "You do get a bit of a haunting feeling," Markusen says. "The Hall of Fame is all about preserving baseball history. What's to say that the spirit of some Hall of Famer may be considering this his second home? What's to say that he couldn't make his presence felt on the premises?"

Sue McLaren wouldn't want it differently. She worked at the Hall and believed there were ghosts in the museum—a conviction she was never embarrassed to share with coworkers and friends. Her job responsibilities included closing the building at the end of the day, starting with the third floor and working her way down. McLaren found it eerie to be alone in the various exhibit rooms and would hear strange noises. "On the other hand, I didn't exactly feel alone," she says. "I felt like the spirits of players were there."

"You always wonder in the back of your mind—with it being a museum," says Rick Peterson, chief security officer for the Hall. "Every now and then, you happen to see lights or something or hear voices and it seems like someone is walking around lost, but you search around and nothing is really there. People have had it happen in every part of the building. Some guys, they get to a point where they don't even bother telling me anymore."

When Kelly first started working at the Hall in 1992, a new wing of the museum was under construction to connect the library with the museum. During nightshifts he would hear what sounded like footsteps. Looking back on it he wonders if it might just have been the building creaking or critters wandering. The building has a larger overnight crew now than when he first started. "Before, when we were on by ourselves the imagination may have run a little wilder," he laughs. "But you never know! It's an old village, and there are stories two blocks from here of different sightings and everything else. Maybe they're spreading into new territory."

Markusen's paranormal tour of Cooperstown includes many of these allegedly haunted locations. With lantern in hand he leads guests down the quaint, tree-lined side streets, past stately eighteenth-century homes with inviting porticos and elegant gardens. Among his stops is the old stone building on Pioneer Street called Smithy, which was formerly a blacksmith shop. Allegedly, passersby hear unidentified wailing sounds coming from within the first floor of the original part of the building. Traveling along River Street, rumored to be the most haunted road in Cooperstown, Markusen pauses in front of a section of stone wall that used to bulge out at times. In the 1950s, a few folks cracked through the wall to determine what the problem was and discovered the remains of a lone Otsego Indian chief, buried in this spot hundreds of years ago. The body was in a fetal position, which is how most Native Americans buried their dead. As word spread through the hamlet about the discovery, some villagers speculated that the chief had been kicking at the wall to protest that the area had been taken over by white civilization.

Further into the tour, Markusen stops across the street from the elegant iron gate of the Otesaga Resort Hotel and passes along stories he's heard from custodial crews, who believe a phantom family of four resides on the third floor during the off-season. In addition to having a prominent role during Hall of Fame Weekend, the elegant resort is well known nationally for its delicious cuisine, finely contoured championship golf course, and gorgeous views of Otsego Lake, the "Glimmerglass" of James Fenimore Cooper's *Last of the Mohicans*. The locals have shared folklore of a Loch Ness–like beast, nicknamed Otsy, that resides in the lake and is rumored to surface during inclement weather.

But for most if not all of the ballplayers who relax in rocking chairs on the Otesaga's back porch during Induction Weekend, staring at the shimmering water and the surrounding hills, tales of serpents and ghosts are far from their minds. Since the mid-1950s, the hotel has housed Hall of Famers for the induction ceremonies. In the early years, anybody could come on the property during the weekend to meet the ballplayers and get autographs. Casey Stengel was known to sit on the couch in the front lobby and tell stories while the public sat and listened. But by the late 1970s and early 1980s, autograph hounds were wandering the property at all hours. "It got to the point where they were up on the floors at two o'clock in the morning, pounding on doors looking for Hall of Famers," says Glenn Schilling, who has worked as a doorman at the hotel for more than twenty-five years. "So that's when we started to close [public access]."

Nowadays, in order to ensure the privacy of players, fans and autograph seekers wait alongside the fence, and Hall of Famers come out to sign for them.

Besides Hall of Fame Weekend, the hotel hosts many other baseball-themed events. Business conventions at the hotel often hire a Hall of Famer to speak in the hotel ballroom. Recent speakers have included Ozzie Smith, Tom Seaver, Don Sutton, and Bob Feller. The hotel also frequently holds meetings for former and present-day managers and owners.

But all the celebrity fanfare does not distract workers from the strange idiosyncrasies of the hotel. Whether it's the nineteenth-century decor of the building interior, the dark lighting in the staff passageways, the way sound carries in parts of the hotel, or a playful ghost, at least a couple dozen present and former staff have reportedly felt spooked in the building.

In her four years working in the downstairs Hawkeye Bar & Grill, cocktail waitress Janeen Whelan estimates that she has heard at least twenty coworkers mention ghostly activity at the hotel—everything from seeing the reflection of a man's face in a glass display case at the base of a mahogany staircase to the sweet sounds of a music box playing in an empty guest room on the second floor on Thanksgiving. Whelan recalls once walking by the Lobby Bar, originally known as the Glimmerglass Lounge, and noticing a man seated at one of the tables near the middle door. To this day she swears that when she walked into the bar, he vanished. Several cocktail waitresses have heard their name called out as they walk down the same hallway. "The thing that creeps me out is that there's nobody there," says one server, who has worked at the restaurant for over four years. "It's not as if there's time for someone to duck into a room. And I think, 'Why is my name being called?' I find no one [nearby] and hear my name, and I'm saying to myself, 'Okay, I'm hearing things?'"

Jean Coloney took matters into her own hands. "Me and one of the other cocktail waitresses at one time had all the master keys and we went to every single closet on all the floors and a big huge storage area. We were looking for ghosts, but we didn't find any."

Coloney suspects that she might be in the presence of ghosts in "the tunnel," the employee nickname for the beverage department office, where she handles requisitions. "I get the reqs every Sunday morning and I see shadows out of the corner of my eye. But you know how you can get like that when you're all alone in a room," Coloney says. "You see a shadow, so you half think someone is watching you and you feel like somebody is there. It's an old building, so you don't know."

Cooperstown history runs far deeper than Colonial America. For hundreds of years prior to William Cooper first setting eyes on the idyllic shoreline of Otsego Lake, the land was occupied by Native Americans who used the lake for fishing expeditions and Council Rock along its shore as a place to rendezvous.

Before the Hall, Cooperstown was already on the baseball map, after a famed sports commission headed by equipment entrepreneur and baseball promoter Albert Spaulding announced to the world that baseball was invented here by Civil War general Abner Doubleday and first played in a Cooperstown cow pasture. Their conclusion has long been discredited by baseball historians, but one of the earliest attractions of the museum was a tattered ball allegedly used by Abner Doubleday.

In the years since the Hall's opening, this pastoral village of only 3,000 inhabitants has attracted over thirteen million visitors. Cooperstown maintains the cozy neighborhood feel of a modern-day Mayberry. But instead of encountering Aunt Bea and Barney, one might find Nolan Ryan eating lunch in a street-side café, or Ernie Harwell in his trademark blue captain's hat, casually chatting with fans. Ted Williams was said to have gone trout fishing on occasion on Otsego Lake. Clete Boyer owned a hamburger joint just up the road.

Nowadays the town is synonymous with baseball. Despite having a world-class opera house, the National Soccer Hall of Fame, the farmer's museum, and a beautiful lake, the largest draw to this inconveniently out-of-the-way little village is the great American pastime.

Markusen speculates that communities that pay homage to the past may not have more ghosts, but may pay more attention to them. It's akin to restored historic homes like Mount Vernon. When people see George Washington's perfectly preserved desk, they can easily imagine him living there, and feel a close connection. In Cooperstown, the old gloves and game-worn uniforms make it easy to believe their former owners can't be far away.

"Baseball is more aware of its history than any other sport," Markusen says. "Baseball honors its dead more so than any other sport. So it's only appropriate that Cooperstown has an attachment to the ghost world."

Chapter 8

Is This Heaven?
No, It's Catalina

Four decades after the Chicago Cubs abandoned their spring training home on California's Catalina Island for the more convenient Mesa, Arizona, one of the island's many loyal Cubs fans felt déjà vu. He encountered what he thinks was a wayward player, in search of his long-gone team.

For twenty-six years, between 1926 and 1951, the Chicago Cubs were annually serenaded by troubadours in Spanish costumes and paraded in tractor trailers or open buses from the steamer pier in dreamily curving Crescent Harbor around Sugar Loaf to Hotel St. Catherine in Decanso Canyon one-half mile away. Islanders had a tradition of grandly welcoming the luxury steamers that carried tourists from Wilmington, then a suburb of Los Angeles, twenty miles across the channel. But the arrival of the Cubs felt like more of a homecoming. The town of Avalon would shut down schools and businesses so residents could greet the ballplayers along the parade route. In early years, William Wrigley, owner of the island and the team, often trailed the procession in a stagecoach. In later years, his son Phillip would greet the team from the saddle of one of his prizewinning Arabian horses.

In Jim Vitti's fine volume, *The Cubs on Catalina*, outfielder Carmen Mauro recalled, "It was a lot of fun to be in Chicago, in that snowy environment, then to step off the train in that sunshine in Los Angeles, then to Catalina—I thought I'd died and gone to paradise."

Wrigley had bought the island in 1919 and was investing millions of dollars in building hotels, a world-class casino, and infrastructure. He brought the Cubs over to train on the island for the first two weeks of spring training in 1921, and the team worked out by hiking for hours along the goat trails that traversed the steep mountains. Legendary hurler Grover Cleveland Alexander told the *Chicago Herald & Examiner* that he was in better condition after just two weeks than he had been the year before at the start of the season. Manager Johnny Evers told the *Los Angeles Times* that Catalina was the "nearest thing to perfection" he had known in his twenty years of baseball.

On the steamer trip over to the mainland, *Chicago Tribune* columnist Robert Edgren overheard Wrigley vowing to make Avalon "the finest home for ballplayers in the world." And he lived up to his word, etching a first-class ball field in Avalon Canyon with dimensions matching that of Wrigley Field. His ballplayers were housed in a luxury resort, or in cozy bungalows just beyond rightfield if they were bringing their families. Under the suggestion of astute team president William Veeck (father of future baseball owner and marketing guru Bill Veeck), a special chef was brought in to prepare meals for the team. The ballplayers basked in the wondrous beauty of a largely undeveloped island blessed with rugged peaks rising to two thousand feet, nearly vertical shoreline palisades, and unique species of wildlife and plants. They mingled with movie stars and the renowned big bands that would come to perform or film a movie. Practices typically lasted only four hours, so the ballplayers spent quiet idyllic afternoons fishing, hunting, playing golf, horseback riding, watching movies, or dancing at the casino to big bands like the Benny Goodman Orchestra. But, as is universal among ballplayers, nothing caught their fancy more than a good old-fashioned prank.

Among the favorites was tricking rookies into thinking there was an animal native to the island called "snipe," which was a cross between a reindeer and a jackrabbit. Players would position the rookies in a gully and pledge to herd the snipe toward them, then go off for drinks while the rookies stood for hours in anticipation. Another popular pastime was placing all sorts of animal and sea life in players' uniforms or lockers. Pitcher Al Epperly opened his locker once and encountered a live stingray. Future Hall of Famer Gabby Hartnett was taking a salt bath in the clubhouse in 1937 when he discovered a live squid in his water. Ronald "Dutch" Reagan, future president of the United States, at the time a young radio broadcaster and sports columnist covering the Cubs in spring training, recorded the incident in the *Des Moines Dispatch*, noting that Hartnett let out a holler "when his unexpected tub mate (in the usual defensive gesture of his kind) surrounded himself and Gabby with a cloud of ink! What the best catcher in the business said then would stunt your growth."

The warm, unassuming hospitality of the town only added to the comfort level of players. Throughout those spring trainings, townspeople embraced ballplayers and coaches as part of the island community, inviting them on fishing and hunting expeditions, carting them around town, and occasionally even inviting them over for dinner. In kind, players bonded with locals. Generation after generation of young men donning the Cubs uniform, including nineteen eventual Hall of Famers, mingled with locals off the field.

They taught the local youth baseball fundamentals, donated worn-out equipment and uniforms, and occasionally treated them to ice cream. The high school kids worked out on the same field after the Cubs finished practices and many of the pros would stick around to give pointers. Cubs practices were often overflowing with kids who would watch the players in awe, retrieve foul balls, shag balls in the outfield, and play catch with their idols.

The overwhelming majority of islanders were endeared to the Cubs. The team eagerly cultivated this far-off pocket of Cubs faithful. Although there were no radio broadcasts of regular-season games on the island, the Catalina harbormaster kept residents informed of how their Cubbies were faring, raising a blue Cubs flag if the team won and a red flag if they lost. (This paralleled a long-standing Wrigley Field tradition, in which the team flies a white flag with a blue *W* over the ballpark after each win, and a blue flag with a white *L* after each loss.)

• ◆ •

The field that the Cubs used is now a multisport youth recreation area appropriately called Field of Dreams. The backstop is intact, but a fire station occupies leftfield. The eucalyptus trees that had bordered the rightfield line at the base of a hill have now overtaken the eroded grandstand. But the clubhouse where players dressed is still a living entity, a sports tavern overlooking the ravine and surrounding hills and golf course. There are photos of Cubs on the wall and a pictorial history of the team within its menu. It's here where the ghosts were rumored to come out and play.

Built in the Mediterranean style, like much of the island architecture, the former clubhouse is graced by elegant archways and columns decorated with florets; much like the rooftops along Waveland and Sheffield in Chicago, the outdoor courtyard affords a quality view of the ball field where the Cubs once played. Dusty Morand, the current Avalon town hall administrative assistant, owned the restaurant for two years in the early 1990s and still remembers a run-in with a spectral ballplayer as if it were yesterday. It was 11:30 one evening and he had already locked the gates and doors in the complex, after checking to make sure it was vacant. He was emptying the trash and put some objects outside and turned around and thought he saw someone. "It was a guy walking across the courtyard. And I looked and I went, 'Oh man, how the heck did you get in here?' And he was a tall thin guy with a baseball hat on. It looked like a grayish baseball uniform—old looking. All I could see was from a quick look. It was a little dark."

Morand thought the gentleman was walking toward the door to the dining office, where the Cubs locker room used to be. The figure was about halfway there when he put the trash barrel down, then turned and saw no one. It was late at night and he was thinking, "I gotta get this guy out of here."

Morand went over to look in the room. The door was locked, and he couldn't get in. He put his ear to the door and heard no noise whatsoever. And he swore to himself that he'd seen the figure walking right toward the door.

"After I walked over there, I went, 'Wait a second. This is impossible. He couldn't have taken two steps before I looked again. Even if he'd run.' That's when I felt the goose bumps run up my arm. Knowing the history of the building and the Cubs, I made the connection."

Morand had heard rumors that the building was haunted. One of his former busboys had refused to go near a narrow

L-shaped cement corridor in the restaurant basement that had served as a storage area for the restaurant. One evening the young man had gone into the "catacombs"—as the staff used to call it—and bolted upstairs shouting that he had seen a ghost. The young man's father had been equally petrified of the building. As a night watchman for the country club, he used to nap in the attic and claimed to have often witnessed mysterious lights and unidentifiable sounds from the clubhouse.

But for Morand, the clincher was the afternoon he strolled through the building with his sixteen-month-old son, Alex, in his arms. His tavern had shut down one year earlier to bring the building up to code after the Northridge earthquake. Morand was giving Robert and Anne Wlodarski, authors of *Haunted Catalina,* a tour of the building and its rumored haunted spots. His son Alex was chatty and playful and seemed to be enjoying himself, but suddenly froze and turned pale as the group passed into the kitchen, which had served as an additional locker area for the Cubs. As they left the room, Alex's cheerful countenance returned, but when Morand headed back into the kitchen with his guests in order to shoot some photos, Alex shrieked in horror and seemed to be staring at someone unseen in one corner of the room. The severity of the toddler's reactions made the group feel so uneasy that they hurriedly exited the building.

Morand has spent very little time pondering about the incidents, but says that other locals occasionally talk with him about it because reference to ghosts on the island is so normal. "I used to work in town at the casino. That had a lot of stories. A lot of buildings in town [have them]."

Given the Wrigley family legacy on the island, it's not surprising that there would be ghost lore attached to their favorite haunt. Shortly after settling on the island, William Wrigley built a lovely Georgian Colonial residence on a hilltop that he named for his wife. Mount Ada overlooked Avalon and the curve of the bay, and from his extravagant perch Wrigley was said to have enjoyed peering through a telescope at the Cubs' practices in the ravine below. Wrigley also hosted American presidents, foreign royalty, and, of course, quite a few baseball meetings at the mansion, including the 1926 annual convention of the National Association of Professional Leagues, at which commissioner Judge Kenesaw Mountain Landis gave the opening remarks.

The Wlodarskis wonder if the building, which is now a luxurious four-star inn, hasn't also played host to "residual energy." In *Haunted Catalina*, they mention mysterious shadows and "the ghostly apparition of a young woman who appears out of nowhere, looks at the guests in their bed, pauses, walks toward the closet, and vanishes."

● ◆ ●

No doubt the long association the building had with the Cubs made Morand's opportunity to run a business more special. When he first moved into the building, some of the original lockers were still intact. Morand recalls the thrill he felt when he first hung pictures of the Cubs in Catalina on the walls. "I've always been a Cubs fan. If you've grown up over here, you were. It's just part of the deal. People that owned the island owned the Cubs. So we always connected in some way."

Morand's close buddies on the island celebrate each other's fiftieth birthdays with a group road trip. When it was his turn, "they asked me where I want to go. I said, 'I gotta see Wrigley.' So they took me to Wrigley for a weekend. People from Chicago, when they found out we were from Catalina, treated us good. They're known to be friendly there anyway, but we got the supertreatment."

Ghosts or no ghosts, the island is brimming with memories and nostalgia about the Cubs era. Just as sure as the Brooklyn Dodgers left an indelible mark on Brooklyn, the Cubs have left stories to be handed down and built a reciprocal affection for the island that otherwise might never have happened. In the town barbershop, longtime barber Lolo Saldana joyfully shares with patrons his memories of playing with the Cubs. During his high school years, he played ball well enough to earn a tryout invitation from Charlie Grimm. Although he didn't win over the Cubs brass that day, he still got to wear the team insignia. Hack Wilson gave him a Cubs uniform that he still keeps in a box behind the barbershop's front door.

"We've got some pretty special memories," Saldana says. "I haven't witnessed any baseball ghosts myself, but I believe the stories and that it's possible. You never know who could be hanging around."

Chapter 9
Land of the
Rising Dead

American Tuffy Rhodes arrived in Japan's Nippon Professional Baseball League as another obscure player-for-hire. Over parts of five major league seasons in the United States, he had hit a meager .224 with eight home runs.

Then he found karma in the land of the rising sun, where Shinto priests bless bats, teams meditate under waterfalls, coaches pour rice wine on the pitcher's mound to ward off bad spirits and ballplayers bow to the diamond as they take the field. Rhodes ultimately would become the most prolific foreign-born home run hitter in Japanese baseball history.

The traditions and mindset of samurai-style baseball run counter to how most foreign imports learned ball in their homeland. Few adapt, and the rest last a season or two. Rhodes quickly learned the language and adopted the culture. He added bulk, developed plate discipline, and in his first three years hit .294 and averaged twenty-four home runs per season. In 1999 he broke out with forty home runs, leading the Pacific League. His monster year would be 2001 when he clouted fifty-five. It tied the Nippon Professional Baseball league record held by the Japanese baseball legend Sadaharu Oh, professional baseball's home run king and a living legend in Japan. (Oh slugged a whopping 868 four-baggers in his career.)

Early on, Rhodes started adhering to Japanese baseball superstitions. He rubbed salt on his bat to get a hit, wore magnetic wristbands, and hung Shinto amulets in his locker, all popular practices in Japanese baseball to "keep the spirits away" and catch good luck.

During the course of Rhodes's historic record-tying season, he added another trick to his trade. "I was with the Kintetsu Buffaloes," Rhodes recalls, "and we put salt on the dugout stairs and we put a little Buddha doll there also. It worked out well for me and for the whole team, so we kept doing the same thing."

The tradition of leaving salt at the entrance to a home or workplace is rooted in Japanese Shinto belief. And its meaning is broadly interpreted, from purifying to prospering, protecting to reversing bad fortune. Groundskeepers will often pour salt on the top dugout step to ward off evil spirits and reverse a team slump. Former Hiroshima Carp manager Marty Brown (now skippering the Rakuten Golden Eagles) says his Carp players "grab the salt and rub it on their body before they start to play. They say it brings good luck and helps them not to be injured."

Jeff Liefer, infielder with the Seibu Lions in 2006, alongside current Boston Red Sox pitcher Daisuke Matsuzaka, recalls his team using salt to open the season. "Last day of spring training camp, there's a big mound of salt that everybody went and got and threw on themselves and I guess that was maybe for health or something."

In 2002, after the Chiba Lotte Marines started the season 0-11, the grounds crew sprinkled salt on both the pitcher's mound and bullpen mounds. They told me, "Make sure you hit a little of that," longtime NPB reliever Brian Sikorski says.

For Rhodes, stories like this don't surprise him. Each team has their own traditions, and the superstitions vary among players.

"Ten years over here is a long time," Rhodes says, "and I've come to consider myself more of a Japanese baseball player than an American baseball player. We Americans have our own superstitions. But I think Japanese are more about using their spirits and stuff like that. Americans do the same things with bats and gloves that they use with their wrist magnets and the stuff hanging from their locker. We're superstitious in one way; they're more superstitious in another."

• ◆ •

And the Japanese way is often more mystical. Just ask the generations of high school ballplayers who describe a "monster force" called *mamono* on the hallowed playing field in Koshien Stadium.

If old Yankee Stadium was a cathedral, then Koshien Stadium is the Vatican. The venerable, ivy-covered baseball shrine is home to the country's second-oldest professional franchise, Hanshin Tigers, and the scene for the country's high school national baseball championships (called Koshien). The most-watched high school sporting event in the world, Koshien—and, in the last few decades, its invitation-only spring counterpart—has been producing national heroes since the inception of a schoolboy national tournament in 1915.

When the summer tournament begins the first week of August at the start of the nation's deeply spiritual O-Bon holidays, the Japanese archipelago grinds to a halt. On any given day, millions of television viewers enjoy seesaw contests with sayonara home runs, squeeze-play bunts, players sliding headfirst into first base even on sure outs, and losing players crying and scooping infield soil into plastic bags to carry off as keepsakes. More than 800,000 fans pass through the Koshien Stadium turnstile during the two-week event. And millions more watch the games live on national television.

The ballpark was built in 1924 to accommodate the masses of fans who traveled from all parts of the country to watch the high school tournament. In the park's early years, there were whispers of a ghost near the scoreboard, says freelance sports journalist and television commentator Masayuki Tamaki. The ghost was rumored to be a farmer who had worked on a rice field and dairy farm where the stadium now stands. One of her chores was to dump honey buckets of manure into a pit, and that's where she fell to her death.

The rumor long ago faded from public consciousness and was gradually replaced by a wider belief that the ballpark holds not so much human spirits, but spirit from the high school game, the essence of emotion or place. Historian Robert Whiting, who has authored the three definitive volumes on Japanese baseball, calls Koshien "a repository of high school baseball fighting spirit and a temple of purity. . . . It's like being in a church—that's the closest thing to it in the West."

And for those who prefer the brick-and-mortar, there's a modest Shinto shrine on the Koshien Stadium grounds where ballplayers, their family members, and fans go for prayer. The small compound features a Zen stone garden and a three-foot-tall stone baseball. According to popular legend, rubbing the stone will bring the Tigers good fortune.

There's also a gift shop that sells Hanshin Tiger *omamori* (amulets with Shinto-blessed prayers inside) and a section reserved for prayers. The heartfelt prayers, which are written on wood tablets called *ema* carved in the shape of a baseball or home plate are mostly for the success of high school squads.

And yet in the minds of Japanese high school ballplayers, there is an ominous, powerful force at work at Koshien that even prayer and ritual can't exorcise.

"Everyone knows about it," says former Hanshin ace Kei Igawa, who is currently in the New York Yankees farm system. "High school players believe there's a ghost on the field —or an unknown force."

"There's always something mystical and magical that happens [during the tournament] at Koshien Stadium," says outfielder Hideki Matsui, who describes Koshien as "a sanctuary for high school baseball." The superstar may have experienced it firsthand. "When I played there in the high school tournament, I was walked five consecutive times. That was unusual."

Although All-Star second baseman Masahiro Araki has never witnessed mamono, he says that the large audience for Koshien games can sometimes draw it out. "I don't believe in superstition," he says, "but it might be possible that something affects games at Koshien."

Veteran Hiroshima Carp catcher Yoshikazu Kura believes that mamono is dependent on what happens on the field. "At Koshien, all it takes is one little play to change for the negative the flow of the game. Players know that if you don't play the game right, if you make a mistake or do something wrong, that minor play will not be overlooked by the baseball gods."

The word *mamono* itself is enough to inspire fear in young ballplayers. Its literal meaning is "ghost" or "apparition." Outside of baseball, it is often used to describe something powerful and downright evil. For instance, Japanese authors will often use it to describe the devil himself or demons in hell.

Pitching legend Masanori Murakami believes the devil is in the details. Having played at Koshien and broadcast tournament games as an analyst for NHK network, Murakami feels that shifting winds create mamono. As the first Japanese ballplayer to play in the major leagues, he also pitched two seasons at Candlestick Park for the San Francisco Giants, another wind-blown feather in his cap. "Koshien is a large, open stadium," he says. "The wind swirls and the fly ball drops in and everybody says *mamono*."

A force that no one debates is the profundity of playing ball at Hiroshima Municipal Stadium. The former longtime home of the Hiroshima Toyo Carp was built at ground zero where a nuclear bomb detonated and 80,000 people died in an instant. The ballpark is across the street from the A-Bomb Dome skeleton and across Motoyasu River from Peace Memorial Park, with its Children's Peace Monument draped with paper cranes, peace towers, peace bells, stone lanterns, a peace fountain, and a burial mound holding the ashes of about 70,000 unidentified A-bomb victims.

Because of its location on the site of unimaginable suffering where block after block was eviscerated, the ballpark was long considered a symbol of the city's rebirth. The intimate, laidback atmosphere of the ballpark only enhanced the experience for the team's passionate fan base. For the generations of ballplayers who played in the stadium, however, it was hard not to think that they were standing at the epicenter of incredible tragedy. After the blast, nearby survivors, many suffering from scorched skin and dehydration, jumped into the Motoyasu River for a relative respite before death.

"A lot of players talk about ghosts along the river," says Makoto Kitoh, who pitched for eleven years with the Carp. "At sundown you see almost like a shadow of people sitting there. Because maybe that's how they died. In only a second and they didn't know they were dead. The spirits never went to the other side."

Kitoh says the ghosts never appear in the ballpark or harm the ballclub, but suggests that they have scared off development along the river. No matter what kind of company tries to open business there, nothing goes right. So it remains open field. It's the only place in Japan where you can buy land cheap."

The ghosts are not just confined to the river, says Carp catcher Yoshikazu Kura, but rather "Hiroshima City as a whole, because there are people who died here and whenever you die against your will there's a chance of you coming out as a ghost."

After learning he would play for the Carp in 1977, long-time baseball man Adrian "Smokey" Garrett was less leery of ghosts than of the reception he as an American might get from locals. "But it couldn't have been further from the truth," he says. "We were treated outstanding and nobody ever came up to us in anger because we were American and we dropped a bomb on them. The main thing I'd heard was if they'd have had it, they would have used it on us. They weren't happy that they lost a lot of life and the city was destroyed, but it ended the war. That was important for them."

Garrett made a lot of friends during his stay in Hiroshima, and he occasionally returns to visit them. He has never encountered a Hiroshima ghost, but was haunted at times about the ballpark location. "That was spooky—just the feeling that you have that something that devastating had happened right there where you're standing. It doesn't cross your mind much as you're playing the game and concentrating on the game, but it was always in the back of your mind."

Former Japanese league and major league starter Darrell May took time during his road-trip stays in Hiroshima to visit the Peace Museum. "Here in the States when you talk about the A-bomb there, it sounds horrific. But when you actually are there and see the photos and [artifacts] and learn what happened there, it's pretty gruesome," May says. As for the ballpark experience, "It's not eerie, just strange. You're absolutely aware of the history."

And for some Japanese ballplayers, that haunting history comes alive luridly. Around two o'clock in the morning one hot summer night in the mid-1980s, as Kitoh was returning to his Carp team dormitory bed after using the bathroom, he felt somebody tap his back. He turned and nobody was there. He got chills and dashed to his futon, dove in, and pulled the cotton duvet over his head. His feet were sticking out and he felt somebody kicking them. He peeked over the duvet and saw a beautiful woman in a kimono sitting bedside. The woman was at a small table and had a bottle of beer. She was trying to pour him a beer. There were only about six inches between the futon and the wall, and yet the woman was sitting right there; he knew it had to be a ghost. She was trying to talk to him and he couldn't hear anything that she was saying. Then, as she sipped from her beer, the A-bomb detonated and she vanished.

At the moment she was there, he wasn't scared, Kitoh recalls. "She was so beautiful I could have fallen in love with her."

Still, the following day he put out a Butsuzo statue (a small statue of Buddha) to keep the spirits away. And for the remainder of his stay in the dorm he slept with the lights on.

The following morning he told the old woman who takes care of the dorm what happened to him, and her comment was, "Oh, you saw that too, huh?"

Kitoh never saw the woman again, but a short while later he was sleeping on the same futon when a male spirit dragged him from under his duvet, then disappeared. Kitoh wonders if that was perhaps an ancient Samurai ghost. "In Hiroshima, they had a lot of war from the Samurai era," he says. "A lot of people committed suicide and a lot of people died."

Kitoh left the dormitory right after that second incident. "I moved into a guesthouse so I wouldn't have to deal with it."

Catcher Yoshikazu Kura had heard rumors from other players about the Carp dormitory ghosts, and understood that the dorm was old and built over a pond. (Many Japanese believe that water attracts ghosts.) But what spooked him most about the building was that in one of the rooms there's an *o-fuda* (a large talisman hung on the wall) placed there to ward off ghosts. "[My teammates] tell me, 'Don't ever touch that, and don't ever remove that.'" Kura hardly needed their counsel—the last thing he'd want to do is share quarters with a ghost.

◆

Professional baseball dormitories in Japan are reserved for younger athletes. Players drafted out of high school are required to stay five years, and can stay longer if they choose. Players drafted from college or the semi-pro industrial leagues must stay at the dorm at least one year. Future All-Star Yoshihisa Naruse fell into the five-year category, which was none too pleasing after he learned that his dormitory had a ghost.

The Chiba Lotte Marines dormitory is relatively modern (renovated in 1998) and is located on a pond near their minor league field in Saitama Prefecture. Before moving in, Naruse was told by teammates that ghosts appear very often at the dorm. He had heard it said further that ghosts are apt to show up near water. And sure enough, after letting him get settled for a few nights, the ghosts sailed in.

He was sound asleep in the middle of the night with his head facing away from the shore when he felt something behind him. He tried to turn but couldn't move his head. Then he broke out in a cold sweat. "I kept trying to move my face," he recalls, "and I don't know why I couldn't—whether I was just scared or something was immobilizing me."

In the weeks ahead, the dorm became even more frightening as more teammates had encounters. Naruse remembers, "One of my teammates was sleeping in the dorm when he heard someone knocking on the door of his room around 3 a.m. He opened the door and as he looked out, a girl's body-less face appeared right in front of his face."

Ghost stories and the Chiba Lotte Marines seem to go back a long way. Naruse played high school ball at Daisuke

Matsuzaka's alma mater in Yokohama. And that school's dormitory too may have been haunted. "I never wanted to be in the dorm by myself, because one of my teammates used to see ghosts. One evening when we were practicing at night, that same teammate ran away from a ghost all of a sudden, which made my teammates and me scared. It seems like the place around the dorm used to be a cemetery and the ghost he saw was an old Japanese military guy."

Marines teammate Shunichi Nemoto shared a similar story about a female ghost in his high school dorm cafeteria at Hanasaki Tokuharu high school in Saitama Prefecture. No bother to him or the ballclub—as team captain, he led his school to their first appearance ever at Koshien.

Former Marines manager Bobby Valentine says he heard none of the ghost stories from players during his two stints running the team—not even the Chiba dorm complaints. But he admits that may be due to the culture rather than players feeling embarrassed. "In Japan players don't usually open up about those kinds of things with managers," he says. He did hear about their superstitions, though. For instance, his All-Star outfielder Shoitsu Omatsu wore pink underwear for good luck. "I heard that you're not supposed to whistle at night here," adds Valentine. An old Japanese superstition holds that night whistling draws out deadly snakes.

Ichiro Suzuki never summoned slithery creatures, but he did accidentally make a high school teammate's skin crawl. In an interview with *Sankei News*, Aikodai Meiden High School baseball coach Takeshi Nakamura recalled practices running until 9 p.m. and Ichiro secretly continuing shadow swings by himself through the predawn hours. The wing of the team dorm where he practiced bordered a cemetery and there were rumors that the site was haunted.

Late one evening, one of Ichiro's teammates heard what he thought was a ghost coming from the wing and bravely headed down to investigate. As he turned a corner, Ichiro suddenly stuck his head out. His teammate's fear was short lived, but down the road, Ichiro's late night practices would help to instill fear of a different kind among pitchers on two continents.

Fortunately, too, fright nights didn't stunt Naruse's development as a pitcher. He made the big club by 2006 and the following year went 16-1 with a 1.88 ERA. It seems that all he had needed was a little bit of ghostly seasoning. For those players who spend restless nights in team dorms, road trips are not necessarily a vacation.

"In America a lot of ballplayers have haunted hotel stories," says former Seattle Mariners import Kenji Johjima. "In Japan, we have a lot of them too."

Wayne Graczyk, baseball columnist with the *Japan Times*, recalls many players sharing firsthand stories with him over the years about the Takezono Ashiya Hotel in Osaka. Former Yomiuri Giants teammates Shane Mack and Balvino Galvez told Graczyk that they awoke one evening because they felt a presence in the room. Other players have reported objects inexplicably moving and televisions randomly turning on and off. Graczyk says that "some players changed rooms or even hotels after the spooky experiences."

Former Yomiuri Giant Brian Sikorski remembers one of his teammates telling him that one floor of the Takezono Hotel was haunted. "But I didn't have anything happen. Maybe they were just messing around telling me that my room was right there and stuff."

"They said the fourth floor is supposed to be haunted," says Matt Winters, who played four seasons with the Nippon

Ham Fighters. "My teammates went up in the room and got cold and everything else and felt a presence in there and they booked out of there."

Three-time All-Star Takeshi Yamasaki of the Tohoku Rakuten Golden Eagles remembers staying at the Takezono when he was in the minors. "We stayed in the annex, and the annex had that ghost. A lot of people talk about the ghost we saw there."

Yamasaki theorizes that the Great Hanshin Earthquake in 1995, which killed more than 6,000 people in the area, may have created the ghost. "The old lady who worked at the Takezono had worked there for a long time," Yamasaki says. "She passed away because of the earthquake. Afterward, the old lady showed up and appeared in the hotel. I heard that she shows up on the fourth or fifth floor."

Veteran hurler Jeremy Powell, who played for several ball clubs in Japan, had heard that there was something strange about that hotel, but he never had any encounters.

Chunichi Dragons All-Star centerfielder Kazuhiro Wada has also heard the rumors. "I haven't seen [ghosts] there, but there was one instance in another hotel we stayed at that I had to change rooms because I felt so uncomfortable." Wada prefers not to mention the hotel by name, but says that it's in Nagoya and ballplayer reports of ghosts are common there. Wada says he himself didn't actually see the ghost, but just sensed something wrong. "I felt very uncomfortable," he explains. "I felt something was bothering me. And as I entered the room, I felt this pressure and then I decided I can't stay in this room."

When fleeing is not an option, there are preferred methods in Japan for keeping ghosts out of sight and out of mind. Players leave food offerings for the spirits or hang amulets on the wall. Orix Buffaloes reliever Daisuke Kato drapes a bath towel over room mirrors that face his bed. "Otherwise I feel wired," he says. "Back in the old days, Japanese used to have triple mirrors for females at each house, and the mirrors were always covered by a fabric when not in use. Because many people believe that a bad spirit comes if it's left uncovered."

•—◆—•

The most commonly told stories are about Okinawa, where American and Japanese soldiers squared off in one of the largest amphibious assaults of the Pacific Theater. During the eighty-two-day battle, the Japanese suffered more than 100,000 casualties and Americans lost more than 50,000 troops.

"In places like Okinawa where the [spring training] camps and hotels are located, there are players who have stronger feelings about spirits," outfielder Takeshi Yamasaki says. "They see people who died in the war. They don't feel comfortable."

Yamasaki cites former teammate, Chunichi Dragon ace Eiji Ochiai, who is often referred to by players as a prolific source of Japanese baseball ghost stories. "He has a sense about ghosts. Every time he goes to Hiroshima, he has headaches and he can't go to sleep. He has a hard time."

One day in Okinawa, Yamasaki asked Ochiai, "Do you really see such things?" Ochiai, who was looking toward a corner of the room, replied, "Yeah, right there! Right there!"

Retired Orix Buffaloes pitcher Shintaro Yamasaki shares a story about Ochiai receiving a phantom bullet. "Ochiai was walking down the street," Yamasaki says. "He felt a sharp pain and fell down. His teammate asked, 'What's wrong? What's wrong?' Ochiai said, 'I got shot by the military.'"

Yamasaki tells a similarly shocking story about a team road trip to Hiroshima. "Ochiai was on the bus headed to the stadium and Ochiai can't see the river next to the stadium. He can't see it because the water color is black, because of the atomic bomb detonation."

Former Dragons teammate Tyrone Woods mentions how Ochiai often used to see a ghost in the hotel lobby in Okinawa. "Ochiai would always tell people when you go to the elevator, 'Hey, you see the little boy? There's a little boy by the elevator!'"

Takeshi Yamasaki remembers the elevator stories clearly because Ochiai was a rookie and mentioned the boy as he first stepped into the hotel. "As I listened to his story, I got kind of scared because I can't see such things. But it's not really meant for me."

●◆●

The very first thing a Japanese ballplayer does as he sets foot on the field is bow. And the last move before leaving the diamond is to bow once more. Starting in the late nineteenth century, Japanese turned baseball into a formal martial art, and martial artists look upon their dojo as sacred.

"Bowing in baseball is the part of old Shinto tradition in Japanese sport," says Marty Kuehnert, senior advisor to the Rakuten Tohoku Golden Eagles. "Bowing occurs in almost any Japanese sporting arena. When you see a swim instructor come into a swim pool, they come in the door and bow. It's all from the tradition of showing respect."

"We do it at an early age," Kei Igawa says. "Taking off the cap and then bowing. Respect for the field."

"The field is sacred," veteran NPB-er Rick Short explains. "American players, we come over here, we chew sunflower seeds, we spit the shells out. That's not allowed here."

Hideki Matsui was shocked when he first came over to the States and saw that American ballplayers don't polish their gloves or, worse, leave their glove unattended on the dugout bench or on the field. In 2009 he told a reporter that occasionally he has to bite his tongue. "When I saw a player spit his chewing gum on the field, I was going to say, 'Hey, wait a minute. Do you know this is *the* Yankee Stadium?' I'm not sure how to explain it, but in Japan we've been told that courtesy and discipline are very important, like, 'Don't spit on the field,' or 'Don't sulk.'" Japanese players show tremendous respect for their equipment. They refer to them as tools, like a Japanese chef might refer to his set of knives.

Ichiro Suzuki famously stores his bats in a humidor. From an early age, his father taught him to take meticulous care of his bat and gloves. And in lectures to Japanese school children, Ichiro teaches young ballplayers that the equipment is an extension of the ballplayers' bodies. When he once slammed his bat down in frustration after making an out, he later felt so bad that he reportedly took the bat into his hotel room that night and slept with it. Ever since, he has not thrown his bat or banged it on the ground. As one prominent Japanese journalist noted, he puts down his equipment as if he's placing a newborn in a crib. Ichiro reportedly refuses to touch a teammate's bat, because he can feel the soul of the person who uses the bat.

Veteran major league outfielder So Taguchi agrees. When a teammate in the minors flung his bat into the outfield as a joke, Taguchi was so angered he wouldn't speak with him for a week. After he calmed down, he explained to the offender that a soul lives inside bats. When he holds his bat, his nerves extend to the tip of his bat. The same holds true with his glove. During an offensive slump, then–Hiroshima manager Marty Brown tried a common American managing technique called "wake up the bats." After a game, he grabbed the teams' bats and threw them onto the clubhouse floor and said, "Okay, let's wake the bats up!"—a lighthearted, fun way to loosen up players. "I did that here and everybody got really offended," Brown says. "It was a really big deal. Equipment at the major league level can be replaced, so it's not a big deal. But here they've been raised with the attitude that what they have to work with as far as equipment is very special to them. They were very silent, very stunned."

Brown sat down with the team afterward and explained that this is a difference between the two cultures. A team representative later said, "We understand what you did, just don't do it again, okay?"

Reverence is also shown toward baseball elders. After a popular Takamatsu Shogyo High School third baseman named Shima died before World War II, teammate and future Hall of Famer Shigeru Mizuhara helped start a pregame ritual. Teammates huddled at third base, took sips of water and poured the water from their mouths onto the bag. (In their eyes, they weren't spitting, but sharing water with a teammate.) "It was done as a sign of respect honoring what Tsuma had done," noted Japanese sports journalist Seijun Ninomiya explains. The tradition lasted over seventy years until the Japanese High School Baseball Federation deemed it a religious ceremony and banned it.

And yet spiritual rituals happen all the time on the diamond—most commonly when Japanese players pray to their ancestors. Boston Red Sox import Hideki Okajima grew up in Kyoto, the most traditional city in Japan, and attended a very strict Buddhist high school, all of which helped shape his approach to the game. "I do believe in many things about Shinto and they are very natural to me," he says. "When I come in the game and run to the mound, after taking my warm-up pitches, I go to the back of the mound and pray. I keep *omamori* all the time in my back pocket and wear *udewa nenju* [Shinto blessed beads on my wrist] before the game and I feel comfortable with that."

• ◆ •

Some Japanese baseball personalities have been nicknamed after supernatural entities. Ichiro Suzuki was referred to as the wizard, Matsui as Godzilla, Daisuke Matsuzaka as Monster of the Heisei Era, and Kazuhiro Sasaki as "Daimajin," a giant monster in Japanese films. Lesser known in American baseball, but highly popular in Japan, was the late Akira Ogi, labeled "magician."

A highly successful and wildly popular manager of the Kintetsu Buffaloes and Orix Buffaloes, Ogi was unconventional even by the more laidback standards of North American baseball. He was a hard drinker and womanizer and permitted the same of his players, as long as they sweated it off on the field the next day. When Seattle Mariners superstar Ichiro Suzuki first met Ogi in winter league ball in Hawaii, the coach was dressed in a white sports coat, white slacks, a white belt, white patent leather shoes, and gold-rimmed sunglasses. Ichiro thought that perhaps he was *yakuza*, a Japanese mobster.

And yet it would be Ogi, as manager of the Kintetsu Buffaloes, who would have perhaps the greatest influence on Ichiro as a ballplayer—advising him on everything from the shortening of his baseball name to "Ichiro" to his crossover to the major leagues. Ogi had even given Ichiro his first legitimate shot in the Japan League. Ichiro's prior manager had discouraged his unorthodox batting stance and repeatedly sent Ichiro down to the minors. Ogi thought that the stance was fine and inserted him confidently into his everyday lineup. Ogi similarly allowed pitcher Hideo Nomo to keep his trademark tornado-style delivery—when almost every other Japanese manager would have tried to make it more conventional—and was credited by numerous other Japanese baseball superstars with developing their careers. Players and fans alike referred to Ogi's track record with players and teams as "Ogi magic."

Orix Buffaloes reliever Daisuke Kato credits Ogi with teaching him how to perform day in and day out without getting injured. He also believes he benefited from Ogi's strong attention to details in how he pitched. "He warned me about flaws in my mechanics that most people don't care about or pay attention to," says Kato. "On the other hand, he always used to find something good in my performance and praise me on [it] even if my total performance was not good. I often remember his feedback and it carries me through, especially when I'm pitching in a clutch game.

"Whenever Ogi took actions, his magic was successful more than eighty percent of the time," adds Kato. "And even if he made a decision that led to a poor outcome, he made everyone think, 'Oh, Ogi must have had some kind of idea.' He used to make a point of ignoring data, for instance. When his team was at the plate at a crucial moment in a game, he intuitively sent in a pinch hitter whose average was only .100 instead of one who was batting .400. Then his intuition succeeded."

After Ogi passed in December 2005, the Buffaloes held a memorial service at Kobe Green Stadium attended by thousands of fans. Ogi's coffin was placed on home plate. On the eve of the service, Ichiro and another Japanese baseball superstar, Kazuhiro Kiyohara, went out drinking in Ogi's honor.

Notably spiritual—famously meditating under waterfalls at Zen temples during the offseasons to fortify his spirit and purify his soul—Kiyohara reached for Ogi magic one more time during spring training 2007. Suffering from torn ligaments in his left knee, Kiyohara uncorked a bottle of awamori (Okinawan rice liquor) that the late Ogi had given him ten years earlier and poured it on his kneecap. Performing the ritual in front of reporters, the slugger said afterwards, "I had Ogi cure my knee."

•◆•

Deep, profound respect for the magical in Japanese baseball even spills over into the business side of the game. Noted sports journalist Masayuki Tamaki explains the traditional Japanese belief in *kotodama*, the idea that the written word or the spoken word comes true. "The living spirit of the word," Tamaki says. "If you use a word that suggests bad outcomes, it becomes real."

When a high school senior is studying for university entrance exams, the student's family don't use words meaning "down"—for instance, the word *skiing*. Similarly, hotels and hospitals in Japan sometimes avoid use of the number four on room numbers. The number four in Japanese is pronounced *shi* in Japanese, which also means "death."

Jackie Robinson's coveted uniform No. 42 is rarely used by Japanese ballplayers, because the numbers four and two are read together as *shi ni*, which sounds phonetically similar to *shi nin*, which means "dead person." *Shi ni* can also be interpreted as "to death." Tamaki says, "Many Japanese people think inside very deeply that all these bad things come true."

Ballclubs often avoid contract language covering negative scenarios. Tamaki offers as an example the absence of injury clauses in the Japanese national team's World Baseball Classic contracts. "In a contract between player and team," he says, "teams don't want to write about negative outcomes—about losing."

And of course Japanese ballplayers have found a way to use word play to their advantage. At the start of every season, teams provide dinners with food considered to impart good luck on players. Kazuhiro Wada says that on opening day his former team, the Seibu Lions, provided bream fish (*tai*, a homophone for the Japanese word for "happy") and *sekihan* (a special occasion good luck dish made from sticky rice and azuki beans).

"I'll eat it at home too for good luck," Wada says. "We [players] all eat *katsu* udon. Katsu means to win—players eat it because they think they can win."

●◆●

NARUSE'S NINE LIVES

At the stadium, Yoshihisa Naruse protects himself from ghosts by carrying an amulet in his equipment bag. He also has cat ornaments in his locker given to him by fans. His nickname is Meow, because his delivery closely resembles the waving motion of Maneki Neko, a porcelain or ceramic welcoming cat found in many

Japanese shops and restaurants. He considers those gifts by fans as protective ornaments, because "he feels his fans' warm hearts."

• ◆ •

FINGER-DIPPING BAD

Twenty-five years ago, Hanshin won its first and only Japan Series, the Nippon Professional Baseball league's version of the World Series, and some fans wonder if Colonel Sanders will ever let them repeat.

Hours after the team clinched the NPB championship, delirious revelers gathered on the Ebisu Bridge in the heart of Osaka's entertainment district. They sang Hanshin player songs and for each Tiger, a fan resembling that player was pulled from the crowd, who then dove into the murky Dotonbori River donning that player's jersey. The crowd paused when they came to the team's biggest star, Randy Bass, a bearded power hitter from Oklahoma. Unable to find a lookalike, fans uprooted a statue of Colonel Sanders from a nearby KFC. The crowd slipped a jersey on him and tossed him in effigy into the water.

In typically polite Japanese fashion, the responsible fans apologized later that night to the restaurant manager and promised to retrieve the statue from the river. The following morning they searched the muddy riverbed high and low without any success. And so began an ongoing mystery that drew more attention with every losing Tigers season. The Tigers have finished in last place in the Central League standings on ten occasions since the Sanders dunking; they have finished second-to-last twice. And boisterous Hanshin fans started to wonder if, in fact, the Colonel's spirit was punishing the team for their mistreatment of a storefront statue.

Not that fans have learned their lesson. In 1993, on the evening the team clinched the pennant, Osaka police estimated that 5,300 fans jumped into the muddy, polluted waters, including one fan who drowned. Area KFCs were prepared for the worst and had already brought their storefront statues inside. Another year there had been a wild rumor among Tigers fans that another iconic statue would be plunged into the Dotonobori. Kuidaore Taro is a national icon, a life-size, mechanical drum-playing clown that had been a restaurant symbol and fixture in the Dotonobori district for decades. "Kuidaore" is an affectionate nickname for Osaka, which prides itself for its culinary uniqueness. The term literally means "ruining oneself by one's extravagance in food." Area business owners met and discussed security measures, including programming the robot so he could swim. In the end they opted for humor deflection, adorning him with a life preserver, goggles, and a sign reading I Cannot Swim.

It seemed that the Tiger fans' prayers were answered on March 11, 2009, when Colonel Sanders's torso was found by divers preparing for construction work in the canal. The next day, the statue's legs were recovered.

"He was apparently found standing upright, which is fitting because although he was a nice man, he could also be strict and demanding," said Sumeo

Yokakawa, a spokeswoman at the company's Tokyo headquarters.

As of this writing, the Colonel is still missing his left hand and his spectacles, probably removed before he was tossed in. And some Tigers fans wonder if the curse will continue until the Colonel is made whole for his damages.

•—◆—•

MONSTER OF A CURSE

When Boston acquired Daisuke Matsuzaka, both signer and signee were in a curse vacuum. Only two years after exorcising their eighty-six-year-old demons, Boston shelled out over $100 million on a player who until just the year before had been living under the shadow of the Daisuke no Noroi (Curse of Daisuke).

As a freshman at Yokohama High School, Matsuzaka was known for skipping practice. But by his junior year he had matured into a hard-throwing ace with a very sharp slider, curve, and changeup. The media dubbed him Heisei no Kaibutsu (Monster of the Heisei Era), a title Matsuzaka lived up to in brutal fashion when he threw a 250-pitch, seventeen-inning game in the Koshien Summer National Championship quarterfinal (after throwing 148 pitches in a complete-game shutout the day before), pitched in relief the following day, and spun a no-hitter in the finale. Matsuzaka's heroics catapulted him to super-stardom.

But what goes up in a hurry often comes down hard. Matsuzaka performed poorly over the next several years in important NPB games in the postseason and the Olympics. The popular sentiment was that one of the most clutch pitchers in recent memory in amateur ball was afflicted by Daisuke No Noroi. Fans also labeled him "Otoko no Gyaku Shiizun" (Opposite Season Man) because injuries often sidelined him during the regular season.

Five years of self-implosions and poor luck culminated in Game Two of the 2004 Japan Series. Matsuzaka had six runs of support, but was knocked out in the seventh inning in a game Seibu ultimately lost 11–6.

Redemption may have come through the titanium necklaces that he began habitually wearing on the mound when he pitched. Thought to improve circulation, flexibility, and the body's healing ability, the necklaces have been popular in Japan since the late 1990s and have more recently gained acceptance in North America. Japanese ballplayers began wearing them with the goal of protecting themselves during the long, grinding baseball season. And like so many other in-game rituals, the boundary has often blurred between usefulness and superstition. Former Orix Buffaloe outfielder Karim Garcia noted, "You see guys wearing the necklaces, different things on their hands, different things on their ankles, bracelets, whatever works for you. I've asked players about it, and I've asked players to give me some, too."

Daisuke Matsuzaka would later tell the *Boston Herald* that the necklace wards off evil spirits.

When Red Sox players sported titanium during their 2004 World Series season championship run, their neckwear and wristwear went relatively unnoticed. But the necklace dangled prominently that same year when Matsuzaka finally loosened the stranglehold of his own big-game losing streak.

In Game Six of the 2004 Japan Series, Matsuzaka held Chunichi to two runs and won. In Game Seven, he pitched in relief and helped Seibu win the Series. In the 2006 World Baseball Classic (WBC), he was a huge factor in Japan winning the championship, for which he earned MVP honors. In fans' minds, Opposite Season Man's curse was reversed.

• ◆ •

SOUTH KOREA—LORD OF THE FLY BALLS

In addition to playing ball in Japan, Tyrone Woods spent five years with the Doosan Bears in South Korea. During his time there, he would observe many rituals such as mounds of salt that he would later see in Japan. He also describes one Korean baseball superstition that few foreigners have witnessed:

"Before the season starts, [the Doosan Bears] like to get a pig head and skin it—it's like a clear pig head, no air, no nothing on it. They say that the pig always has to be smiling. They will go take that pig head and place it on a table at home plate. Then they serve rice wine. Each player has to drink a little bit, make a wish, and pour it over the field. And then [players] would pull money out of their pockets and put it in the pig's mouth or stick it in the pig's ear. The ritual is to pray for a championship."

● ◆ ●

TAIWAN—SPREADING THE GAME

Chengqing Lake Stadium in Gaoxiong County, Taiwan, was completed in 1999 and built over an unmanaged graveyard. Shortly after the Taiwan Major League franchise Gaoxiong Fala started using the ballpark and lost their first several home games, rumor spread that the venue was haunted. A Daoist psychic advised head coach Xu Shengin that the ballpark ghosts did not understand baseball. He suggested burning a baseball rule book so the ghosts would learn. The next day, the Fala fan association burned incense to worship the sky, the land, and the ghosts. At the same time, a rule book was burned. That day Fala won 12–2 against Taipei Gida at home.

Chapter 10
The Wild Frontier

Like many minor league parks, Frontier Field—the home of the Rochester Red Wings, Triple-A affiliate of the Minnesota Twins—is always looking for ways to generate some income in the off-season. In 2004 the park became home to Fear at Frontier, an annual Halloween celebration that runs several weeks in October. Makeshift haunted houses are erected in the stadium, and vendor booths are set up with food and games.

Minor league affiliates for the Orioles, Devil Rays, Cardinals, Phillies, and Yankees host similar October events, as do major league teams like the Rangers, Red Sox, and Royals. No one considered Frontier Field a truly *haunted* location, but to help promote the event, the team invited local ghost hunters to visit the park and check for wayward spirits.

To the club's surprise, the investigators claimed to find some. In fact, they found hundreds. "Basically these things were coming out of the woodwork," says J. Burkhart, the director of Rochester Paranormal. (The *J* is for Joe, but he uses the initial "just to give myself a little distinction.") Burkhart's group had already heard stories from fans that indicated something was up at Frontier Field. "People reported unusual activity," he says, "like feeling someone pushing them from behind, or hearing someone talking to them and turning around to find nobody there. Other times people said they actually saw the apparition of a woman or a man walking about." Burkhart himself had visited the park and taken a photo of the ticket booth in front of the stadium. "When I processed the picture later, there was what appeared to be a ghostly woman emerging from the glass."

But when Burkhart and his associates came in for a midnight investigation, they found more than one or two mischievous spirits. "We took a slew of photos and basically in quite a few of them, stuff came out. I think my favorite was the disembodied head that's floating out of one of the dugouts." A year later, the group returned to the field for an ESPN piece on the haunted park. This time they reported gaggles of ghosts in the stands.

Chuck Hinkel, the team's director of media relations, was there for the midnight stakeout. "We were standing in the outfield and the people from the paranormal group made their calling for the ghosts," he remembers. A big wind kicked in at just that moment, a synchronicity that some witnesses found eerie and the investigators found affirming. "At one time they said there were about 200 of them flying around us," Hinkel recalls.

Why so many? Most teams would like to attract the living as easily as the Red Wings are packing in the dead.

According to Burkhart, ghost crowds are nothing new. "There are places where you can find them concentrated," he says, citing examples like houses, wooded areas, and graveyards—and yes, even ballparks. "When people pass away, those things which they actually experienced the bulk of their life in, that's what they gravitate back to because that retains the strongest life memory."

•◆•

For many Rochester citizens, Red Wings baseball would certainly qualify as a "strong life memory." The city takes tremendous pride in its baseball heritage, which stretches back at least as far as the early nineteenth century, when a primitive form of the game was played on Mumford Meadow along the banks of the Genesee River. Professional baseball came to the Flower City in the late 1870s, and by the turn of the century a minor league team called the Bronchos was formed. The club took on the moniker Red Wings in 1928 and soon after started long affiliations with the St. Louis Cardinals, and then the Baltimore Orioles. In 2003, they signed on with the Twins.

To date, eight Hall of Famers and several hundred major leaguers have donned the Red Wings uniform. Over the years, the team has blossomed into one of the most storied franchises in minor league baseball, and has developed rich traditions and a loyal following, prompting *Baseball America* to name Rochester the best baseball city in the minor leagues in 1998.

Local residents have always supported the team. When Hall of Famer Red Schoendienst played his final game for the 1944 Red Wings before heading off to World War II, fans passed around a cap and collected nearly $500, which they presented to the young second baseman. The following decade, when the St. Louis Cardinals announced they were selling the Red Wings, fans from all over the city pitched in and collectively purchased the team.

If some of those departed stockholders are lingering here, maybe they can't resist Frontier Field, where the team moved in 1997. It is known as one of the more endearing smaller ballparks in the country. With the Art Deco Kodak building visible above the leftfield seats and freight trains passing behind the rightfield fence, the stadium captures an old-time feel in a modern facility.

Or maybe the wandering spirits are sticking around for the ballpark's concessions, which offer an impressive menu with local flavor. Among the highlights: Cheddar prime rib sandwich, turkey club crepe, chocolate-dipped cheesecake on a stick, and the ever-popular white hots, a Rochester variation on the frankfurter.

In recent years, the ballpark has hosted sleepovers, which can accommodate up to 1,500 tenters. Wide-eyed Cub Scouts file into the ballpark after the game with sleeping gear and flashlights. A video board shows cartoons, then the campers retire for an evening under the stars . . . and, in the view of some, a canopy of ghosts.

•◆•

It's also possible that some ballpark ghosts are holdovers from the previous tenant. Prior to housing Frontier Field, the plot of land on which the stadium sits was home to Alling & Cory, a distributor of paper and packaging products. Their building was said to be haunted by a janitor who died there. Legend also has it that when the park was built, construction crews unearthed some human remains at the site. Frontier Field itself has hosted two ceremonies in which the cremated ashes of baseball fans were spread on the field.

For Nick Sciarratta, the Red Wings director of corporate development, it makes sense that a ballpark would attract spirits. "There's all kinds of strange beings both earthly and otherwise that inhabit a baseball park in the course of the baseball season, times [twelve] seasons," he says, referring to the number of years Frontier Field has existed. "And then you have probably some carryover from the [previous stadium] that made its way over to here."

Sciarratta was not on the field when the group conducted its investigation, but he has seen pictures from Burkhart's team, which were posted on the Fear at Frontier Web site. "Very clearly there's something in some of those photos," he believes. "They are kind of convincing."

If nothing else, the publicity around the "haunted ballpark" has made some Red Wings employees jumpy. Kevin Johnston, the team's clubhouse manager, recalls that after the ESPN story aired—which was the first time he had heard anything about ghosts in the stadium—he was suddenly aware of stray noises when riding the freight elevator or walking alone through the locker room. One night, when the team got in late from a road trip and Johnston was laundering uniforms until 3 a.m. in the clubhouse, the nocturnal noises got his imagination going. "If there was a camera there, you might have seen me walking around with a baseball bat," he says with a smile.

Sciarratta can relate. He and his daughter and her friend were in the park one fall afternoon when they heard strange voices. "They were very scared and I was very scared because we were the only ones in the ballpark at the time," he remembers. The trio immediately thought of the now-famous Frontier Field ghosts. But when they cautiously investigated, they discovered a more benign culprit: Someone had left a radio on.

Gene Buonomo, on the other hand, never found a simple explanation for his spooky experience. Buonomo, the head groundskeeper at Frontier Field, was alone one morning in his office, a room just off the garage located behind the rightfield foul line. He heard a loud slamming noise that seemed to emanate from the area behind his office.

"So I came out, because I could have sworn somebody was there," Buonomo remembers. He walked around the concrete walls of his office to the space behind it, a small work area with cabinets, a sink, and a washing machine. No one was there. But he saw what he describes as a shadow—in this windowless and unlit environment—that seemed to recede into the locked door at the end of the work area.

Investigating further, Buonomo unlocked the door and entered the room, a small storage space filled with grounds-keeping supplies. Again, no one was there. He left the room, the door locking behind him. "I said, 'Well, it's my imagination,'" he recalls, though he still felt certain he had heard a loud noise and seen a bizarre shadow. Standing just outside the storage room door, he began straightening some items and making a pot of coffee, when noises emerged from the storage room. "It sounded like someone was going through the shelves or something," he says.

Buonomo again entered the locked room he had just exited and again found nobody. Now he was thoroughly scared. "I ran," he says, still jolted by the recollection. "I got out of there!"

Buonomo, who has been with the club since 1992, never experienced anything like that before and considers himself a skeptic for the most part. But he grew up in the neighborhood and vividly recalls a haunted house story from a nearby street (a father repeatedly tempted by a "little man" in the attic to jump out the window to his death) that he swears is true.

If he has any fears about being alone around the park at night, it's usually not about ghosts. "I'm more scared somebody is going to mug me," he says. "My father always said you gotta be more scared of the living than the dead."

Burkhart describes the area surrounding Frontier Field as "very violent," which he thinks explains why "some of the entities that I encountered there were violent.

"They basically get into your face," he says of the ballpark spirits. "They swoop up on you. You'll hear voices screaming at you. There's times when you can actually feel something taking a swing at you. They never connect with you, but your body goes on full alert for a brief second."

In this way, Burkhart says, the spirit world "is just like the world of the living. You have those that are loving and you have those that are filled with spite and hatred."

•◆•

Indeed, J. Burkhart has experienced both the affection and the scorn of the living world. His paranormal investigations have earned him a reputation in this upstate New York community.

"Basically, I'm Rochester's whack job," he says. His supernatural claims have made local headlines, and he sometimes pays a price. Two days after the Frontier Field story aired on ESPN, Burkhart was fired from his maintenance job. Other reasons were given, but he feels certain the paranormal publicity was the motivation.

Nearly a year later, Burkhart was still looking for a job. "I've been trying like hell to find work. Nobody wants to hire the freak that certified Frontier Field and was on ESPN. It's like I'm being punished."

In fact, Burkhart notes that while his efforts have helped Frontier Field promote its annual Halloween festivities, he hasn't seen a cent from it. That applies to all his supernatural investigations. "I've never made money off doing this, ever. Everybody else makes money off me doing it for them."

Now in his mid-forties, Burkhart has felt connected to the paranormal all his life. "I attract the stuff. It's almost like you're selected; it's like a door in your mind has been

opened and you can never close it. Things come to me. Sometimes I'll see them. Sometimes I'll sense them. Sometimes I'll
just kind of get an image in my mind. When I was younger
it used to intimidate the living hell out of me."

Burkhart found few established avenues to pursue his
interest in the supernatural, so he started his own stud-
ies, while paying the rent with stints as a bounty hunter
and private detective. He took on the name Lord Archaeus
(reflecting his belief that supernatural events are rooted in
"the molecular cohesion of subatomic elements"), which he
still uses professionally today. He founded Rochester Paranormal in 1986 and maintains the group's very active Web
site, with regular updates on new finds, strange sightings,
and ongoing investigations.

The *SportsCenter* feature was the group's biggest media
coup and generated a lot of feedback and attention. "We
were immensely proud to be the first team of freaks that
actually were shown an interest by ESPN," says Burkhart
with a chuckle.

He acknowledges that "there are a lot of quacks out
there" in the paranormal community, charlatans trying to
make a name for themselves. But, he adds, "There's a lot of
weirdness in this world. There's a lot of unexplained stuff.

"We're kind of an unusual paranormal group. Our intention is not to cram down people's throats what we think is
real. We just report the facts as we know them and let the
public decide for itself."

• ◆ •

Gene Buonomo, still riled by the odd noises in the storage room, has decided for himself. "I believe there is something," he says. "Definitely *something*." Chuck Hinkel says

that all the publicity "was good exposure for our organization," but adds, "I personally don't believe in it."

Don Barone, who produced the piece for ESPN, had fun with the story and was impressed by the coincidence of the large gust of wind that kicked up when Burkhart summoned the spirits. But did he come out of the experience a believer? "I came out believing that people who want to believe, believe," he says. "I didn't experience anything."

Very few players have either. Of the few who know anything about ghosts at Frontier Field, utilityman Tommy Watkins is typical. "I heard this field is haunted," he says. Did he have a strange experience? Hear stories from other players? Catch wind of an odd encounter from locals or stadium personnel? "I saw it on *SportsCenter*," he explains.

Outfielder Michael Ryan, a former Red Wings player now in the Marlins organization, also learned about the alleged ghosts from the ESPN report. But once he did, he reevaluated his playing days there. "There were times when we got back on the bus late from a road trip—like three in the morning. Walking from the clubhouse to our cars you could hear things being slammed, like doors and stuff." He wonders now if it might have been ghosts.

Even without firsthand player testimonials, though, it is easy to imagine the story of Frontier Field ghosts spreading in clubhouses, and growing along the way. Ryan says that when he saw the *SportsCenter* feature, "I was surprised. I didn't know it was an old graveyard, the field." He pauses. "I think that's what they were saying."

In fact, nothing of the kind was said in the segment. But stories, like ghosts, have a life of their own.

Chapter 11

Mickey on
the Mantel

For some players, baseball memorabilia is a means for achieving a kind of immortality: As long as people collect their cards, photos, autographs, and other items, their names are remembered and their legacy continues. And indeed, the market for sought-after baseball collectibles is always strong. Recent years have seen phenomenal bids for items like Roger Maris's 1961 batting helmet ($40,000), Joe DiMaggio's 1947 MVP Award ($281,750), and Shoeless Joe Jackson's "Black Betsy" bat ($577,610). In 2007, an anonymous Southern California bidder paid $2.35 million for the Holy Grail of baseball memorabilia: a Honus Wagner T-206 baseball card circa 1909, one of fewer than sixty known to exist.

But for every high-stakes bidder, there are millions of everyday fans like Ben Blake who collect just for the fun of it, to create another connection to the game they love and to their baseball heroes of the past. Like many memorabilia enthusiasts, Blake started by collecting cards as a kid. He'd clip them to his bicycle spokes to create that motorcycle sound, trade with friends, bundle them in rubber bands, and store them in shoeboxes. He took a break from the hobby when he went to college and joined the service, but resumed his passion in the late 1980s.

Today, in his late 40s, he estimates he owns half a million baseball cards. "It's like an addiction," he says. The cards and other objects—signed balls, bats, pennants, figurines, as well as memorabilia from other sports and hobbies—fill a small den in Blake's home in Rapid City, South Dakota.

As an adult, Blake became more selective about his purchases. "I kind of moved away from the packets and saved up a little bit of money and bought one or two choice items, like the Babe Ruth cards," he says.

The "Babe Ruth cards" is an uncut sheet of nine different cards, with the Babe in various poses. Printed in the 1920s, Blake picked it up at a small town auction for $50—a steal, since he estimates it is worth about $300. When he got home and hung the sheet on his den wall, he quickly noticed something odd about it.

"You'd go in there and it was almost like you'd catch something in the corner of your eye. I wouldn't see a ghost, but it was like a presence. It was so weird and it just drew me to that picture. I'd look at it and it was almost like, in some of the photos, the eyes followed you. Turn to the left, they'd be looking at you. Turn to the right, they'd be looking at you."

Then the picture itself would move. "I'd come in and it would be tilted. I had it mounted on picture wire with two nails in the back. How does that tilt? It moved more than three inches." Blake quizzed his wife and daughter—had they been in the room, slammed a door, done anything that might account for the picture's movement? They said they had not.

The picture's eerie feeling and odd movements continued for years ("It was just something that I learned to live with"), but things got livelier when Blake added two signed baseballs to his collection. The first was a 1958 Yankees ball, bearing twenty-eight signatures, including both Mickey Mantle and Yogi Berra on the sweet spot. Blake put the ball in a Plexiglas case and displayed it on a shelf in his den.

He left for a few months on a military assignment in Cuba. During his absence, nobody entered the sports room; in fact, when he returned, it was as if the door had been "nailed shut." But the '58 Yankees ball was gone from the shelf. It was lying on the floor, its Plexiglas case in pieces around it.

Looking at it closely, something seemed different. "The Berra signature didn't look right. Before, the Mantle signature was dark and the Berra signature was just lighter. Now you could barely see the Berra signature at all. You can still see the impression because it's an old leather ball. But it's very faint."

Blake could not imagine what had happened. What could knock the display case off the shelf? What could cause the Berra signature to fade while the Mantle signature stayed visible? He bought a new case for the ball and returned it to the shelf, but the eerie feelings were starting to grow in the sports room. "I didn't even want to go in there," he recalls.

• ◆ •

Two years later, Blake picked up another prized piece, an authenticated ball with signatures from Sandy Koufax and Mickey Mantle. He gave the ball its own Plexiglas case, and set it next to the '58 Yankees ball on a shelf in the sports room.

An hour later, the family's dinner was interrupted by the sound of a large crash. Blake raced to the room to discover that the entire shelf—which had stood for years—had collapsed. The L-shaped brackets that held it were completely folded down, and the shelf's contents were strewn across the floor.

Blake tried to keep his imagination in check. "Maybe that was the ball that broke the camel's back," he reasoned. As unlikely as it seemed, perhaps the weight of that one small item somehow was too much for a shelf that had borne an entire set of encyclopedias for years, without so much as bending.

He rebuilt the shelf that night, with new twelve-inch brackets, and reassembled the memorabilia and decorations. He put the two balls next to each other, and then headed off to bed.

The normally sound sleeper "tossed and turned all night long," Blake recalls. He took sleeping pills at 11 p.m., but they didn't help much. At 4 a.m., he was not only awake but was also feeling somehow drawn to the sports room, with a kind of eerie apprehension. He made his way to the room, opened the door, and was shocked at what he saw.

"It's like a poltergeist has been there. The '58 team ball is hanging off the edge of the shelf. The new ball is further down the shelf, also hanging over the edge. I had put them next to each other, but now they are about a foot apart, with something else between them. It was like something had picked it up and moved it. I know damn good and well I wasn't the one who put it there."

As if not to be outdone, the Bambino got in on the action too. "The Babe Ruth sheet was upside down on the wall," Blake says.

In addition, the Koufax ball, which had been displayed with the pitcher's signature facing out, had turned so that Mantle's signature was now front and center. Another ball, signed by Astros pitcher Roy Oswalt, which had been stored in a closed box with other memorabilia under the desk, was now lying in the middle of the floor. "I don't know how that got there," Blake says.

Blake again quizzed his wife and young daughter, but neither had been anywhere near the room. Could the family cat have snuck in and disrupted the shelf? "The door was closed and it's got one of those old-time locks you have to turn and then push," Blake explains. "Besides, we have three cats and none of them will go near that room." (The cats also react to the card collection. "They will bite your hand and run away" if you come at them with the cards, says Blake.)

Blake was, to say the least, thoroughly spooked by the situation. He was hesitant about even entering the room for a while. "It was like a cold feeling. I wasn't afraid to go in there, but I was cautious. You look behind yourself. I would peek in first. I would see if there was a mop hung on the wall that was going to swing down and hit me or something."

But he handled the situation like a manager presiding over a team whose players don't get along. "I thought, 'All right guys, we gotta talk. We gotta rearrange things here.' I separated them. I put Ruth on one wall. I've got Mickey on a shelf on another wall. I've got Mickey and Koufax on another shelf on another wall. I've got them separated now."

Giving these baseball greats their own space in the sports room seems to have done the trick—all has been quiet in the Blake collection since then. But what conclusions does Ben draw about what was going on?

"I go to church. I'm not, like, a person that likes *The X-Files*. But I believe in ghosts, I really do. I'm open-minded." He jokes that being out of the military has made a difference. "These are things I would never say if I had to re-up my security clearance!" he laughs.

He notes that his rural house, which has a view of Mount Rushmore, is on Native-American ground, and may have a spiritual history of its own. "I know for a fact there is a lady who died and she had her ashes scattered back there on the next parcel, and some of them blew over onto our land." Blake plans to have a medium visit the house soon, to see if he detects any presences.

But for the most part, he's comfortable now that Ruth, Mantle, and the others are getting along. "If we live in a haunted house, it hasn't affected me. I don't think it's a malevolent presence or anything." Just a baseball fan with a definite decorating point of view.

Chapter 12
Viva La Fantasma!

Latin-American ballplayers have always had a reputation for leaning heavily on superstition. Some of it has been borne out of caricatures like Pedro Cerrano, the voodoo-practicing Cuban refugee ballplayer in the movie *Major League,* and some from the noteworthy rituals of a handful of players, such as Panamanian Julio Zuleta, who blessed the bats of his Cubs teammates with an assortment of fruit in 2001, seemingly halting an eight-game skid and sparking a twelve-game winning streak. In 1978 the Dominican outfielder Rico Carty burned five roman candles in his hotel bath tub, toilet tank, and sink in the hopes of getting five hits in that evening's game. The following year, fellow Dominican reliever Pedro Borbon reportedly placed a decade-long curse on the Cincinnati Reds following his release from the team. And Puerto Rican shortstop Julio Gotay was reportedly so fearful of crosses, he twice refused to field throws to second from catcher Elrod Hendricks because someone on the opposing team had strategically fashioned a crucifix with chicken bones near the second base bag.

In general, Latin player superstitions are more noticeable because of an often very open spirituality—for instance, making the sign of the cross before stepping to the plate or pointing to the heavens after a hit. Most Latin-born players grew up in poverty, and some credit religion or spiritual forces for helping them to escape.

Several current Latin stars of the game carry talismans in their back pockets or consult spiritualists in their home countries. (Of course, in just about any big-league clubhouse there are naysayers. Pedro Martinez, Omar Vizquel, and Ivan Rodriguez all say they don't heed superstition.)

There is also a vast body of superstition that swirls around winter-league ball. Atlanta Braves manager Bobby Cox saw his share when he played and coached in Latin America in the 1960s and 1970s. "There's voodoo every-where—Venezuela, the Dominican, absolutely," he says. "They believe in that too—I mean current players."

The most infamous tales migrate north from Mexico.

"A lot of people in Mexico—and I've seen it firsthand—believe in witchcraft," former major leaguer Karim Garcia says. The Mexican-born outfielder says that the owner of one of the Mexican League teams he played for, which he prefers not to name, was called a witch lady. His teammates would regularly go to witch doctors and "cleanse themselves" and the team often brought "somebody in the clubhouse that comes and reads your hand or rubs your feet and tells you about your life."

"That kind of thing happens and they are right," Garcia says. "I had one person when I was on the team that came and stared over my fist and told me about my life and I was like, 'How the hell does she know?'"

Mexican players call it Magia Blanca (White Magic). And Garcia says its intent is harmless. "Tell your future and stuff like that," he says. "A lot of guys in baseball still believe in that stuff."

And just like in the States, a lot of ballplayers in the Mexican league are wary of hotel ghosts.

"You gotta overlook a lot when you're playing in Mex-ico," former Phillies outfielder Glenn Murray says. "The hotels in Cancun and Monterrey are good. But those away from the large cities or tourist areas, forget it. Just a mattress and a box spring. Then you gotta deal with bugs and sometimes the AC won't work. And El Rancho in Navojoa is the worst hotel ever. The town is awful. It's in the middle of the desert. For entertainment, locals ride around in circles. The hotel is a cave. You could shut your door and shut your shade and go to sleep and never know it's morning. One night as I was lying in bed about ready to shut off the lamp, I looked up and a scorpion was on the wall above my head."

The scorpions were nothing compared to the rumored ghosts.

"The stories of El Rancho are legendary," retired third baseman Jeff Cirillo says. "That place is definitely haunted."

Mexican-born utility player Benji Gil also heard the rumors often during his seven years in the league, but had to experience it himself to believe it. "The room had window shutters, and one day it was really windy and all of a sudden the shutters just started snapping open. I had latched them and I don't care how strong the wind is, it's not going to pull that latch open. After that, we got together and convinced the team to actually put us up in another hotel."

"You hear a lot of weird noises that you never hear anywhere else," pitcher Scott Chiasson says. "Just like, the AC makes weird noises. The shower got on once, and we didn't know how it got on. I came home and it was on. The TV would click on. Just a lot of weird stuff.

"Rumor is something happened at a hotel connected to it," he adds. "Some guy killed two people during a wedding or something."

Phillies outfielder Matt Stairs, who played six seasons for the Mayos de Navojoa, had heard that a local bar owner's son was murdered outside the hotel. "People say the son was coming back to haunt people," he says. "You hear a lot of different stories. A lot of it is just stories and I don't know if guys are drinking a little bit too much or too much sauce or what it is when it happens."

The ballclub takes its name from the Mayo Indians who settled on the Gulf of California Plain in the 1700s. They took up agriculture, fishing, and artisanship. And while holding on to their traditional culture even after Spaniards settled into the area, they ultimately fell head-over-heels for baseball. The team was founded in 1959 and purchased by its current owner Victor Cuevas in 1987. Cuevas later told *Sports Illustrated* that he wanted to make sure professional baseball stayed in Navojoa because "the people need it. They have two things here: religion and baseball."

Los Angeles Dodgers screwballing icon Fernando Valenzuela was born and raised on the outskirts of the small, agro-industrial city. A promising nineteen-year-old speedster named Rickey Henderson earned the respect of the locals, helping the squad to its first championship in thirty years. They were also charmed by his late-night hunting for hare. In the late 1990s, Stairs became a local hero because of his charitable work with impoverished children in the city's sprawling slums. By age twenty-seven, he became part-owner of the team and the following season he served briefly as manager.

Murray, himself, enjoyed the local hospitality. But he would just as soon not have heard the local ghost stories. "They always said the back side of the hotel was haunted, which has the bigger rooms for families. The back side also has a nightclub that is loaded with stories, and they say something happened in the club and there are still ghosts in there."

Three-quarters of the home team's players and usually the visiting team roomed at the hotel. And according to Murray, there was nothing to do in town except visit the night club if they were home on a Friday evening. Late in the 1993-94 winter season, Murray was at the club with teammates Tyrone Horn, Derek White, Troy Rikers, Joey Eichman, Tavo Alvarez, Hector Alvarez, and Hector's wife. They were all on the dance floor when Hector's wife suddenly fainted. As the players nervously waited for paramedics, the music stopped abruptly and the room lights started blinking. "And there was no DJ or worker controlling the lights," Murray says. "For me, it was like, 'We're in Mexico. It just happens.' But you could see everyone else was scared. So we cleared out of there as fast as we could."

Stairs recalls a similar incident at the hotel bar's grand opening a few years earlier. "People came running out of the hotel bar" thinking it was the ghost of the owner's son.

Murray notes that even before this incident, DJs were afraid to play at the club. "The more you heard the locals talk about it, the more you thought something was there. You wouldn't see a lot of town locals coming there. Maybe only fans and ball teams."

"My birthday was around the time the bar incident happened," he adds. "And I'm like, 'Ah, I'm ready to go home.' I stayed for another month and during that time they never had another function in the club. They usually did every Friday and Saturday. They were scared of it."

Former Milwaukee Brewer Angel Miranda had heard rumors about the ghosts of Pancho Villa's soldiers underneath his hotel when he played for Algodoneros de Union Laguna (now Vaqueros Laguna) in Torreon. Local legend was that the hotel was built over the ruins of a residence of

the legendary Mexican Revolutionary general. Villa had con-
quered Torreon in 1910 and waged three more battles for the
city over the next few years. "They hear a lot of horses in a
tunnel underneath the hotel and see blood," Miranda says.
"I never went in the tunnel, but that's what they say when
I stay down there."

• ◆ •

Angel Miranda hails from Puerto Rico, where a ghost is
thought to court local ballplayers, a phantom Baseball
Annie whom players encounter during the drive to Isidoro
Garcia Baseball Stadium in Mayaguez. She's spotted hitch-
hiking in the resort town of Guatajaca Beach and is said
to be stunningly beautiful. "I hear a lot of people talking
about it," Miranda says. "I don't know how they see her.
They're scared, they're scared!"

Miranda recalls the story of one player who stopped to
pick her up. He gave her a lift to her parents' home, where
she said she would run in and get some money to go out. She
entered the house, but never returned. The driver exited his
car and shouted, "Is somebody there?" An old woman came
out of the house and over to the car. The driver asked, "The
girl who went into the house, is she coming back?" The old
woman said, "Okay, I know what you're talking about. This
isn't the first time this has happened. She's an evil spirit."

"All the players from all teams in Puerto Rico take that
road when we play in Mayaguez," says Miranda. "We drive by
that spot. It's right by the water, by the beach. It's beautiful. At the same time, at night it's very dark. I know a lot of
the stories from players, so if I see somebody there, no way
am I going to stop. I'll go real quick, because she will come
after you. The place is scary."

Most Boricua ballplayers familiar with the stories echo Miranda's fear, although some tell different versions. "There's a few of them," former utility player Felipe Crespo says. "A recent one has somebody crying and she is sitting on top of the bridge wearing a white dress. I never encountered that. But I know recently they had a girl who died in a car crash on that main road to Mayaguez."

"I heard that one, but thankfully it's not the road I use," pitcher Jose Santiago says. "I go all the way from my home to Mayaguez by highway."

Woody Huyke had heard the stories four decades ago when he was a player. "You're driving, you see a woman, and stop. The woman gets in your car and is talking to you, and all of a sudden she disappears. I know that people are very afraid of that road. People won't take a chance."

The stories are reminiscent of local Taino folklore about *maboya*, a nocturnal, evil spirit that eternally wanders the jungle or beaches in search of spirits to prey on. In San Pedro de Macoris, the famous baseball-crazed city in the Dominican Republic, there are parallel legends about shape-shifting demons and a phantom woman who flags rides from unsuspecting taxi drivers. (The stories are shared in detail by pitcher Miguel Batista in *Haunted Baseball*.)

"There are a lot of similar tales in Puerto Rico," Huyke says. He recalls a Puerto Rican pitcher from the Yankees system in the 1960s, James Horsford Gillman, who routinely put water in his closet for the spirits. He swore by that, Huyke says. "I've seen players and coaches still do that. Not necessarily the newer generation but the older one ahead of this one."

Huyke recalls a lot of "weird stuff" as a child growing up on the island. A good friend of his father, who used to play ball with the both of them, would point out rabbits at night and say they were spirits. Huyke says the island is deeply rooted in different spiritual traditions, with voodoo and Santeria widely practiced in the localities neighboring Carolina, Roberto Clemente's home town, and witchcraft famously practiced in the town of Guayama.

Legend has it that Guayama's nickname Pueblo de Brujos (City of Witches) grew out of the locals' deep affection for early-twentieth-century hometown pitcher Marcelino Blondo, who was better known as Moncho el Brujo (Moncho the Witch) because his father was a medicine man. Local historian Adolfo Porrata-Doria argues that the town name instead derives from a local tradition starting in the 1920s, where fans brought to the ballpark lit candles and pointy leaves of a native bushy plant commonly known as *brujo*. Fans strung the leaves from posts and wires with the intent of spooking the visiting team's players into believing that the leaves would curse them and bless the home team. According to Porrata-Doria, it was all in good fun, but the visiting team assumed that fans had magical powers.

Similar pseudo-voodoo still occurs in Latino baseball-loving regions such as Cuba, where fans have been known to burn life-size effigies of a visiting team's players or manager, and on the Atlantic Coast in Nicaragua, where fans good-naturedly hold processions replete with coffins, toads, and candles to cast mock hexes on the local team's opponents.

Guayama fans' magic spell may have carried over to Los Brujos (Witches) of the late 1930s, which won back-to-back Puerto Rican winter league championships in the league's inaugural two seasons. The immortal Satchel Paige led the local nine to the second title and to that year's ERA title, all the more impressive given that the fireballer was spooked by the city's supernatural reputation. Paige was notoriously superstitious to begin with, and according to Porrata-Doria in his book *Guayama: Sus Hombres Y Sus Instituciones*, he was known to practice various rituals, including bathing with aromatic leaves and receiving massages "designed to ward off evil spirits." One afternoon he was spinning a no-hitter through five innings at home when an opposing Ponce batter approached him and, perhaps to unnerve Paige, said that he saw the ghost of Moncho el Brujo standing near the pitcher's mound as Satchel was pitching.

"Paige was struck silent; he couldn't utter a word or make a move," Porrata-Doria writes. "He headed toward the locker room, showered, got dressed and went home. No one could change his mind. He gave no explanation. He only said he did not want to continue playing."

• ◆ •

More than six decades old and often overshadowed by winter ball in other countries, the Venezuelan Professional Baseball League has more recently become the preferred winter league for some major league organizations. Over the years, the league has exported exceptional talent to the majors, including the likes of Luis Aparicio, Dave Concepcion, Ozzie Guillen, and Andres Galarraga, but in the last two decades the number of Venezuelan stars making headlines in North America has increased tremendously—Francisco Rodriguez, Omar Vizquel, Johan Santana, and Miguel Cabrera, just to name a few.

As for how superstitious those ballplayers are, it depends who you ask.

"I think our superstitions are the same ones you see in the States," says Seattle Mariners outfielder Franklin

Gutierrez. "A lot of players have necklaces, a lot of things they think are gonna help them play. But it depends on you personally."

Longtime backstop and coach Randy Knorr, who played four seasons with the Cardenales de Lara, says all of Venezuela is swarming with superstition. "I believe the whole country is haunted," he says. "They believe in spirits and ghosts more than Americans do. So they talk about it all the time. You hear more about it down there than in the States. I've talked to ballplayers—when I told them about my own ghost encounter, they said, 'Oh yeah, somebody dies, they're always around and they're always behind you and some days you can feel them.'"

Knorr had his run-in at the Hotel Principe in Barquisimeto. Two days after Knorr arrived in town, the Cardenales went on a four-day road trip. He returned to his fifth-floor room to find that all the clothes he had unpacked were folded and back in his hockey bag, which was sitting by the door. He went down to the front desk and said, "Hey, listen, tell the maids that I'm going to be there for a while. Don't pack my stuff." The clerk smiled and said, "Okay." Following the next road trip, he returned to his room and his belongings were packed again. He went downstairs again and said in broken Spanish, "Hey man, come on. Don't do that. Stop packing up my stuff." The clerk called the maid over. "Are you packing up his stuff?" "No." She told the clerk that when she was cleaning his room, she had noticed that his bags were already packed and thought he was checking out. Soon after, his wife visited and they were asleep when Knorr suddenly felt somebody sitting on the end of the bed. He'd had a couple of drinks and was groggy, but was alert enough to see a gentleman by his feet. "He's got these coveralls like a mechanic would wear. So I'm shaking. And my wife goes, 'What are you doing?' 'There's someone on my bed!' And she goes, 'Shut up and go to sleep. You've had too much to drink.'"

As they were speaking, the image faded away.

Knorr headed downstairs in the morning and said to the front desk clerk, "What's going on in my room?"

"I don't understand."

"I swear there was somebody in my room last night."

"Oh, it's your imagination."

Over breakfast in the hotel restaurant, Knorr shared his story with teammates. Knorr recalls, "One of the waiters who spoke English came over and asks me what floor I'm on and in what building. 'Are you in 501?' And I said, 'Yeah, I'm in 501.' And he said, 'That's bad.'"

The waiter told him that years earlier, a mechanic had killed his wife and her lover and then shot himself in the room.

"So I guess maybe whatever is in there is still in there," Knorr says. "Sometimes my toiletry bag would be packed. I woke up the next morning and it had my stuff zipped up and just standing there. So whoever that person was, he must have been a neat freak."

Braves manager Bobby Cox, who managed the Cardenales de Lara in the mid-1970s, had bigger problems to worry about than Felix Unger–esque ghosts. Members of his team "would drive home at night—we'd take the bus—I had native Venezuelan ballplayers that would swear up and down they'd seen a spaceship. The sky was wide open there—completely black."

Not that the team bus was immune from the mystical. "On road trips we would often drive by one of these blessing areas in the mountains," Cox says. "The bus had to stop before we proceeded any further. It was a shrine with a waterfall behind it, because so many people were killed up in there—car wrecks. So that was a tradition. The bus would not go another inch until we did that."

Asked if it was out of respect for the dead or out of fear, he replied, "Fear, I think. Then respect. Fear first, respect second."

Chapter 13

Crazy '08

Anybody can have a bad century.
—CHICAGO CUBS ANNOUNCER JACK BRICKHOUSE

Chicago Cubs fandom is all about delayed gratification. The team has not won a World Series since 1908. Ever eager to end the skid, some Cubs faithful—and maybe even the team itself—turned to the supernatural for a little bench support in 2008. The Cubs season began with a séance and ended with what some believed was an exorcism.

That kept the season in perfect accord with its predecessors, especially the last Cubs team to win the championship. The 1908 team was a superstitious bunch. Manager Frank Chance looked for four-leaf clovers prior to a game's start. Pitcher Ed Reulback worried that striking out the first batter portended losing the game. Centerfielder Frank Schulte—whose dog had become a good luck mascot for the team—believed it was lucky to find and pick up hairpins on his way to the ballpark. He even had a detailed code worked out whereby the size of the pin and the angle of its prongs indicated the kind of hit (single, double, triple, home run) the talisman would bring.

Many fans are aware of the Cubs' most famous legend: the Curse of the Billy Goat, which alleges that local tavern owner William Sianis successfully jinxed the club when he and his pet goat were kicked out of a 1945 Wrigley Field World Series game. (Chronicled in detail in *Haunted Baseball*, Sianis's proclamation that the team would lose that championship and never return to the Fall Classic has so far proven accurate.) But few fans realize that Sianis's goat was not the first barnyard visitor to a Cubs game. That happened in—of course—1908. After an August victory at the West Side Grounds, the team's home from 1893 to 1915, the *Tribune* noted "One happy rooter proudly escorted a diminutive goat off the field of battle after it was over under the impression it would be accorded the place now occupied by Schulte's bull pup as mascot."

Many fans considered the 100th anniversary of the last championship team to auger well for the Cubs, so hopes were high for the 2008 season. The previous October, anonymous fans had attempted to break Sianis's hex by leaving the butchered remains of a goat on the statue of longtime Cubs announcer Harry Caray, just outside Wrigley Field. (The grisly act was repeated with a severed goat's head prior to the team's 2009 home opener.) This was done just in time for the Cubs' playoff series against the Arizona Diamondbacks. The result? Chicago was swept in the series three games to none.

During spring training of '08, Cubs fan Mike Reischl had another idea. He had heard the story of Billy Jurges, the Cubs shortstop who, midseason in 1932, was shot by a jealous girlfriend a few blocks from Wrigley Field in the Hotel Carlos, then a popular residence for Cubs players. Reischl found Jurges an interesting figure. He was born in 1908. He is often considered one of the inspirations for the character of Roy Hobbs in *The Natural*. (The other was former Cub Eddie Waitkus, also shot by a woman in a Chicago hotel.)

The incident is even rumored to have motivated Babe Ruth's famous—and disputed—"called shot." After Jurges's injury, the Cubs acquired Mark Koenig to take his place.

Koenig had been the starting shortstop on the great Yankees teams of the late 1920s. He hit .353 as Jurges's replacement in 1932, helping the team reach the World Series, and was indignant that the team only voted him a half-share of the postseason bonus. Legend has it that Koenig complained about this to his former teammates when the Yankees came in for the World Series, and the New York team razzed the Cubs about being "cheap" throughout the games. When Ruth came to bat in the fifth inning of Game Three, some say he wasn't pointing to the outfield spot where he intended to deposit the next pitch (which is just where the ball went) but was instead pointing at the Cubs' dugout and complaining about the treatment of his friend Mark Koenig.

"So I was thinking to myself, wouldn't it be interesting if we could go into that hotel room with a psychic and talk to Billy Jurges and find out, one, what's going to happen this year with the Cubs, and two, did he think that Babe Ruth called the shot?" Reischl says.

He brought the idea to his friend, *Chicago Sun-Times* columnist Dave Hoekstra, who was looking for a fun article to kick off the season. The pair set up a "séance" in the room where Jurges was shot (Room 509—coincidentally, Jurges's birthday was May 9) and brought in medium Rik Kristinat to conjure the Cub.

"I work with spirits," says Kristinat, a fifth-generation medium who is also an ordained minister for the Spiritualist Church. Kristinat is in his mid-fifties and says he communicates with the dead via an intermediary. "I have a spirit guide named Running Deer who helps me out. I found out about him when I was nine years old."

Kristinat begins his communication by meditating. "I just ask spirit to come around and to help me and to put into my head what I'm supposed to know. I open myself up to the vibrations that surround me. Spiritualism is just understanding vibrations and trusting your intuition." Sometimes he achieves "a moment where something is very, very present." Other times the images are "foggy," he says, but Kristinat focuses on outlines until a picture starts to take shape.

"For example, if a person is blonde, I'll sense that they are blonde and I'll say, 'I see a blonde person standing next to me.' I don't necessarily *see* the blonde person, but I sense that the person is blonde."

Reischle and Hoekstra told Kristinat only that they wanted to contact a Cub named Billy who had been shot in that room. When Kristinat walked in and began meditating, he got more hits than Pete Rose.

"I kept getting the sense of lilies of the valley," a fragrance Kristinat's grandmother used to wear. He told the folks in the room that a woman was involved and "her name could be Rose or Scarlet."

The name of Jurges's assailant: Violet Valli.

Kristinat began sensing where Jurges had been shot. "I knew there wasn't a death involved, because I would have felt that," he explains. He felt a pain in his left hand and identified that as the site of a bullet entry.

Jurges's wounds were to his left hand and his buttocks.

Kristinat said he smelled alcohol. Valli explained to police that she shot Jurges "over love and too much gin." (Or perhaps the medium was picking up on the bottle of Tanqueray Reischl had brought along to ensure that spirits of one kind or another were present.)

Kristinat said he heard a voice with a distinctive accent. "It was definitely one of those *dese-dem-dose* guys—like a Bronx kind of voice." Jurges's hometown? The Bronx.

Kristinat said he felt that the departed Cub had been poor and was pushing a product. In his youth, Jurges was employed by a grocery store, delivering packages via horse and cart.

Kristinat had an accurate image of the middle-infielder Jurges at the ballpark. "I'm looking down the diamond and I want to say he played in the center—shortstop or second base."

"It was really kind of spooky, to be honest with you," Reischl recalls. "He said that Billy Jurges was in the room and he was talking to Billy." The medium also related the events of the shooting. "He said Jurges and the girl were fighting, and that [Jurges] said he had turned and the girl came out of the bathroom with a gun."

For Reischl and Hoekstra, the eeriest moment came toward the end when they asked Kristinat if any particular Cub was going to do poorly or well. "All I could see was a lightning bolt," the medium says. He asked, "Who's called the Lightning Bolt? Does that mean anything?" At which point, Brian Bernardoni, another attendee, opened a bag he'd brought with him. In it was a replica Roy Hobbs jersey from the movie *The Natural*. On one of the sleeves is a patch with a lightning bolt.

"I brought out the jersey and lay it on the bed," Bernardoni says. "And the whole room freaked out. No one knew I had that jersey with me."

Even Kristinat was impressed. "I thought that was pretty cool," he admits. "Even I still get shocked when I say things."

As for the 2008 season, Kristinat quoted Jurges as saying that if the team really wanted it and really tried hard, they could do it. Kristinat also said that the departed Cub was "worried about money. Worried that if the players play the game for money, they're not going to win."

"He didn't come up with anything on the Babe Ruth angle," Reischl says. "We kept asking is there anything with the Yankees. He wasn't hitting on that."

Still, the folks in attendance were impressed. "He was actually pretty close about some things," Bernardoni says.

If nothing else, Bernardoni and Reischl enjoyed a unique window on Cubs history, a shared passion of theirs. The two worked for years to get a memorial plaque put up on the location of the West Side Grounds, the Cubs' pre-Wrigley ballpark and the site of the team's last World Series, in 1908. The marker was officially installed in 2008. Both men are longstanding Cubs fans who believe in honoring the history and traditions of baseball. Bernardoni says that the spirit of the game can inhabit old ballparks in both literal and figurative ways.

"There have been stories of ghosts around the old West Side Grounds. People say they've seen people playing catch [at the site]. There was a death at that ballpark—a little boy fell off a rooftop building while reaching for a home run ball. There is evidence of a baby being born there."

Bernardoni believes the energy of a ballpark makes it a prime attraction for supernatural forces. "Ballparks are sacred places, hallowed ground," he says. "You can't have a place where forty to fifty thousand people gather x times a year and celebrate or mourn and *not* have it carry with it some kind of karma. It just isn't possible."

Reischl says he puts no faith in Sianis's hex. Bernardoni is more open to it. And what about Kristinat, the medium who talks to dead Cubs via a spirit named Running Deer? What does he make of the curse?

"I don't believe in that," he says. "I don't believe in curses. I believe someone has to lose, and it just happens to be their luck."

A BLESSING AND A CURSE

If Kristinat's channeling of Billy Jurges was correct, the Cubs must have really wanted to win, because they did a lot of it in 2008. They led not only their division, but also the National League, for much of the season. They sent eight players to the All-Star Game, tying a league record. Pitcher Carlos Zambrano threw a no-hitter in September. The team ended the regular season with a record of 97-64, tops in the NL and the club's highest number of wins since 1935. All looked good for the first round of the playoffs, the NLDS matchup against the Dodgers.

But fans who tuned into TBS on October 1 to watch that first postseason game were startled to see the opening footage for the pregame show. A man in religious robes was walking through the Cubs dugout, just hours before the game. He was waving a small branch and reciting something as he went. Cubs chairman Crane Kenney accompanied him and was seen pouring some kind of liquid out of a small glass bowl and onto the dirt around the dugout.

Before long, commentators and bloggers and news headlines were blaring an attention-getting announcement: the Cubs were holding an exorcism in Wrigley Field to remove the demons and curses that have plagued them, just in time for the postseason.

The episode began when Father Jim Greanias received a call from Kenney. "The way he explained it to me, he and another guy from the Cubs were talking about maybe bringing a priest in to bless the field. They contacted our local church near the ballpark, which is St. George's. And the priest there said anything you want to do with the Cubs, you gotta call Father Jim Greanias."

For Father Jim, of St. Iakovos Church in Valparaiso, Indiana, the Cubs have been a lifelong obsession. "I'm a diehard Cubs fan. I grew up on the south side of Chicago. I got beat up a lot of times!" Greanias's fandom has even bled into his calling. "I have pictures of me wearing a Cubs hat at the end of a liturgy. I have a collar with the Cubs logo on it—somebody made it for me. In my office I've got icons on one wall and Cubs paraphernalia on the other.

"Both my children are adopted from Russia. And they know that they can rob a bank or murder somebody and Daddy will always love them. But if they ever come home White Sox fans . . . the first plane back, baby!"

So when Kenney proposed a blessing of the field, he didn't have to wait long for a reply. "The priest in me was like, 'Okay, cool.' But the little boy in me was jumping up. 'Yeah! Sure! No problem!'"

Father Jim did make a request of his own. "I said I don't want the media involved because I don't want anything being mocked with the church." Greanias was well aware of the hoopla surrounding the curse and the odd theories people hold about breaking it. ("I've heard you're supposed to sacrifice a goat on the ground, with the blood running onto the field," he cites as an example.) Kenney said the team wanted no publicity either and the two established a time to bless the park.

Was the famous goat curse the reason for the blessing? "Whether there's a curse or not, who knows?" Father Jim recalls Kenney saying, "But if nothing else, let's ask God's blessing." Kenney did acknowledge that the team was seeking a Greek Orthodox priest for the ceremony because William Sianis—who invoked the original curse—was Greek.

The two men generally agreed on a better-safe-than-sorry policy: "*If* there's something happening that we don't understand, the best way to deal with it is through prayer and blessing," Greanias says.

"So we went there and we were going to bless the whole field," Father Jim recalls. But while in the dugout, Kenney spotted members of the press who had arrived early for the game, and he got cold feet. "Would you mind just doing the dugout?" he asked Greanias. The priest was thrown. "We usually bless everything. But I was nervous. I said fine, we'll just stick with the dugout."

Greanias conducted the ceremony. He had no idea a cameraman was catching the action. But on TV that night, there he was, reciting his prayer and walking the length of the dugout, while Kenney poured holy water over the gate.

Father Jim was surprised when, sitting in the stands for the game, he started getting phone calls from friends around the country who saw him. He was even more surprised when his ceremony was characterized as an exorcism.

"In no manner was it an exorcism," he insists. "We do have prayers against the Evil One, against possessions, but I didn't use that one at all.

"The whole deal was, we live in an immediate world and part of the deal is we have to learn how to transcend this world for a spiritual world. So *if* there's something going on spiritually, *if* there's something happening, let's just offer a blessing. It won't hurt."

Over the years, Father Jim has blessed everything from restaurants to junkyards. A relative once asked him to bless the horses he bet on at the racetrack. Some people request blessings of houses they think are possessed. "I will include words like 'Get out of here,' 'I command you to leave hold of this building,' if there's anything Satanic-feeling going on," he says. "But in no manner did I use the word *curses* or acknowledge that [at Wrigley Field]."

Occasionally, the priest has been asked to cast out demons. In one home, three-year-old twin girls said they saw "Uncle Bobby" lurking in various rooms. The parents dismissed it as an imaginary playmate. "But then things started happening at home," Father Jim relates, "like a picture flew off a table while the family was eating dinner. And the kids' stories started getting scary. They said, 'Uncle Bobby said he's going to come take us with him.'" One morning, the girls' mother saw the initial *B* etched deeply into an end table. She called Father Jim to bless the house.

"When I was going through the house, [the girls] didn't say anything. When we got in the basement, they simultaneously said 'Uncle Bobby's behind the air conditioner!'" Father Jim cast some holy water in that direction. "Then they both said, 'Uncle Bobby just ran out of the house!'"

Despite all this, Father Jim says he is not a big believer in possessions and haunted houses. But, he admits, "I believe in the spiritual. And I believe there are things that we don't understand. So when people tell me stories about ghosts and all that, I never discount that stuff."

And what about his beloved Cubs' famous hex? How much validity does he give it?

"As a man of God, none," he says flatly. "As a Cubs fan . . . there's something funky going on there. One hundred years and you haven't won . . . there's too many 'Cubbie Occurrences' that go on. It just makes you think there's something happening here."

"But," he re-emphasizes, "that's purely as a Cubs fan."

After the incident became public, Greanias got mostly positive emails and phone calls. Even manager Lou Piniella reportedly found the incident funny. For the priest, it ended up a positive experience. "As a Cubs fan I was in the dugout four hours before the game. As a dad I had my ten-year-old with me who said 'Thanks, Dad, for the greatest day of my life.' And as a priest and as a Christian, it was an act of faith. So for me it was a win-win-win."

That is, until Crane Kenney started giving a different version of the story. At the Cubs' 2009 fan convention, he called the blessing "one of the dumbest things" he ever did, claimed that Greanias had contacted the team—not the other way around—and said that the priest was simply grubbing for free tickets.

"That upset me. I don't want anyone who knows me thinking I'd use my priesthood for that purpose." Nor does he need to. "I haven't paid for tickets in twenty years! Everybody wants to go to heaven so they give me tickets!"

Even more upsetting to the man of the cloth is the notion that God somehow failed the team. The Cubs lost Game One—and Game Two and Game Three—and were quickly out of the postseason, a hasty and anticlimactic end to what was supposed to be their magical year.

"A lot of people say it didn't work. That only bothers me from the standpoint of I don't want God getting a bad rap. Certainly in no way did I pray for the Cubs to win. I've been a priest for thirteen years. If I had that kind of power they would have won thirteen years ago.

"We didn't pray for the Cubs to win and the Dodgers to lose. We prayed for everybody. I prayed for the health and well being of the players, the staff and administration, all those who work here, and all those who attend games—the fans.

"And to be truthful with you, it was a prayer for protection. Nobody slipped or bumped their head on the dugout, did they? So that part worked!

"All things are in God's hands, including whether or not the Cubs will win the World Series. God doesn't cause it and God doesn't stop it," Greanias says. But, he adds, he can envision his team in a classic World Series Game Seven scenario:

"It's gonna be top of the ninth, two outs, bases loaded, Cubs ahead by three runs, two strikes. And the closer is going to throw a ball straight down the middle. It's going to be a strike and about halfway to the plate, the Second Coming's going to happen. And the Lord's going to come down, and then we'll never know. And I'll turn around and say something to the Lord—I'll get mad at Jesus and I'll end up in hell for all eternity just because of the Cubs."

Worst of all? "I'll never know if the Cubs win the World Series."

●◆●

HOW MANY CURSES CAN
ONE TEAM STAND?

The Cubs' infamous Billy Goat Curse is the most famous hex said to befall the team, but hardly the only one. In addition to the Curse of Fred Merkle (chronicled in *Haunted Baseball*, it holds that the century-plus of losing is attributable to a dirty-tricks play the team made to get to the 1908 World Series), there's also the Curse of the Totem Pole, which states that the

Kwagulth Totem Pole just down West Addison Street from Wrigley (at the intersection of North Lake Shore Drive) is bad luck for the team. Legend holds that the crests on a totem should be positioned to face one's enemies. The images on the Kwagulth Totem Pole are aimed right at Wrigley.

In early 2008, new Cubs catcher Geovany Soto was told of the so-called Curse of the Rookie. The past three Cubs to win the NL Rookie of the Year Award met bad luck shortly thereafter. Second baseman Ken Hubbs, who won the honor in 1962, was killed in a plane crash less than two years later. Jerome Walton never again came close to the impressive numbers that brought him the 1989 award and was out of baseball by 1998, averaging just thirty-seven game appearances in his last seven seasons spent with six different teams. Dominating pitcher Kerry Wood, the 1998 honoree, missed the entire 1999 season after requiring Tommy John surgery, one of eleven trips to the DL he made before being recast as a relief pitcher in 2007, having never regained his initial glory.

"I don't care about that," Soto told the *Chicago Sun-Times* during spring training 2008. "I don't believe in all that stuff." Soto went on to win the award. The following year, he tested positive for marijuana prior to the World Baseball Classic (and was banned from international play for two years as a result), spent time on the DL with a muscle strain, and suffered a major power outage, ending the season with a .217 batting average.

In their 2008 book *Hoodoo: Unraveling the 100-Year Mystery of the Chicago Cubs,* authors Grant DePorter,

Elliott Harris, and Mark Vancil note that Murphy's Law (the adage that anything that can go wrong, will go wrong) has a particularly literal application to the North Siders: the name Murphy has been conspicuously present during some classic Cubbie Occurrences. Charles Murphy was the much-loathed owner of the team from 1906 to 1913. (Among other transgressions, Murphy was reviled for mistreating players, ignoring league rules, and scalping 1908 World Series tickets to his own team's games.) The goat William Sianis brought to Wrigley in 1945—and which was subsequently kicked out, prompting the tavern owner's curse—was named Murphy. The Mets broadcaster who called the notorious "black cat" game at Shea Stadium in 1969 (in which the harbinger of misfortune ran on the field and hissed at the Cubs dugout, presaging the team's fall from first place) was Bob Murphy. Leon Durham's infamous error that cost the team a trip to the 1984 World Series was made at Jack Murphy Stadium in San Diego. The authors even claim to have found several "local celebrities" and "high-profile Chicagoans" named Murphy who attended the 2003 Bartman game and other prominent Cubs losses.

Chapter 14
Going . . . Going
. . . GONE!

What goes up must come down—usually. Players at a pro ball game in Florida in 1974 might disagree. They still talk about that day when Joe Wallis hit a routine pop-up that headed for shallow rightfield . . . and then disappeared.

"It was the weirdest thing I ever encountered," Garry Templeton says. "The ball never came down."

It was August 6, 1974. The Key West Conchs, the Class-A affiliate of the Cubs, were hosting the St. Petersburg Cardinals in an evening game at Wickers Field, their home park. A number of future major leaguers, including Templeton, Tito Landrum, and eventual Hall of Famer Bruce Sutter were on the field that day. Donnie Moore was on the mound, pitching his last game for the Conchs.

In the bottom of the first inning, rightfielder Wallis dug in at the plate. Cardinal pitcher Lonny Kruger delivered, and Wallis connected for what everyone thought was a simple fly ball that would just clear the infield.

"I remember the second baseman started back," recalls Ernie Rousseau, who was in leftfield for the Cards that day. "I remember the rightfielder coming in." Rousseau moved in to back up second base, as is customary for that play. But when he looked to the infield, "there was no play."

At about the time the ball should have come down, rightfielder John Crider ducked, indicating he had lost sight of it. Second baseman Jimmy Williams did the same. Claudell Crockett in centerfield shrugged his open hands helplessly.

"There were twenty-five guys going, 'Where the heck is that ball?'" Rousseau says.

"We ran back for it, and it just disappeared," marvels Templeton, who was playing shortstop. "It was the damnedest thing I've ever seen."

Wallis was clearly perplexed too. He stopped at first, but was waved on to second by the coach. He paused there too, before haltingly advancing to third. With no ball in sight and no play in the works, he finally bounded for home. The umpires declared the hit a home run.

"And that's when all hell broke loose," Rousseau says. The Cardinals vigorously protested the call. But the two-man umpire crew had limited options. No one felt that the ball had been heading for foul territory, and no one could find the ball on the field or make a play.

"Produce the ball! Produce the ball!" the umps told the Cardinals, Rousseau remembers. "Nobody ever found that ball. The final word was, '[there's] no ball to tag out the runner.'"

The Cards gave a good search, though. "We looked all over for that ball," Templeton says. "We spent a good ten minutes. Everybody combed the field; we sent guys outside the field. No ball."

It seemed to have disappeared into thin air.

In the wake of the mystery, a few theories began to develop. The most obvious was that the wind had somehow taken the ball. *St. Petersburg Times* reporter Eric Lincoln, whose account of the event nearly two weeks later is the only contemporaneous reportage of it by someone who was present, says the winds gusted up to twenty knots that day. But the players disagree.

"There was no unbelievable wind or Gulf Stream that day," insists Rousseau.

"I know it was a pop-up for sure," Templeton adds.

Others looked to supernatural explanations. Key West has a reputation as ghostly, and Conch owner Julian DePoo told Lincoln that "Papa has that ball," referring to the ghost of famed Key West resident Ernest Hemingway. "His spirit is everywhere around here."

Templeton suggested that a UFO intercepted it. Others credited the Bermuda Triangle—infamous for odd disappearances—a corner of which encompasses Key West.

All these years later, Conch manager Q. V. Lowe doesn't recall the incident in detail, but does believe the ball went out of the park. "There was not much question in my mind that ball was hit out there behind the rightfield fence," he says. "The lights weren't good and sometimes you get a little fog moving in. I remember several people hitting a ball and everybody's looking for it."

But Lowe appears to be the only one who thinks Wallis hit a dinger.

"I've never heard anybody who was on that baseball field say it was a home run, because it was a pop-up," says Templeton. "It went straight up."

"There was no way that came within 150 feet of the fence," Rousseau insists. "I saw a lot of fly balls. I know judgment and depth. It was not a fly ball."

The Conch players laughed at the whole episode from their dugout. As the Cardinals filed out of the stadium afterward (losing 7–4), fans ribbed them about the disappearing baseball, chanting, "No ball! No ball!"

The Cardinals players found the experience eerie ("We were happy to get out of that ballpark," Templeton recalls) but within days were joking about it on the bus. "We talked about it for a couple of years," Templeton says, "but then people thought we were crazy so I didn't say much else about it."

But the event was so unusual—so inexplicable—it has stayed fresh in players' minds. "I can remember the play like it was yesterday," Rousseau says. "Because it was the most bizarre thing I've ever seen."

He doesn't claim to understand what happened, but Rousseau knows that the ball Wallis hit did not go foul and did not clear the outfield fence. It simply went up and never came down.

"It was a fair ball that was never found, and it was not over the outfielder's head. That I can swear to God," he says. "The rest, I have no clue."

Chapter 15
Charmed

Baseball and superstitions go together like a hand and batting glove. While hundreds of major-leaguers subscribe to their own personal rituals and routines, sometimes good luck charms become a team event, with players, managers, and fans believing in the power of unlikely amulets and mascots.

GNOME FIELD ADVANTAGE

The 2008 Los Angeles Dodgers were slow out of the gate. After the first three weeks of the season, the team many had expected to lead the division was a dismal 7-11. It was their worst start in twelve years. Perhaps it was inevitable that such an "ignominious" situation would be cured with a relatively unusual good luck charm.

"We had a little gnome with an LA Dodgers hat on it," Matt Kemp says. "We had him in the locker room and the dugout. And he was good luck for us."

"I don't really know how it started or what caused it," Blake DeWitt recalls. "Somehow we got a gnome and somehow it became a good luck thing. It kind of happened out of nowhere."

Actually, it happened out of the bullpen, where a relief pitcher brought in a garden gnome as a good luck charm after the pitching staff got off to such a rocky start. "Every day they'd bring it back and forth to the bullpen and it had its little spot that it just stayed in," All-Star catcher Russ

Martin recalls. "I think they might have moved it around if somebody got on base."

The gnome seemed to deliver. "The bullpen started doing great," Martin says. "And then we started struggling at the plate, and we're like, 'We need to get a hitting gnome.'"

On April 21, the Dodgers rolled into Cincinnati fresh from being swept three games straight in Atlanta, where the team had managed just one run in each game. Pitcher Joel Beimel gave Martin a computer-printed image of the bullpen gnome. Martin wrote Hitting Gnome. Rub Me Here for Hits on the picture and taped it to the back of a dugout bench.

The team's anemic bats came alive, pounding fifteen hits in a 9–3 victory. Several players rubbed the gnome for luck on their way to the plate, including third baseman Nomar Garciaparra, who went two-for-five with a home run and three RBI, and Martin himself, who was three-for-three on the night, his first three-hit game of the season.

Pitcher Brad Penny got the win and despite the fact that he wasn't wild about the new talisman ("I don't like gnomes," he was quoted as saying. "I don't want to touch one. Keep that thing away from me. They're evil-looking") he also knew better than to mess with success. "It worked," he told reporters afterward. "We better have him in there again."

Two days later, when the near-last-place Dodgers defeated the Arizona Diamondbacks, who had the best record in baseball, Russ Martin was seconding Penny's comments. "The gnome can't really hit for us," he said at the time. "But if we keep winning, I guarantee you he will be out there."

By the time the team returned home, the paper image of a hitting gnome had been replaced by the real thing. "We got one," Martin says. "Somebody heard about it in the newspaper and I think a fan made one or something and sent it to us." (Actually, the hitting gnome was an official Los Angeles Dodgers garden gnome. Yes, the team already had a licensed gnome product—multiple ones, in fact—on the market.)

For the next two-plus weeks, the hitting gnome seemed to work its magic. The Dodgers embarked on an eight-game winning streak, and went twelve and four overall. Martin recalls players joking about "the power of the gnome." Noticing a resemblance to the Dodgers' legendary manager, the team had T-shirts printed that featured the gnome with Tommy Lasorda's face superimposed on it. In the dugout, the hitting gnome had become the twenty-sixth man. "It was on the bench, as part of the team," says Martin.

"I thought it was fun," Kemp recalls. "It worked, for a little bit."

When the winning streak ended, the hitting gnome made its exit. It was starting to crumble, and attempts to restore it ("We patched him up and put him in surgery," Blake DeWitt recalls) were not successful. Eventually, Martin says, "we just lost faith in the gnome."

"Poor little guy got us through our rough patch and that was about it," Delwyn Young says. Indeed, the turnaround made a difference in the team's season. The Dodgers were one game out of last place when the gnome came in, and the club ended 2008 winning its division and proceeding to the postseason.

The whereabouts of the hitting gnome today are a closely guarded team secret. Martin hints that "it might still be in LA somewhere," while Young says, conspiratorially, "I can't tell you [where he is now]. Just cherish the memory."

"It was just a fun thing for a little while," Martin says. "We needed something to get us going."

"It was just something to go with," Young adds. "It's a gnome and it's a way to get hits. It's all part of baseball."

• ◆ •

DODGING SPIRITS

The gnomes' mystical power was not out of place in the Dodgers organization. In *Haunted Baseball*, workers described the team's ballpark as haunted, an opinion shared by players. "There's lots of creepy stuff in Dodger Stadium," Delwyn Young says, citing the batting cage as a particularly spooky spot. "I'd hear all these random noises but there'd be nobody in there. You can feel something—you know, like somebody's standing behind you and you turn around? Like you're being watched. There's eyes in the cage—always."

The gnome story is reminiscent of the team's 1993 Sod Squad: After the team went 0-9 on artificial turf that season, players bought some strips of Kentucky rye-blue grass from a Pittsburgh nursery and brought it to Three Rivers Stadium for their series against the Pirates. They won the first game, and kept the sod in the visiting clubhouse shower room overnight. They brought it out the next day and won again. The team dropped the last game of the series, but flew the two-and-a-half square yards of sod on to their next series in St. Louis, which they also won.

Over the course of their next six artificial-turf games, the team went 4-2. The victories contributed to an eleven-game winning streak, the team's longest in seventeen years.

Pitcher Orel Hershiser, the self-proclaimed head of the Sod Squad, promised to keep the grass with the team "until we lose," but later admitted that "it's really starting to stink." He planned to bring the grass back home "where we can water it, fertilize it, keep it ready for our next trip." But by the time the turf made it to Los Angeles, groundskeeper Al Myers found it beyond salvation. He got some replacement sod in time for the team's mid-June series in Cincinnati—again, the Dodgers lined the front of their dugout with strips of real turf—but when LA lost the series, the charm seemed to have wilted right along with the original grass.

ANIMAL ELECTRO-MAGNETISM

It is not uncommon for enthusiastic fans to give good luck pieces to favorite players—many major leaguers' mailboxes are full of them. But when Dyar Miller was pitching for the Baltimore Orioles in 1976, he got a present that was unusual even by baseball standards.

"We were in Milwaukee and I was walking through the bullpen after the game and some fan handed me this little shoe box. I open it up and there was a little bird in it. Come to find out it was a baby turkey." The fan was clearly thinking it would be good luck to give a bird to a player on a team named for a bird. "It had a little Oriole helmet on it," recalls Miller. "It was painted up like a little bird, an Oriole."

Miller found the gift odd and didn't know what to do with it. "So I took it home on the plane that night." The team was heading back to Baltimore for a home stand and decided to keep the turkey in the clubhouse for a while.

"We started getting on a win streak and [manager] Earl Weaver wouldn't let the turkey out of the clubhouse." As an old-time baseball pro, Weaver knew the value of a good luck charm—even if it posed certain logistical problems in the locker room.

"The thing got big!" Miller remembers. "It was running loose in the clubhouse." The team gave it a name, which Miller can't recall, and clubhouse manager Clay Reed was responsible for its feeding and care. But when it reached full growth, Miller says Reed took it to his farm. Though Hall of Famer Brooks Robinson warned that the bird's trip through the airport X-ray scanner would render it inedible ("We can't eat that bird," Miller recalls him saying. "It will be screwed up!"), the turkey eventually became Reed's Thanksgiving Day dinner.

• ◆ •

Sometimes teams adopt animal mascots, and sometimes animal mascots adopt teams. That was the case in 2007 when a squirrel decided to make Yankee Stadium its home. Although every ballpark has its share of birds and rodents and who knows what else, Lucky (as he came to be known) was something of a grandstander: He perched himself atop the rightfield foul pole, seeming to watch the game and lord over it at the same time.

The bushy-tailed charm first appeared on Opening Day and presided over the team's 9–5 defeat of Tampa Bay. Not realizing the squirrel's good luck powers—and confirming most stereotypes about New Yorkers—fans in rightfield who spotted the animal high atop the pole reportedly yelled out for it to jump.

But Lucky paid no attention and was next caught by cameras on June 8, when the Yankees topped the Pittsburgh

Pirates 5–4. By the time he was broadcast on the scoreboard during the team's August 28 victory over the Boston Red Sox (5–3), he was greeted with an enormous ovation. Yankee outfielder Johnny Damon, who said that he fed Lucky sunflower seeds prior to that game, pounded a home run into the upper deck that sailed right over Lucky's head.

By this point, a new wrinkle was added to the squirrel's legacy: Some claimed the new mascot was the reincarnated spirit of Yankee legend Phil Rizzuto, who had died a few weeks earlier, on August 13. After all, Rizzuto was known as the Scooter and as anyone who has ever seen a squirrel can attest, the nickname certainly fit Lucky. (The fact that the rodent had appeared prior to the Hall of Famer's death did not seem to detract from this theory.)

By the time Lucky made his last recorded appearance in his sky-high seat on September 4—a 12–3 victory over the Seattle Mariners—fans were wearing T-shirts with his likeness and Yankee hats with stuffed squirrels perched atop them. He was never spotted again, but his record was intact: The Yankees won every game at which the animal was seen sitting on the pole.

But was he really good luck? After the Boston victory, a piece in the *New York Times* warned that the squirrel might actually portend ill for the Yankees: Its actions recalled those of Ratatosk, a squirrel from Norse mythology that carried insults up and down a tree that represented the world. The animal goaded a rivalry between the evil dragon at the bottom of the tree (here, the Red Sox, according to the *Times*) and an eagle at the top (the Yankees). In the Norse myth, the dragon destroys the world, leading the paper to conclude that Lucky "just might have foretold that the Yankees will not prevail over the Red Sox this season."

And indeed, Boston won the division by two games over the Yankees . . . and then went on to win the World Series.

•◆•

But the Red Sox had some mascot magic of their own.

The notoriously superstitious Boston bullpen had adopted a pirate's theme that year, dubbing the pen the Black Pearl, with a Jolly Roger flag draped on the wall, code names for each of the players, and a secret handshake. Mid-season, Mike Timlin's wife, Dawn, added to the decor by purchasing Parlay the Parrot and presenting it to the crew. The stuffed bird sat on Jonathan Papelbon's shoulder for a couple of games, before finding a permanent perch on the bench. For good luck, Hideki Okajima and a few of his mates would rub Parlay's head right before entering a game. So naturally, more than a few relievers' feathers were ruffled upon discovering that Parlay was stolen late at night following Boston's Game Seven victory over Cleveland in the ALCS.

Mike Timlin made a humble plea to Red Sox Nation for the bird's safe return. "It kind of started as a little joke type thing—'Oh, we really need him back,'" the veteran reliever told Boston's WBZ-TV, "but we *really* need him back. He's an integral part of what's going on out there [in the bullpen]."

Timlin described the bird as looking like a macaw with a green tail, brown plastic legs, and "elastic coming out of his feet."

"He's kinda beat up," he added. "He ain't pretty because he's been out there all year long, but we just need him back."

Two Northeastern University students dropped the parrot back off to a Fenway bullpen attendant just in time for Game One of the World Series and were rewarded by Boston sportscaster Bob Loebel with tickets to Game Six or Seven of the Series, treasure which ultimately proved to be worthless after Boston swept the Rockies. Derek Tarsy and Brian Holt explained that they had found Parlay in their apartment freezer the day after a party celebrating the Game Seven victory. They claim that they hadn't stolen the parrot, but someone had brought it there during the party. After seeing Timlin's appeal on television, they knew they had to bring it back. "We're both big Red Sox fans," Tarsy said, "and we're not trying to jinx the [team]. We want the Red Sox to win."

Which they did. At the championship "rolling rally" parade, Timlin and Okajima perched the bird on top of a speaker on their flatbed truck for all the land lovers to see.

A THONG AND A PRAYER

In the 1989 movie *Bull Durham*, phenom pitcher Ebby Calvin "Nuke" LaLoosh goes on a winning streak when he begins wearing a black garter belt underneath his uniform. This is no case of Hollywood exaggeration: A number of players have developed a belief in unusual undergarments as a means of invoking the baseball gods. Itinerant reliever Rob Murphy often donned a pair of women's black silk panties on the days he took the mound, joking that he wore them to convince his girlfriend that they were his after she found them in his glove compartment. (In fact, a friend gave him the panties; he wore them as a gag one day and pitched well, thereby starting a personal ritual.)

Slugger Jason Giambi goes Murphy one better: He not only believes in the magical power of his skivvies—he shares their winning ways with his teammates.

The underwear in question is a leopard-print thong with black and gold lining. It is not what one expects a hulking, six-foot-two, 200-plus-pound power hitter to slip on before

a game. But the AL MVP and five-time All Star has been rely-
ing on the thong since 1996. When a player is in a slump,
the thong is a mystical cure. "Every person who's worn it has
never not gotten a hit that day," Giambi insists.

"It started as a joke," he says. "The guys who make all
my underclothes are buddies of mine." Giambi quipped that
he avoided tan lines by lying out in a thong. "It became a
joke and then they made it."

Giambi kept it in his locker. One day a teammate was in
a slump and said to him, "I need to get a hit—gimme the
gold thong."

"I gave him the gold thong and ever since that day it's
never not gotten a hit."

Giambi is not the only believer. His former A's teammate
Johnny Damon went through a period where "I couldn't buy
a hit." Giambi told him it was "guaranteed" to end his slump.
"I wore it . . . and that was it." When Damon reunited with
Giambi on the Yankees in 2006, he again availed himself of
the hit-helping thong. "It gets your mind off of baseball and
it gets you thinking about the tight underwear you're wearing and you play much better," he says.

In addition to Damon, Giambi is known to have shared his
slingshot with Yankee teammates Bernie Williams, Robin Ven-
tura, and Derek Jeter (who wants it known that he wore it *over*
his shorts, but also says he hit a first-pitch home run when he
donned the lucky lingerie after an oh-for-thirty-two stretch).

The thong is so powerful that even the suggestion of
it—or, perhaps, fear of it—can work some magic. In 2008,
Yankee second baseman Robinson Cano was in a hitting
slump. "I told him, 'Hey, if you don't get a hit today, you're
wearing the thong tomorrow,'" Giambi recalls. "He ended up
getting a hit. Sometimes the thong is motivation in itself."

While the notion of a community thong might sound a little uninviting, Giambi assures that it is washed between wearings. In his days with New York, the underwear had his No. 25 stitched on it, indicating that the team laundry took care of cleaning duties. (And presumably guaranteeing that they didn't confuse it with other players' leopard-print gold thongs.) And, he says, it is worn only in extreme circumstances.

"Only when you're really struggling can you put that on," Damon says. "You can't do it if you're just going oh-for-five. You need to be really struggling. Then he would offer it to you."

Desperation is Giambi's barometer for when it's time to go to the thong. "It has to be something where you can't figure it out. When you've tried everything else," he holds up the magical undergarment, "this is it."

• ◆ •

ADULT CHARMS

The thong is good clean fun, players insist, but clubhouse superstitions can veer into questionable adult territory. In May 2008, the struggling Chicago White Sox drew the ire of fans and the commissioner's office when players put two inflatable female dolls in their locker room in Toronto. One doll had a bat inserted from behind, allegedly to stand it up. Signs on the dolls read LET'S GO WHITE SOX and YOU'VE GOT TO PUSH (the latter had become a catchphrase for the team during spring training). Players were encouraged to point their bats at the dolls in an effort to invigorate the team's offense. Not only was the incident decried as sexist and demeaning, the attempt to turn around Chicago's then five-game losing streak also failed: The Sox lost that day, and again the next. Centerfielder Nick Swisher—identified as the protagonist of the poor-taste talismans—eventually apologized for any offense.

The Goddess Lounge in Baltimore has a storied baseball past: Babe Ruth bought the bar for his father in 1916. An old photo shows the pair behind the bar, ready to serve thirsty patrons. The elder Ruth ran the place until 1918, when he was killed on the street corner outside, stabbed while breaking up a fight. Today the establishment—just a few blocks from Camden Yards and from the house in which Ruth was born—is a strip club frequented by both visiting and home-team baseball players. They've developed a superstition based on a poem that appears on faded yellowing paper taped to the wall of the bar's back office. Entitled "The Babe," it consists of several stanzas of nondescript pulp. Its power lies not in its poetry, but in its presence. A number of major league players believe that touching the poem will cure a hitting slump. "Several players swear by it," says the bar's co-owner, who is obviously willing to suspend the establishment's "no-touching" policy for at least one Babe in residence.

A CHARM WITH SOME HEART

In addition to his gold thong, Jason Giambi also wears a necklace for good luck. "The daughter of my strength and conditioning coach made me these beads," he says, proudly displaying them. "I've worn them for thirteen years now.

I've restrung them. I take it off in the off-season and I wear it every day during the season."

Necklaces and bracelets are common good luck charms for players. John Buck wears wristbands for each game, but replaces them when their luck runs out. "Once I go oh-fer, after the game I'll just throw it to a little kid. It's not me that went oh-fer, it's the wristband."

But perhaps no good luck jewelry ever had as much of a meaningful impact as the bracelet Brett Gardner keeps in his locker. It worked its charms not only on the Yankee centerfielder, but also on the special fan who gave it to him.

Like many players, Gardner believes in giving back to the community and using his celebrity to help those in need. On May 15, 2009, he made a visit to New York Presbyterian Morgan Stanley Children's Hospital in Manhattan. He was not scheduled to play that night, so he stopped by to read books to sick kids. The visit was arranged by Project Sunshine, a not-for-profit organization that brings volunteers to children's hospitals.

One of the children he met there was Alyssa Esposito, a Long Island eighteen-year-old with a history of health problems. At three months old she was diagnosed with leukemia. At fourteen months, she had a bone marrow transplant. Now she was seriously ill with a badly inflamed heart. She had spent the last 107 days in the hospital, desperately awaiting a heart transplant. From her wheelchair in her ninth-floor hospital room, she would look out the window each night at the distant lights of Yankee Stadium.

So when Alyssa heard that a Yankee player was coming to the hospital, she joined the children eager to see him. And she brought Gardner a special gift: a Project Sunshine friendship bracelet. She told the outfielder that when he

wore it, he would "hit a home run in every at bat"—a prediction a bit extreme for any player, but particularly outra-
geous for the speedy but light-hitting Gardner.

"I thought to myself, 'Yeah, right,'" Gardner later told
reporters. "I didn't want to say anything when she gave it
to me, but I'm not really a home run hitter." He's not kidding: In his major league career to that point, Gardner had
hit exactly one home run.

But it was to be a night of exceptional occurrences. It
started in the third inning, when New York's game-starting
centerfielder Johnny Damon was ejected for arguing a called
third strike. That put Gardner in the game. In the seventh
inning, he blooped a pitch down the leftfield line. The ball got
past Minnesota Twins outfielder Denard Span. It kept rolling
and rolling and Gardner kept running—all the way around
the diamond. It was the first inside-the-park home run in the
new Yankee Stadium, and the first by any Yankee in ten years.

"I didn't really think about it as I was running around
the bases," Gardner said afterward. "I just assumed the guy
made an error. I didn't know it was a home run until I got
back in the dugout."

After the game Gardner, who also had a single and a triple on the night, shared the story with locker-room reporters. "A little girl gave me a bracelet," he said, marveling
at its power. "I had it in my locker and I'll take it with me
everywhere I go."

But the Yankee player's big moment was soon out-
shined by his benefactor. While the game was going on—
possibly around the same time he was racing round the
bases—Alyssa's family got the call for which they'd been
praying for more than three months: a donor heart had
become available. The next morning, she was in surgery.

When she awoke, her family played Alyssa a tape of Gardner's home run. "He's running for me," she said with a smile.

The operation saved her life. "She was very, very sick before her transplant," juvenile cardiologist Dr. Linda Addonizio told local news station WPIX. Two weeks later, the teenager was "doing fantastic" and well enough to go home.

In mid-June, she and Gardner were reunited at the hospital to tell their amazing story. "It's cool how it happened," said Alyssa, while smiling for the cameras and wearing Gardner's pinstriped jersey, "that it happened on the same day." Alyssa was invited to a Yankee game a few weeks later, where she visited the dugout and met Yankee players. Alex Rodriguez gave her his batting gloves.

"If we make it to the playoffs and into the World Series, we might have to see each other every day," Gardner quipped.

Today, Alyssa is hale and increasingly energetic and doctors expect her to lead a normal life. Gardner says he keeps the bracelet with him at all times, a link to a special friend with whom he shares what is literally a heartwarming story.

Chapter 16

A Song for
the Ages

"Music," William Congreve wrote, "hath charms to soothe the savage breast, to soften rocks, or bend a knotted oak."

And, some Red Sox fans insist, to win the trophy.

The song in question is a turn-of-the-century ditty called "Tessie," which the Boston faithful credit with all seven of the team's world championships. If it seems unlikely that a number originally written for a modest Broadway musical and sung to the lead character's pet parakeet would become a magical good luck charm for a major league baseball franchise, consider the stats:

- The Sox have never won a World Series without "Tessie" performed live at the ballpark. (The same held true for the Boston Braves, prior to their move to Milwaukee.)
- In the World Series games during which the song has been played, the team has often rallied from behind or won in dramatic fashion.
- During the fifteen-year span that "Tessie" was played live at the ballpark in the postseason, Boston won five World Series titles, with a win-loss record of 25-7.
- From 1919 through 2003, the song was never played live and Sox fans suffered eighty-six years of heartbreak.
- Since the revival of "Tessie" in 2004, Boston has won two titles. In both Series, the song was played live.

(The song was not performed in the seasons the Sox failed to win rings.)
- In the modern era, the Sox have been 5-0 in games when the song was performed live at Fenway Park, four of which were won by walk-off hits or game-winning home runs.

Shortly after Red Sox ownership changed hands in 2002, longtime baseball marketing guru Dr. Charles Steinberg was brought in. Steinberg had a reputation for preserving old baseball traditions and honoring them anew. In Boston, he fell into a bowl of chowdah.

Steinberg discovered "Tessie" and its association with the World Series titles through 1918 and the drought thereafter. He had never heard it. Thanks to a colleague, he found "Tessie" online. It was a 1902 recording for the Broadway musical *The Glass Slipper*, and it was about a woman who tells her secrets to a pet bird. To her horror, the bird blurts out those secrets at a social gathering at her house. The recording was scratchy and the song sounded almost operatic.

During the 2003 off-season, Steinberg pondered how he might use "Tessie" or make a re-creation of it. Enter Jeff Horrigan, who covered the Red Sox at the time for the *Boston Herald*. Horrigan is co-founder and director of Hot Stove Cool Music, a concert series that raises money for the Jimmy Fund to help strike out cancer. At a January 2003 event featuring the Celtic punk band Dropkick Murphys, Ken Casey, lead vocalist and bassist, mentioned to Horrigan that the band members were all Red Sox diehards and would love to find a way to connect themselves with the Sox. A couple of weeks later at spring training camp, Steinberg was chatting with Horrigan and fellow *Herald* reporter Steve Buckley and said, "I don't know why no one has ever rerecorded the song. If a good version of it was done, we would probably play it at the park."

The Dropkicks were on tour in London. Horrigan went to the press trailer and sent Casey an e-mail with the ancient recording. The band gathered around to listen to this operatic song about a bird. Although it was typical for the band to take old Irish folk songs and give them a modern kick, Casey told Horrigan this one wasn't going to make the cut. He cited the band's reputation, "because you can't do a song about birds." He added, "If you want to write a new Tessie, maybe we'll record that."

A couple of days later, one night before he went to bed, Horrigan wrote a song basically about the song.

•◆•

And a song-worthy history "Tessie" is. Although it was born on Broadway, and was popular in its day, it rose to new meaning when a gang of prominent, baseball-crazed Irishmen calling themselves the Royal Rooters adopted it as their war song. It was not their first theme song and by no means the only tool in their arsenal.

The Rooters were clever, witty, and gleefully off-their-rockers. They first made headlines in 1897 when they followed the Boston Beaneaters, predecessors of the Braves, to Baltimore for the Temple Cup, an exhibition postseason tournament pitting the top two finishing teams in the National League. Congressman John Francis "Honey Fitz" Fitzgerald, future grandfather of President John F. Kennedy, hosted the Rooters and led the procession to the ballpark.

When the American League formed in 1901, and a second Boston team lured away some of the National League's biggest stars, the Rooters switched allegiances. By the time the first World Series was born with the Boston Americans, forerunners of the Red Sox, squaring off against the NL's Pittsburg Pirates (spelled back then without an -*h*), the Rooters were a well-organized, highly spirited outfit. They headquartered at Third Base Saloon—part sports bar, part baseball museum, part gambling hall, and full-time haven for fans and players. Baseball arguments were presided over by Mike "Nuf Ced" McGreevy, saloon keeper and baseball fan extraordinaire, who always gave the final word, then ended discussion by pounding his fist on the bar top and exclaiming "Nuf Ced!" Along with Honey Fitz, Nuf Ced was ringleader of the Rooters. Both home and away, he famously led a procession of Rooters into the ballpark, marching around the outfield sporting Continental Special bowler hats, high white collars, cowbells, tin horns, wooden rattles, megaphones, bass drums, and brass cymbals. In later years, the Rooters were bedecked even more colorfully—sporting badges with red stockings, sashes of stitched-together red socks, American flags, or headbands proclaiming OH YOU RED SOX!; once they paraded onto the Polo Grounds diamond holding lit torches. And during the games, the local press seemingly reported their every move, as Rooters hollered through tin megaphones, sang incessantly, ran up and down the aisle in a tizzy, opened and closed miniature parasols to music, and danced the jig on the roof of the Boston bench.

In the postseason, the Rooters hired bands and during a rain postponement off-day in Pittsburgh during the 1903 World Series, Nuf Ced sent Rooter Tom Burton to the music store to find a new score. Burton came back with sheet music for "Tessie." The next day, with the Sox down 5–1 in the ninth inning of game four, Nuf Ced passed out song cards for "Tessie" to his peers in hopes of rallying the team. And sure enough, the Sox came charging back scoring three runs and falling just short of victory. The Rooters set to work writing versions that would flatter the Bostons and, according to McGreevy, "charm the Pittsburgh players so that when they hear [the lyrics], their eye will lose its keenness and their arms their brawn." For the legendary Pirates shortstop Honus Wagner, they wrote:

> *Honus, why do you hit so badly?*
> *Take a back seat and sit down.*
> *Honus, at bat you look so sadly,*
> *Hey, why don't you get out of town!*

Years later Wagner admitted that the song did indeed distract and unnerve him. Pittsburgh third baseman Tommy Leach told Lawrence Ritter in *The Glory of Their Times* how the Rooters' melody shifted momentum. "They must have figured it was a good-luck charm, because from [Game 5] on you could hardly play ball, they were singing 'Tessie' so loud."

A different "Tessie" refrain targeted Brickyard Kennedy, and the Bostons shelled the Pirates starter on his thirty-sixth birthday, 11–2.

However, Rooters did not hedge their bets solely on the power of Tessie. Louis P. Masur, in his book *Autumn Glory: Baseball's First World Series,* describes how prior to Game Five, the Rooters had swept off a Pittsburgh street a seven-year-old African-American boy named Hiram and brought him to the game for good luck. "The Rooter tied a horseshoe around the mascot's neck and claimed that 'each player of our team on going to bat rubbed his hand on the kinks of that black head and drew forth skill, strength, and certainty.'"

The racism inherent in such gestures is apparent today, but in the late nineteenth and early twentieth century, it was popular for teams or players to recruit African-American boys as mascots. Most famously, Ty Cobb would rub the head of "Lil Rastus" before at-bats during the 1908 season. Adults with physical disabilities and mental illnesses were also used. Among the celebrity mascots of the era were Louis Van Zelst, a crippled person of short stature whom Connie Mack and the Philadelphia A's relied on for one season; Eddie Bennett, who was associated with pennants for the Dodgers, White Sox, and Yankees; and Charlie "Victory" Faust, who inspired the New York Giants to a pennant in 1911.

Pittsburgh fans tried to disrupt Boston's karma in Game Six by repeatedly showering Boston starter Bill Dineen with confetti as he pitched. But Dineen kept his focus as the Royal Rooters egged him on with "Tessie." Following the team's 6–3 win, team captain and manager Jimmy Collins said, "I do not know what I would have done without [the Rooters]. Their aid in encouraging us to victory has meant a lot to us in these games. They share in the victory with us."

Mounting concern over the impact of "Tessie" inspired the Pittsburgh faithful to form their own organized chorus for Game Six that they had dubbed the "Champion Rooters." Stepping it up a notch for Game Seven they hired their own band whose sole mission would be "to drown out the strains of Tessie." Louis P. Masur writes, "Pittsburgh fans believed that the song was the Pirates' 'death knell,' and they instructed the band to perform a 'program of antidotes' for 'Tessie' that included 'Hail, Hail, the Gang's All Here,' 'Down, Down, Down Where the Wurzburger Flows,' and 'The Smoke Goes up the Chimney Just the Same.'"

Boston won that afternoon and took the best-of-nine contest the following day. Following the series-clinching Game Eight, popular *Boston Globe* scribe Tim Muriname wrote: "['Tessie'] will go tunefully tripping down the ages as the famous mascot that helped the Boston Americans win three of four in Pittsburgh, capture the final game in Boston and with it the title—champions of the world. Sang by the thundering ensemble at the Huntington baseball grounds yesterday afternoon, 'Tessie' was there when anything worth doing was done . . . the words of the song have about as much to do with baseball as they did to the operation of stoking in the roundhouse across the field. But the effect is the thing; so 'Tessie' is a four-time winner."

After winning four of the next fourteen World Series, the Sox and their aging Royal Rooters learned that all good songs must come to an end. Eighty-six years without the chorus of "Tessie" at Fenway; eighty-six years without a championship.

Although hardly the only team dithering in a long championship drought, the Red Sox certainly made late-season losing a gut-wrenching art form. Dropkick Murphys bassist Ken Casey had grown up with it. His granddad had a couple of friends who worked in Boston, and in 1975 started taking the six-year-old Casey onto the field before and after games and into the clubhouse. He would dive in the right field and pretend he was Dwight Evans. Longtime Red Sox fixture Johnny Pesky got him a ball signed by the whole team. Casey took it home and played baseball with it out in the rain. "I tell you, my backside was sore after then," he recalls. Not as painful a memory as watching the Sox fade in Game Seven of the 1975 World Series.

That Fall Classic was his introduction to the heartbreak of supporting the Red Sox. Casey was at the home games in the '86 World Series (in which Boston was one out away from winning the championship before a famous error turned the tide for the Mets) and glued to the set for the games at Shea. "Just watching Game Six destruct and everything and how it all happened," he recalls. "It definitely came on in '86—believing in the curse, for sure."

As with most New Englanders, '86 didn't dampen his loyalty, but deepened his support. He stoically endured the season-ending collapses and wore these losses like battle scars. He admits that part of his inspiration for forming the Dropkicks was to make connections with the Sox and score better tickets. "Having an in with the team and getting into the games," he says. "It was as simple as that. When it comes to baseball, we're still kids at heart. Do something that gets us into the park? Sure, we'll do it. Getting us on the field? Even better."

So when Jeff Horrigan sent him revised lyrics to "Tessie," Casey was flat-out sold.

The band was still in Europe, so on opposite sides of the Atlantic, Casey and Horrigan refined the song. Both transcribed the original scratchy recording and faintly made out the nonsensical lyric, "Tessie is a maiden with the love." They ended up using it in the lead-in, then the band started putting the song together. The key was B flat, which suited the band's bagpipes. Red Sox players got involved, with Johnny Damon, Bronson Arroyo, and Lenny

Dinardo agreeing to do backup vocals. "Twice we had different studios reserved," Horrigan recalls, "and each time was after a grueling, excruciating Red Sox loss, and afterwards, no one wanted anything to do with it. We reserved Woolly Mammoth Studios next to the Old Baseball Tavern. They won that game and we were able to get a bunch of guys just to come on over."

In the liner notes for the EP that was released in June 2004, Casey went out on a limb and wrote that the intent of the song was "to bring back the spirit of the Rooters and put the Red Sox back on top." It was by no means the first prediction that a revival version of "Tessie" would break an eighty-six-year old curse. Noted Red Sox historian Glenn Stout, who had once curated the McGreevy Collection at the Boston Public Library, wrote an article in 1986 reminding readers that no Sox team had won a World Series without "Tessie" and urging a revival. Unfortunately, a George Vecsey article later that year, suggesting a curse of the Babe, had more traction. Author John Holway was more blunt in 2000 in his well-researched *The Baseball Astrologer*: "The nose-dive in the fortunes of the Red Sox has been blamed on the Curse of the Bambino. Nonsense. When the Fenway organist strikes up a happy, lilting rendition of 'Tessie' again, I believe, the Red Sox will return to the glory days of old."

There were Red Sox executives who were aware of the success rate of the song. Of them, Steinberg was among the most vocal. "Every time a new demo came out or an updated version," Horrigan says, "we would give him a new copy and he would all but force Red Sox employees to listen to it saying, 'This is the song that is gonna do it.'"

And yet Steinberg was as jittery as any of the Fenway faithful, who had had the proverbial magic carpet pulled out from under them year after year. "You don't have the right as a forlorn Red Sox fan to believe something magical is happening," Steinberg says, "until you've waited the requisite number of moments after the Red Sox World Series and you realize that it has really happened. With other franchises, you think you can feel it. You say it's happening. You couldn't do that in Boston, because you had to wait until that final out was squeezed in Game Seven in St. Louis."

Ken Casey's faith solidified on July 24, 2004. The Dropkicks had performed "Tessie" live from centerfield in a soggy Fenway Park. Then, after a fifty-four-minute rain delay, the Sox-Yanks tilt was underway. The Red Sox, nine-and-a-half games behind the Bombers in their division, had fallen behind 3–0 in the top of the third when Bronson Arroyo threw a curveball that plunked Alex Rodriguez and incited a brawl that started with Jason Varitek throwing a glove in A-Rod's face. Most Red Sox fans considered that moment the turning point of the season, although the momentum shift wasn't immediately reflected in the score.

"I had already shot my mouth off quite a bit," Casey says, "and the Sox were just getting killed [down 9–4 in the sixth] and I'm thinking, 'Oh my god, it's over before it starts. They're gonna get creamed in the first game.' Then the Sox come back, and Bill Mueller hits a walkoff home run on the same day that the song was debuted. That's when I started to go, 'Whoa, maybe there is something to this.'"

The Sox further backed him up, winning twenty-two of twenty-five games in late summer, then in the historic run in the playoffs. On two occasions when the Dropkicks performed "Tessie" at Fenway in the postseason, the Sox won with late inning rallies: first, at Game Three of the Division

Series, when David Ortiz hit a series-winning, tenth-inning walkoff; then in Game One of the 2004 World Series that the Red Sox would ultimately sweep.

Dr. Charles Steinberg made sure that the band got to all the postseason home and away games that season. Red Sox players warmly greeted the band on the field and always made them feel welcome, and Casey drew from it that players thought the band was bringing the team good luck. "They were buying into it a little bit," Casey says. "I'm just basing that on the fact that they were treating us well and they just felt like we were kind of, in some small, small way, a part of it."

Casey also got a rise out of seeing fans at Fenway sing along to "Tessie" on the PA system after David Ortiz's walkoff home runs in the ALCS. But for him, the most profound moment occurred in the moments after the Sox defeated the Yankees in Game Seven. He joined a stream of Red Sox fans making their way down toward the Red Sox dugout. "All these kids we grew up with and all these people we knew, so there's this whole crowd of us," he says. "I happened to be with my friend Tim Brady, who was with me at all these World Series games in '86. And here we are eighteen years later and kind of getting to see the Sox turn it around. It was pretty awesome."

Before Game Four of the World Series, Steinberg told Casey, "If they win, go wait by the Cardinal dugout and I'll come find you." And sure enough, after the final out Steinberg pulled Casey and a friend onto the field, advising them to blend in because MLB had not issued them a pass. "We got on the field," Casey says, "and we ran and the first thing we did is try to pull the rubber from the mound, so then we filled our pockets with all the dirt from the mound and we're trying to pull up the bases. We were behind every news television camera in the background of every interview— being the morons on the cell phone. Hey, you wait eighty-six years, and then not be an idiot when the time comes?"

For reasons unbeknownst to the band, the Dropkicks were not brought in to perform "Tessie" at Fenway in 2005 or 2006. Their next invitation occurred during the 2007 postseason, the next year the Sox won the Series. They performed at Game Seven of the ALDS, as Daisuke Matsuzaka warmed up behind them in the pen, and then the Sox completed another improbable come-from-behind series victory.

Casey remembers the even warmer reception that players gave him as they came off the stage onto the field, with several players hugging them as if they were teammates. Ortiz greeted the band with, "Hey man, it's the rock 'n' roll band!" Even Curt Schilling came over and said, "Hey, thanks for the good luck," and hugged band members.

Tim Wakefield says it was mostly veterans like himself who were aware of the history of the song and association with good luck. The younger players were more just admirers of the band. "They thought 'Tessie' was a pretty good song," he says, "but only some of the guys understood the basis of the song and the Royal Rooters."

Jonathan Papelbon had become one of the band's biggest backers. With Pap's assistance, Casey and baseball historian Peter J. Nash opened a modern-day McGreevy's Third Base Saloon in Boston. Papelbon used the band's tune "Shipping Off to Boston" as his entrance song and danced a jig to it throughout the 2007 season and in a kilt on the Dropkick Murphy's float during that year's championship "rolling rally" parade.

Tens of thousands lined the three-mile-long parade route, and the city-wide celebration was uncannily similar to the Boston Red Sox first rolling rally in 1912. Following Boston's defeat of the New York Giants in the 1912 World Series, the Royal Rooters led a procession of open convertibles carrying players through downtown Boston and a crowd of thousands.

Social boundaries between player and fan were more informal in the early twentieth century. Team owners packed as many fans as possible into the ballpark, and as a result standing-room sections were allowed in the outfield and rules were changed to accommodate. Balls landing in the crowd were ruled automatic triples. Ken Casey thinks that level of closeness may have helped "Tessie" catch on, although he doubts the new version could become fan-driven like in the old days. "If you look at those old pictures of the Royal Rooters, they're right down on top of the field," he says. "And that's why I think Fenway has a step up on other parks. But the more that you remove the fans from the game, the more sedate they become. You want them to stand five feet from first base, sure then they'll be screaming and singing louder than they are now."

A bit of that raw potential for magic still lingers at Fenway, the oldest ballpark in the country and still the preferred destination for descendants of Boston's Royal Rooters. Ballpark architect Janet Marie Smith, who oversaw the design and completion of Camden Yards, Petco Park, and Turner Field before helming widely acclaimed renovations on 4 Yawkey Way in Boston, says that the warmth and charm of Fenway is in the details.

Smith notes that all of the factors that go into making a new ballpark more comfortable—wider aisles, smaller sections, shorter rows, vendor aisles—also create such a leisurely, laid-back, remote feeling from the game that fans never get the energy that they would at Fenway Park or Wrigley Field. "The older ballparks essentially hold more energy," she says. "You've got the same number of people, but fewer square feet per person. So if someone stood up in front of you, as they do at Fenway now, the whole section stands up. There's a wonderful natural camaraderie from that kind of seating arrangement, where you're forced to stay tuned to the game."

Accordingly, every player ever to put on a Sox uniform has his stories about the Fenway faithful.

Jason Bay recalls his first games in Boston after his mid-season trade from the Pirates: "There were 35,000 people into the game at Fenway versus 15,000 in Pittsburgh just watching. It was as if we were in the playoffs every night. That's when it felt especially magnified."

"You could see it all the way down in the minors," Justin Masterson says. "I started out in Lowell, and every game the ballpark was sold out. Everyone knew my name and all about me even when I'd just started with the club."

Jacoby Ellsbury started noticing early on that baseball fans understood small ball. "They know the game very well," he says. "The simple things—the hustle plays. Beating out a ground ball to prevent a double play. Moving a runner over. They appreciate the little things on the field—not just the home run."

The appreciation occurs not just at home, but on the road. Cries of "Let's go, Red Sox!" can be heard at ballparks around the majors. Modern-day Royal Rooters, minus the pomp and circumstance.

Following a game in Baltimore where visiting Sox back-ers made more noise than the hometown fans, Mike Lowell told the *Boston Globe*, "I don't know if it gives you an advantage, but it makes you feel good. It's never bad to have people cheering for you on the road."

Tampa Bay Rays first baseman Carlos Pena told the *Globe* that he was almost thrown out on the base paths because of Boston's fan presence at the Tropicana Dome when the Red Sox visited. Pena was on first base when a teammate lined a shot to then Sox leftfielder Manny Ramirez. Pena heard the crowd roar and assumed that the ball got past Ramirez. He was rounding second when he realized that the crowd was cheering because Ramirez had caught the ball. Luckily Pena beat the throw back to first. "We know not to read anything by the noise the crowd makes when we play Boston," he said. "It's crazy. They're one of those teams that has world-wide fans."

Red Sox players admit that in the curse years, the influence of fans was sometimes counterproductive.

"It was always the Curse of the Babe," Lou Merloni says. "It started putting a little pressure on the guys. We start thinking, 'Jesus, we're trying to win a damn championship and people are coming to us over and over asking if we believe in the Curse.'"

Derek Lowe wonders if it wasn't intentional. "In a strange way, a lot of Red Sox fans like that attachment to the fact they hadn't won. They talked about it every year. 'Oh, this isn't the year. To heck with these guys!' It went hand in hand. Red Sox fans—misery. I tell you there's something that they enjoyed about it."

Mike Timlin recalls the 2004 Red Sox tackling the issue head-on: "In 2004 we kind of sat down as a club and said, 'We need to see if we can convince everyone outside of the clubhouse.' Because we knew we could win the World Series, but we had to convince everybody outside of the clubhouse—and that means our fans, front office, everybody. And we had to exude that type of energy to them. Then they finally started picking it up like, 'Wow, these guys can really do it.'"

Of course, the exposure players have to fans and vice versa is all relative to the era. Even with an old-style ballpark, players are more celebrity-oriented and earn amounts that would have been unfathomable back in the early twentieth century. Ballplayers are protected by bodyguards, and old-style social forums for baseball have been eroded by online social forums, blogs, sports talk radio, and other forms of social media. Even Red Sox Nation is now a team-run club rather than something that rose up grassroots from the community. The old-time organ at Fenway has given way to loudspeaker music, and fans sing along to their songs, as opposed to the old-fashioned lyrics of "Tessie."

Still, even now, when fan-player interactions are limited to a quick greeting when a player signs an autograph seeker's ball, fans still believe that their support for a team matters. There is no better example of this than the resurrection of the song "Tessie" and, in 2008, McGreevy's Third Base Saloon. The bar was the brainstorm of author and filmmaker Peter J. Nash, who had once been known in the music industry as rapper Sinister Prime Minister Pete Nice, and is now as deeply respected as a baseball historian as he was as a musician. An active member of the Society for American Baseball Research since he was twelve, Nash is author of a volume of photography of the Royal Rooters (*Boston's Royal Rooters*) and a history of the Greenwood Cemetery in Brooklyn, New York, where many of baseball's early pioneers were laid to rest. Nash also produced the film *Rooters: The Birth of Red Sox Nation*. But his material pride and joy is his astounding collection of baseball memorabilia from the late nineteenth and early twentieth century. And much of the Rooters-related artifacts has found a home in the bar on Boylston Street in Boston. In fact, the bar itself holds many of the objects that were in Third Base Saloon, including life-size replicas of a baseball mannequin (called The Baseball Man) that once stood on the roof of the original saloon and ceiling light fixtures made out of actual players' baseball bats. Nash used to have a replica of the bar in a former gas station that he converted into the Baseball Fan Hall of Fame in Cooperstown, New York. But Nash is quick to point out that the actual Third Base Saloon had many incarnations, as Nuf Ced had moved it twice before Prohibition closed the final location near the corner of Tremont Street, which was closer to Fenway Park. In eulogy of its closing, the *Boston Traveler* reported, "The room . . . where the strains of 'Tessie,' the old Boston Baseball war song, made the rafters tremble; that room is now strangely silent—almost deathlike."

The reopening of the saloon was, as Casey described it, a "no-brainer."

"It just seemed like a home for the story," Casey says. "Somewhere to go to see ['Tessie'] in action and tell them about these characters from the Rooters and just the legend of the place. Here's Pete making a replica of a bar in upstate New York. Why not make a replica of a bar that actually pours beer and make a real one."

Casey is proud just to carry the torch of history. "I think the coolest thing is being part of that fan tradition in Boston," he says. "We're reading about 'Tessie' in books from almost a hundred years later. And we're kind of finding us a place in history and we'll be a footnote in a couple of books that there's this rock band tagging along with the [future champion] team through the year trying to claim they had something to do with it. Like in the sense of trying to bring their spirit, those guys were beating on bass drums and yelling through bull horns—kind of what we were doing."

Dr. Steinberg says that what he draws from "Tessie" is that when fans are positively engaged in the atmosphere in the ballpark, their effect can be powerful. "The Royal Rooters thought of that. Honus Wagner acknowledged that in defeat for the Pirates. I think that's one of the most gratifying elements of going to a ball game is that you matter."

Chapter 17

Ghost Check
in Aisle 3

Walk through the Potrero Hill Shopping Center in San Francisco's Mission District and you'll see the typical sights of
a strip mall: the coffee shop, the pharmacy, the gym, the
clothing store, and the like. The parking lot is large and filled
at any given moment with mothers carting kids in SUVs to
pick up something for dinner or rent a video for the weekend.

There is nothing here to indicate that the asphalt and
tar were once an expanse of perfectly manicured green
grass, encircled by 18,600 seats that were often filled to
capacity. Nothing to indicate that this was the home of the
San Francisco Seals, one of the most successful and best-
loved minor league teams of the twentieth century. A team
whose roster featured future Hall of Famers like Joe DiMaggio, Lefty Gomez, Harry Heilmann, Earl Averill, and Tony
Lazzeri. A team that won an impressive eleven championships in its fifty-five seasons, more than any other Pacific
Coast League team.

With not so much as a small plaque to mark the location
(let alone a statue, or a sign bearing the name or logo of
the great team), it's no wonder that few people working or
shopping here have any idea that this was the site of many
memorable baseball moments—not only for the Seals, but
for the San Francisco Giants, who played in Seals Stadium
when they first moved to the West Coast. In two generations'
time, the legendary team has been all but forgotten by

current Potrero Hill residents—with the exception of some strange goings-on at one of the shopping center's stores.

• ◆ •

Ross Dress for Less is one of those chain discount retailers that carries everything from clothing to housewares to shoes to linens to jewelry, all in a large, cluttered, fluorescent-lit retail floor. The branch at Potrero moved into the mall in 1996. It wasn't long before workers started noting some odd experiences.

Lianna Peña worked the upstairs cash office. "I'd be sitting working on my paperwork and then papers that were on top of the safe would suddenly all go down on the floor," she recalls, adding that there was no breeze or force in the room to account for this. On other occasions, "Things would disappear from my office, like reports that I know I left there. I would ask everybody, 'Did you take this?' and they said, 'No, no, no.'"

Sometimes Peña would get to her office to discover a mess that hadn't been there when she left. She would walk in cautiously, announcing to any spirits, "Okay—I don't have time to play with you! Get away from here!" She laughs at the recollection now, admitting, "I was scared, but I couldn't show it to the ghost!"

Vilma Peraza, who manages the store, had her own office scare. "I was upstairs at night, sitting at my computer," she remembers. "And I felt someone touching my back. When I turned around, there was no one there." She describes the sensation as a very distinct tap that couldn't be accounted for by air-conditioning or a lump in the chair she sat in. "I ran downstairs!" she says. "I was very scared." For a long while after that, Peraza would not go up to the office alone.

Vilma also recalls the time she and a security guard were leaving the building. She turned back toward the store and saw a figure moving like a flash through the aisles. She thought it was simply an employee . . . and then realized that nobody was left in the store. (Assistant manager Antoinette Torres had a very similar experience working alone in the store after hours. A figure flashed by quickly in the aisles, she says, though she notes that she had been up all night with no sleep and it might have been her mind playing tricks on her.)

Several employees have heard odd noises on their break. "The office is directly above the break room," Yadira Lopez says. "You hear people walking. Or a chair rolling, like someone is sitting up there. You think, 'Antoinette's up there—let me go tell her something.' But you go up and there's nobody there."

For Alfredo Hernandez, a supervisor at Ross, the overnight shift (required occasionally for inventory, or to oversee off-hours maintenance crews) is anything but quiet. "I've done maybe three or four overnights by myself. You hear something way on the other side of the store. You go over and there's no one there, and things will be scattered on the floor.

"It happened again just a few weeks ago when they waxed the floor. I was here by myself, working in the stockroom. I let the workers out for their meal break, and I had the whole store to myself. Then I heard a noise like somebody was working with the polishing gun. I thought, 'Didn't I let them out?' I went over and there was nobody."

The stockroom itself is a spooky spot for Hernandez. "You hear stuff, like a banging on the door. And then when you look outside and turn on the light, there's nobody there." Hernandez also describes an eerie feeling that someone is in the room with you, a hair-on-the-back-of-your-neck sensation other workers say they've experienced too.

Hernandez has occasionally heard words being spoken, including his own name—so distinctly that he has walked to the front of the store, thinking he's been paged, only to discover that no one has said a word.

And so the stories go. Motion-detector alarms going off when no one is around. Towels folded neatly on shelves at closing, discovered strewn across the floor the next morning. Security gates pulled down over the front door, only to be found up again moments later.

By all accounts, the "ghosts" at Ross Dress for Less are friendly sorts. "They never do nasty or really scary stuff," says Peña.

"It doesn't bother me," Lopez agrees. "It's like an ongoing joke." Lopez even gave the ghost a playful name: George.

"When something happens we'll say, 'Oh, George is here.' Someone will say, 'I have so much work to do,' and I'll say, 'Oh, let George help you. He needs to earn his keep.'"

While there are many stores in the shopping plaza, George—and any other spirits—seem to favor this location. Prior to Ross, this storefront housed a Safeway grocery store where items mysteriously fell off the shelves late at night, and employees talked of ghostly ballplayers roaming the aisles. The Safeway moved just a few doors down in the same mall (part of an expansion plan); since then, they report no strange activity.

Meanwhile, employees at the retailer have wondered why their store might be haunted. There has been much speculation over the years, and rumors have started that the land was once a cemetery, or that a customer may have died at this spot. The fact that Seals Stadium once stood here is news to the folks at Ross Dress for Less.

●◆●

Across the street from the Potrero Hill Shopping Center is a neighborhood bar and eatery called the Double Play Restaurant. Founded in 1909, the Double Play is a Mission District institution that still attracts blue-collar regulars, particularly for breakfast, lunch, and happy hour.

It is also a virtual shrine to the San Francisco Seals. Memorabilia and photographs line the walls of the three main rooms; the large dining room is decorated with huge murals depicting Seals Stadium. Here's a photo of the 1931 team, which won the pennant in their inaugural year at the stadium. Here's Lefty O'Doul managing the 1949 squad that played a sixteen-game Good Will Tour in Japan, the first baseball team to visit after WWII. (They went at the request of Douglas MacArthur, who regarded the trip as an important piece of international diplomacy, and who urged the team to "please win every game"—which they did.)

All three DiMaggio brothers—Dom, Vince, and Joe—are represented on the walls of the Double Play; all three played for the Seals. In 1932, Vince convinced the team to let his younger brother Joe fill in at shortstop for the last three games of the season—an inauspicious debut that would lead to a legendary career. Among Joe DiMaggio's many major league achievements with the Yankees is his famed 1941 fifty-six-game hitting streak, a record that still stands today. But in 1933, DiMaggio strung together a remarkable sixty-one-game streak while playing for the Seals.

Don Russo grew up in the neighborhood and remembers first going to the stadium when he was four or five. His father would put newspaper under Don's coat to keep him warm, and carry the sleeping child home after the game. As a teenager, Russo attended games on his own. Kids were let in free after the seventh inning, and if they helped pick up cushions afterward (which fans rented to soften the stadium's wooden seats, and threw back on the field as they exited), they were given a pass for free admittance to a future game.

Russo went on to play rookie league ball himself. When the opportunity came later in life to co-own and run the Double Play, Russo jumped at it. It was he who put the mural in the back room and added much of his personal memorabilia to the restaurant's decor. He wanted to re-create the feel of the great team's great stadium.

"It was a real gem," he says admiringly of the long-gone ballpark. "Somebody did a book on the ten greatest stadiums of all time—places like Fenway and old Yankee Stadium. Seals Stadium was the only minor league park in the book."

The Double Play is where the true "spirit" of the Seals—ghostly or otherwise—seems to reside. The older patrons here are probably the most devoted Seals fans left, a friendly group of locals in their fifties, sixties, and seventies who remember the homey culture of a stadium where usherettes wore uniforms like flight attendants, kids sat in trees outside the park to watch the game, the grounds crew maintained a garden in the back of the field, and women were admitted for free one night of the week. "It was a perfect little stadium," one barfly recalls.

These aging fans also remember great Seals players like Lew Burdette, Ferris Fain, Frank Malzone, Ken Aspromonte, Albie Pearson, Smead Jolley, Paul and Lloyd Waner, and Leo

Righetti, whose son Dave would become a pitcher and coach for the San Francisco Giants team that forced the Seals out of town.

The Seals won the PCL championship in 1957 and then left San Francisco for Phoenix in 1958 to make way for the major league team that had emigrated from the East. The San Francisco Giants occupied Seals Stadium for two years while Candlestick Park was being constructed; afterward, the stadium had no professional team and was eventually torn down in 1962 and converted to commercial use. Prior to the current shopping center, a car dealership occupied the spot.

In the decades following the Seals departure, former players would often stop in at the Double Play to talk with fans and reminisce. But fifty years later, few of these players are still around. In the summer of 2006 alone, three beloved former Seals (Con Dempsey, Dino Restelli, and Tom Del Sarto) all died within one month of each other. The fraternity of Seals players—and its auxiliary club of fans—is steadily dwindling.

The Double Play is changing as well. In January 2006, new management took over. The deal allowed the previous owners to take 40 percent of the Seals memorabilia with them; some patrons calculate that more than that was removed, including some of the more valuable pieces. Although the walls are still fairly full of Seals souvenirs and photos, for younger customers these are abstract museum pieces.

"It's like anything else," Russo says. "The times are changing, and they're changing so quickly. We're a society that moves on to the next. After me, and the people around my time, people won't even remember the stadium."

Today the Potrero Hill Shopping Center bustles with steady traffic, in a smooth flow of commerce. Like most modern-day malls, it is serviceable and soulless, efficient and impermanent.

Except in one store, where some unusual noises, bizarre occurrences, and unsettling events lead people to suspect that this is a site with a restless past, a noteworthy history that demands to be acknowledged.

Chapter 18

Minor Leagues,
Major Ghosts

Like all visitors to the Lackawanna Station Hotel in Scranton, Pennsylvania, the first thing that Philadelphia Phillies pitcher Roy Halladay was struck by was its beauty. The massive building, which began life as a train station in 1908, still bears the unmistakable look of a grand railway terminal, the kind constructed at the height of the railroad boom in the early 1900s. From the outside, Doric columns stretch up seventy feet to support an entablature above the main entranceway, an ornate clock flanked by sculpted eagles. In the lobby, a mosaic tile floor and marble walls transport visitors back to the early decades of the twentieth century. A barrel-vaulted Tiffany stained-glass ceiling adds to the effect, creating a space as lush as it is quaint.

But while the opulence of the grand hotel formed Halladay's initial impression of the place, it would not be the most lasting one. That had to do with the odd goings-on in his room.

It was the summer of 1997 and the future Cy Young Award winner was a young Blue Jays prospect with the Syracuse SkyChiefs (currently known as the Chiefs). The team was in town to play the Scranton/Wilkes-Barre Red Barons, the Triple-A affiliate for the Philadelphia Phillies. (In 2006, the Scranton team became the Triple-A club of the New York Yankees.) Halladay was drained from the nine-hour road trip and eager to get some rest. He had just faded to sleep when he was startled by the sound of water gushing full force from the bathroom-sink faucet. At the same time, he noticed the television—turned off when he fell asleep—was now inexplicably turned on. And, he says, a "putrid smell" suddenly filled the room.

Dismissing the oddness as a function of his groggy state, Halladay closed the faucet, turned off the TV set, and returned to bed. But as he started dozing off, more strangeness ensued. The toilet flushed on its own and the room lights came on. Now he was spooked. "I don't know what it was," Halladay says. "But I called the front desk to change rooms."

It was the pitcher's first visit to the Lackawanna Station Hotel, and in many ways, a fitting initiation. Dozens of players have similar stories from their stays there; hundreds of others repeat those stories to teammates and others around the International League. The Lackawanna is probably known as the most haunted road hotel in the minors.

"That was the rumor," remembers Mets star David Wright, who passed through Scranton playing for Norfolk in 2004. "It kind of creeped you out just to think about it while you were there. You know, old hotel . . . a lot of creepy things. That's a little bit spooky, especially after you hear the stories."

Take, for example, television sets turning on and off. Former Syracuse SkyChiefs roommates catcher Randy Knorr and infielder Eddie Zosky left their room for breakfast one morning and came back to find the set was on. That night they fell asleep with the set still on (their typical practice) only to wake up and find it was off and pushed back into its cabinet.

Veteran reliever Tyler Walker had a similar experience. "I was asleep one night and the TV just came on out of nowhere. I turned it off, and a little while later it came back on." John Foster, a pitcher in town with the Richmond

Braves, also had his set turn on and off on its own. During a stay in 2005, Louisville manager Rick Sweet could not get his set to turn off. "The clicker wouldn't work. The set wouldn't work." He called downstairs and the hotel staff came up and unplugged the television—and still it stayed on. "I changed rooms," Sweet says.

Then there are the stories of being locked out of one's room. Veteran pitcher Kane Davis's experience is typical: He left his room to visit some friends and came back to find that the door was dead-bolted from the inside. At first he thought his roommate had returned, but he knocked and got no response. Then he went back down the hall to call his room—again, nothing. He returned and tried his key again. This time, it opened a bit—the dead bolt was undone—but the flipper latch was shut and prevented the door from opening all the way. Davis summoned the hotel staff, who finally opened the door with a special tool. "They said that happens all the time. I said that *doesn't* happen all the time—I've stayed in hotels my whole career and that's *never* happened."

But it has happened to other players at the Lackawanna Station Hotel. In July 2006, pitcher Phil Stockman's flipper latch mysteriously locked itself and he had to be let into his room by security. (For good measure, Stockman awoke later that night to find all the lights in his room turned on.) In 2005, pitcher Chris Booker spent nearly half an hour trying to help a teammate get into his room. The key didn't work, and then when it finally did, "We tried to push the door, but it was like someone was holding it." Eventually, the force relented and they got into the room.

• ◆ •

If there are ghosts in the International League, Scranton seems just the place for them. The city is something of a ghost town itself, a prime example of the Northeastern Rust Belt—mining towns (iron and coal, in this case) that were at their zenith in the early 1900s, but which have become economically depressed in the wake of that industry's collapse. In the mid-1930s, Scranton's population peaked at around 150,000. Today, it is less than half of that.

The Delaware, Lackawanna, and Western Railroad rose and fell with the city's fortunes: It was the life beat of the local and regional economy for decades, and the rich design of the train station (its French Renaissance exterior, its two-and-a-half-story waiting area of Sienna and Alpine green marble) bespoke its prominent stature. But by 1960, the railroad's decreasing popularity forced a merger with the Erie Railroad. Ten years later passenger service stopped altogether, and the DL&W declared bankruptcy in 1972.

But the building was preserved, and after several suggested uses (including as a shopping mall, a museum, and a restaurant complex), it was converted into a Hilton hotel that opened on New Year's Eve 1983. Today, it's part of the Radisson chain.

The careful restoration of the hotel adds to the impression that it is of another time and place. The decor is steadfastly early twentieth century; all the original designs—even the original brass fixtures—have been lovingly restored. Stepping in the lobby is like stepping back in time. Several ballplayers liken it to the Overlook Hotel in Stanley Kubrick's horror film *The Shining*.

Various touches add to the haunted atmosphere. The area above the lobby's atrium is open space all the way up to the sixth (and top) floor; as a result, the fourth-, fifth-, and sixth-floor hallways essentially wrap around this empty space and look down upon the stained-glass archway that covers the lobby. Stories abound of people leaping off the ledges on these floors and falling to their deaths in the lobby below.

The open space also allows music and other noises from the first floor to waft upward. The lobby contains a baby grand piano at which a pianist sits in the evening, playing music to accompany the dining crowd in the lobby's restaurant. On the higher floors, the drifting music takes on an eerie, distant quality, adding to the haunted effect.

Some visiting baseball players claim to have seen the piano playing by itself late at night, another of the many Lackawanna ghost stories. Athletes also claim that the hotel's staircase—which winds around an old wrought-iron service elevator, and is used mostly by staff—is haunted. The basement of the building, currently housing offices and meeting rooms, is rumored to have served as a morgue during the Civil War.

Even the elevators are considered spooky. Their three interior walls are covered in mirrors, creating an eerie effect in which the image of the passenger recedes into infinity, becoming a ghostly blur at the end. "People who have had rooms next to the elevators hear people laughing and talking," says pitcher Chris Michalak, who had the experience himself. "And they go out and the elevator doors will open right in front of their faces and there's no one there."

• ◆ •

But the stories of odd noises and automated TV sets and lights and faucets can't compare with the tales of ballplayers who say they have actually seen or felt ghosts in their rooms.

Louisville catcher Dane Sardinha awoke at four in the morning to the sound of banging at his door. He yelled at his roommate Steve Lomasney to be quiet. A little later, "I woke up and saw someone sitting at the end of my bed, facing the other way." This time he knew the culprit wasn't his roommate. He had heard rumors of ghosts in the Lackawanna, "so I tried to kick him off the end of my bed." The strategy worked . . . temporarily. "Maybe thirty minutes later I saw him between me and my roommate's bed." This time, Sardinha "started swinging and yelling." Lomasney "heard my yelling but he hid underneath his blanket and pretended like nothing was going on."

Journeyman outfielder Ernie Young's first night in the hotel was equally memorable. He awoke to discover "there was a hand over my mouth. I couldn't scream, I couldn't yell or anything. There was nothing I could do about it." He never saw whatever force was clamping his mouth ("a presence or something," he says), but the experience lasted from fifteen to twenty seconds. When it ended, he turned on the TV and woke up his roommate, needing a little company to quiet his nerves.

J. D. Durbin, however, got a very good look at the spirit in his room. He and fellow Rochester pitcher Travis Bowyer were sound asleep in Room 418 when Durbin awoke to a cold shiver. "I turned my head and saw a guy in green-and-white striped long-sleeved shirt, spiky blondish hair, laying on his back on the bed with his elbow by my face. He was looking at me with big eyes. I started yelling 'Travis! Travis!' but my roommate was snoring like a buzz saw. As I turned back, the man was getting up to leave. I closed my eyes tight and reopened them and a heavyset African-American woman in an old purple dress was standing by the door. Then she sort of faded out." Bowyer awoke moments later and suggested the two sleep with the lights and television on for the rest of the night.

Perhaps the pair should have done the same three weeks later, when they were back in Scranton for another series. This time in a different fourth-floor room, Durbin recalls nodding off when Bowyer suddenly started talking out loud and laughing in his sleep. "He sprang up, turned on the light, and started freaking out," Durbin says. "He said he saw someone [in the room]. He started searching the bathrooms and different rooms. At first I thought he was just messing around, but he was pretty freaked out."

Louisville pitcher Joe Valentine was freaked out when he heard whispers in his room in the middle of the night. They woke him, but he put them out of his mind and went back to sleep. A little later they started again. "I got up and turned the light on and looked in the room to see who was there, and I was by myself." The next morning Valentine asked at the desk who was in the room next to his, and he was told it was vacant. "I thought, 'All right, something is going on.'"

In 2005, something *was* going on in Room 624. Buffalo Bisons trainer Todd Tomczyk dropped his luggage off in his room and then headed to the ballpark. When he returned, he discovered one window was wide open—a window that had been locked and bolted shut, impossible for guests to open. Having already heard about the legendary Lackawanna Station Hotel ghosts, Tomczyk was shaken. "I almost slept on the bus," he recalls.

The next night, Tomczyk's electricity went out. He called the front desk and was told that there was a thunderstorm. "No, there wasn't," he insists, noting that the electricity was on everywhere else in the hotel. Tomczyk stepped into the hallway, reluctant to go back inside. Outside his door, he encountered Bison infielders Jake Gautreau and Jeff Liefer, and accused the pair of playing tricks on him. "How are we going to control the power in your room?" Gautreau asked.

As the three discussed the odd phenomena in Tomczyk's room, the door to Room 620 opened and a strange-looking teenager emerged. His skin was pale and long black hair hung in front of his face. He walked with a cane and had a large scar on his left leg. "He was walking real morbidly— sinisterly," Liefer recalls. "Real skinny. He just didn't look healthy. He looked kind of like what you would imagine a ghost would look like."

The trio called out to the boy, who didn't respond. He slowly walked down the hall, passing right by the group at one point and disappearing into the stairwell. "All of us were scared and freaking out," Liefer says. Gautreau remembers a brief exchange as the boy walked by. "We said, 'Hey buddy, isn't it a little late for you to be up?' It was probably a little past midnight. And he said, 'I don't sleep.'"

Some minutes later, the boy re-emerged from the stairwell and again walked past the group without making eye contact. Then he looked back at them and said, "You guys want to see something weird?" When they said yes, the boy reached his hand around his neck and pulled his head 180 degrees.

"He turned his whole head around!" Gautreau recalls, still astonished by what he saw. "Everyone just had their mouths on the floor." Liefer recalls hearing the *crack-crack-crack* noise as his neck pivoted. Tomczyk yelled, "That's not anatomically possible!" But the boy repeated the move.

The men spent the next few minutes talking with the teenager, whose name was Thomas. They asked him questions, and he responded with what Liefer calls "real weird answers." At one point he drifted toward the ledge that overlooks the atrium and they thought he was going to jump. But he continued to respond almost absentmindedly to their questions. "I shouldn't be here right now," he told the group. "I should be dead." When they asked why, he said that he had been in a car crash. "So the first thing you're thinking, if you believe in ghosts, is that this kid died in a car accident," Gautreau says. "He's got a broken leg. He turned his head all the way around. You take it for what it's worth."

The story quickly made the rounds of the league. Today, Gautreau says he thinks the kid was real, though he allows that "there's still a 5 to 10 percent chance it could have been [a ghost]."

• ◆ •

If Thomas were indeed a ghost, he joins a long list of the hotel's more permanent residents. Pitcher Chris Michalak heard of the ghost of a little boy who haunts the third floor, as well as a hotel butler who is said to inhabit the fifth floor.

Many alleged ghosts come with rumors of accidental deaths and suicides. Reliever Gary Majewski was told that "a girl fell off the fifth story and her ghost is roaming around there somewhere." Jeff Liefer heard it was a man who fell off the fifth floor and now haunts it. Richmond pitcher Matt Wright heard of a man who jumped off the fourth floor and a woman who jumped from the sixth floor, both suicides.

Liefer also heard "another crazy story" involving someone in a wedding party, who likewise fell to his death. Todd Tomczyk's version of the wedding story claims that "a woman got kidnapped on her wedding day, and now the entire wedding party haunts the fourth floor." Tomczyk also heard that a man fell off the sixth floor back when the building was a railroad station, and now "his wife and kid haunt the sixth floor." That sounds like a variation on the story first baseman Kevin Witt heard, in which the man who "completed" the construction of the train station climbed to the top of the building and jumped off. On the one-year anniversary of his suicide, his wife jumped off the same spot and killed herself.

Outfielder Alex Rios heard that a man was actually killed there—deliberately thrown off the sixth floor by an assailant. When Rios stayed on that floor, he heard noises in the night and thought someone—perhaps the murdered man—was in his bathroom.

With so many legends making the rounds of clubhouses and team buses, some of the more intrepid players have taken it upon themselves to do a little ghost hunting at the hotel. Majewski would stay up late with the lights out just waiting for some otherworldly visitors. "I like freaked-out stuff," he says. "I'd love to see things like that."

Perhaps he should have joined third baseman Joe Crede and his buddies. In town with the White Sox Triple-A Charlotte affiliate in 2002, they did a little late-night snooping on the third floor, which they had heard was haunted. "It was three o'clock in the morning. We were walking around being real quiet," Crede recalls. One person in the party felt a strong chill; just after that, they heard loud creaking noises, which sent a scare through everyone. "We bolted out of there."

A year or two later, another group of Charlotte players, including catcher Jamie Burke, set off on their own after-hours ghost hunt. "We tried to go and find the room that some things happened in," says Burke. The group had heard stories of sheets being pulled off people's beds in the night, and TVs and lights turning on and off by themselves. The teammates ducked into a storage room at one point and someone shut the door behind them, enclosing them in darkness. But they never came upon any actual ghosts. Burke suggests the size of the party may have scared away the spirits. "I don't think anything's going to happen when you've got ten or fifteen guys standing around late at night," he laughs.

• ◆ •

Despite all these stories from different players staying at the hotel at different times over the years, when you ask the staff about rumors of ghosts at the Lackawanna, the response is nearly unanimous: There's no such thing. What's more, many insist that baseball players are the only guests who claim the place is haunted. Clerks at the front desk, servers in the bar/restaurant, and maids in the hallways all say that ballplayers pull pranks on each other (see Chapter 19: Pranks, Hoaxes, and Jokes) and love to tell stories, but that none of their claims is based in fact. "I've been here thirteen years," says one maid. "And if it were haunted, I wouldn't work here."

Sameer Ali, marketing director at the hotel, says that every odd occurrence has a perfectly simple explanation. Some of the television sets are old, for instance, and don't work properly; hence, their odd behavior. Ditto for the lighting and plumbing irregularities: The building is old, but they are continually working to upgrade systems. Glitches occur along the way. "These things happen in all hotels," Ali notes, adding that the active imaginations of some players—occasionally fueled by a few drinks in the hotel bar—lead them to ascribe more to it than meets the eye.

Visiting athletes have also complained that the hotel smells like a funeral home—there is a strong scent of flowers, but no flowers to be seen. Ali says this is simply a floral spray and deodorizer used by the cleaning staff. Catchers Chris Snusz and Brian Schneider, roommates on a 2000 road trip to Scranton with the Ottawa Lynx, claim they heard the sound of a train in the early morning, as if it were right beneath their room. Ali says that trains do pass near the hotel regularly—there are still tracks just behind it—and that accounts for any railroad noises.

As for the rumor that the station used to house a morgue in the Civil War era, this seems unlikely. The site was not a train station during the Civil War (though train tracks may have run nearby). It is true, however, that trains running through the station sometimes carried dead bodies to be buried elsewhere. These cadavers had to be stored while waiting for the appropriate trains, and an area in the basement was used for this purpose. Not quite a morgue, but a temporary storage area for bodies awaiting transport. Which, for many baseball players, is ghoulish enough.

●◆●

If it's all based on misunderstandings and innuendo, where did people first get the notion that the Lackawanna Station Hotel is haunted? One longtime bartender at the hotel says the ghost stories began with a woman named Sylvia who worked on the waitstaff for years. Sylvia wanted to be a writer, and when a local paper run mostly by volunteers started up, she began penning a regular column that discussed goings-on about town, her opinions on various subjects, and other random themes.

In one edition, she wrote about an experience she claimed to have had at the hotel. She was picking up room-service trays in the halls late at night when a ghostly woman whooshed down the hall, moved past her, and disappeared through a wall. Sylvia claimed it was the ghost of Phoebe Snow. Snow was a kind of spokesperson/mascot for the railroad, who resembled the "flying lady" hood ornament on a Rolls Royce. She wore a white Victorian dress to emphasize how clean the anthracite fuel was and would stand at the front of the train waving to people and welcoming them aboard. Sylvia's story was picked up by some train magazines and the legend of the haunted hotel began.

Sylvia is not, however, the only hotel employee who says strange things go on there. One person currently on the waitstaff says that when delivering room service, he sometimes hears his name being whispered or called out in the hallways. Another bartender has his own variation on the death/suicide tales: A woman died of a heart attack on the fourth floor, he says. Shortly thereafter, her despondent husband killed himself by jumping from the sixth floor down to the lobby. Their spirits haunt the building.

Whatever the truth, there's no doubt that the Lackawanna's reputation precedes it. Athletes hear the stories before they ever set foot in the place, and are jumpy from the start. Players who typically room alone will often try to find roommates for their nights at the Lackawanna.

When major league outfielder Matt Diaz first arrived in Scranton with his Durham Bulls teammates, his roommate, infielder Jason Smith, who'd been with the team for a couple of years, told him, "Dude, whatever we do, if our room is on the fifth floor, we're switching."

Ottawa Lynx second baseman Luis Figueroa was in town in June 2002 when a minor earthquake shook Scranton. "My roommate, Dicky Gonzalez, and I thought at first it was the ghosts that everyone is always talking about. We grabbed our knives and went under the covers, because they're ghosts and they can be inside the covers, too."

Louisville infielder Matt Kata, citing the advice of popular psychic Sylvia Browne, makes a habit of entering his room, acknowledging any ghosts, and firmly telling them to leave him alone. Richmond second baseman Jon Schuerholz does just the opposite. "I'll walk in and say, 'If there are any spirits here, I'm not trying to piss you off. If you'd like to come into my room, come into my room.'" The invitation is genuine. "Everybody says they see ghosts. I'd like to see one."

At least Schuerholz—unlike many nervous players—is finding a way to enjoy the historic building, with or without unintended guests. Looking back on his experience, Roy Halladay now appreciates the special beauty of the Lackawanna Station Hotel.

"It's a lot nicer than the newer chain hotels I stayed at in the minors," he says. "I found it really interesting and memorable just to stay in such an old hotel. Even with the strange stuff that happened to me."

Chapter 19
Pranks, Hoaxes, and Jokes

From giving the classic "hot foot" to sticking chewing gum bubbles on player's caps to putting hot dogs in the fingers of baseball gloves, ballplayers are known for practical jokes and good-natured teasing. With so many ghost stories and haunted legends running rampant throughout baseball culture, it's no surprise that guys routinely pull pranks to scare one another—usually the rookie. While many players believe wholeheartedly in ghosts and curses and things that go bump in the night, some learn quickly that not every eerie occurrence is the result of a malicious spirit. Every once in a while, it's the work of a mischievous teammate.

The frequency of these pranks—and the fact that they are so often successful—is a testament to the special place ghosts occupy in the baseball imagination. In addition to being a source of wonder and fear, ghosts have become a source of entertainment in the fraternity-like atmosphere of the typical clubhouse.

Probably the most common ghost-related prank is the "haunting" of a player's hotel room. It works best at hotels that already have ghostly reputations, like the Radisson Lackawanna Station Hotel in Scranton, Pennsylvania (see Chapter 18: Minor Leagues, Major Ghosts). Players with extra time on their hands and an irreverent sense of humor find it easy to prey on their teammates' paranoia.

Roommates Kevin Witt and Tom Evans, infielders with the Syracuse SkyChiefs, decided to have some fun with their teammates on a trip to Scranton in the late 1990s. "We took the room list and just started going to people's doors and scratching the door or jostling the handle," Witt says. "Some of the doors are kind of loose and you could just push them a little bit. We went to everybody's rooms on different floors and just messed with people."

More convincing, of course, are the "special effects" that go on inside the rooms. Players will sneak in to write creepy messages in blood-red lipstick on the bathroom mirror, or rearrange the furniture. Tampa Bay Ray B. J. Upton recalls the time that teammates wanted to scare pitcher Tim Corcoran. "They put grape juice in his toilet to make it look like blood."

Very often, roommates are the source of the gag. Richmond Braves pitcher John Foster decided to "mess around" with his roommate, Kyle Davies. "He'd be sitting there watching TV, facing the other direction, and I was on the other bed. And I'd throw a sock over and act as if I was asleep. And he'd be like, 'Holy smokes! Did you see that?!' And then he'd tell everybody."

Like so many players, Davies does believe the Scranton hotel is haunted, and even today tells of how he would "close the shades at night and in the morning they were open." But he seems to have caught on to his prankster roommate. "It might have been John just messing with me."

•◆•

Many practical jokes are much more elaborate than Foster's errant socks. Players will go to great lengths to set up and pull off a convincing room haunting.

First baseman Andy Abad was with the Pawtucket Red Sox when he heard what he considers a genuine ghost story: A rookie came out of his hotel room claiming that while he was sleeping, a ghost picked up his bed and slammed it down. Checking it out afterward, Abad looked at the legs of the bed and discovered that they were about half an inch off their indentations in the rug—seeming confirmation that the bed was moved.

The next night, Abad—who likes to fish on the road and had fishing line with him—decided to use the story to frighten a teammate. "We got a guy's room key and we went in there and rigged the whole hotel room—like the doors for the TV cabinet, and the lamp, and the drapes. We rigged it all." That night, Abad hid by one side of the bed while a confederate was in the closet. They waited for their mark to fall asleep. "And then we started pulling the strings."

The drapes rustled, the lamp fell over and broke. The cabinet doors opened. "The guy freaked out and he ran downstairs," recalls Abad, laughing. "'You gotta change my room! The room is haunted!' he told the lobby staff."

Abad is an inveterate prankster, and often repeats the room-rigging stunt, especially for the benefit of rookies. He knows that a careful and thorough setup is the important first step of a good ghost prank. In 2006 he told infielder Jeff Bannon about the moving bed well before their Louisville Bats team got to Scranton. When they checked in, Abad and Bannon's roommate, outfielder Chris Denorfia, banded together to get Bannon.

Denorfia slipped Abad his room key and then went to dinner with Bannon. When the two returned, Denorfia said he was going to stop in the bar for a drink and would be up shortly. Bannon went up to the room alone.

"I open the door and it's pitch black," Bannon remembers. "The air conditioner is all the way full, so it's freezing. They had unscrewed the light bulbs, so the light switch didn't work. And they left the water running in the bathroom."

Entering a cold, dark room spooked Bannon right away. "I'm thinking, 'Oh my God. This is weird!' I started freaking out a little bit." Bannon finally turned on a light and then saw the rest of Abad's handiwork. One chair had been stacked upon another, and both were on the bed. On the table, a beer can was open, with a half-full glass of beer beside it. A partially smoked cigarette lay in the ashtray.

Telling the story today, Bannon says these touches were over the top. "Right there I'm thinking, 'Okay—this is too much.' I may believe in spirits and whatnot, but I personally don't believe that ghosts are gonna pick up and move furniture. And physically smoke a cigarette and drink a beer."

Bannon went down to the front desk. "I asked them is there a way that they can track if someone else got a key to get into my room, or if someone else's key went into it." They promised to look into it, and Bannon then went into the bar and told his teammates what he'd experienced. "I said, 'You'll never believe it! My furniture's stacked, et cetera, et cetera.'" While he was telling the tale, the hotel staff approached and told him that there was no need to investigate his room lock: One of the maintenance workers had heard a teammate say that he was going to "haunt" the room.

Bannon insists today that he quickly realized it was a prank and he wasn't too scared. But Abad claims he was "really freaking out" and teammate pitcher Chris Michalak says, "He was very upset. He was very disturbed. He couldn't deal with it." Michalak says Bannon wanted the locks changed on his room. Even hotel staff recall the incident and say that Bannon was panicked and anxious.

Bannon says he pretended to buy into it, and he had a reason for doing so. "I never let on to the other guys that I knew, because . . . I'll get them back!"

Abad's pranks are the equivalent of whistling past the graveyard, because he does believe ghosts exist, and that the Lackawanna Station Hotel in particular houses some. "I do, I really do," he says. "When you walk in the place you get a sense of it. It almost feels like a haunted ghost ship, like the *Titanic*.

"Guys like us hype it up and have fun with it. But then again, you're looking over your shoulder. 'Cause it was spooky, too. You gotta sleep with one eye open."

●—◆—●

As inventive as Abad and his cohorts are, they are only continuing a much larger tradition of room rigging. Tom Evans recalls a group of teammates pulling a similar prank on a SkyChiefs rookie in 1998. "They had a string tied to a lamp," Evans recalls. Once again, a complicit roommate had supplied a key to the "ghosts" while the target of the joke was out. "They were in the hallway, and they pulled the string and pulled the lamp off the bedside table. The guy hopped on the bed and was freaking out!"

Veteran minor league pitcher Kevin Tolar and friends considered rookie-room-rigging something of a sport. "We went to Wal-Mart and bought some fishing line and different things and we rigged the room up for a rookie that had just come up and scared him flat to death. Making the doors move, and the windows shake, and curtains move, and all that stuff." It worked so well that "we did it for a couple years in a row."

Tolar says the secret to pulling off such a prank is lots of setup, to get into the head of the rookie well before the hotel visit. "About two weeks before we went we'd start telling him [hotel ghost stories] and we'd have it set up good for the first night."

• ◆ •

Baseball players aren't the only ones occasionally duped by an invented ghost story. In 2005, ESPN ran a Halloween feature on a Gettysburg College professor named Peter Stitt who had a fantastical story to tell. He had lived in a house once owned by Hall of Fame pitcher Eddie Plank, the first lefty pitcher to win 300 games. On February 24, 1996, Stitt was awakened by his dog, alerting Stitt to strange sounds emanating from the first floor, a "woosh-and-thunk kind of noise." Investigating over the next few days, Stitt discovered that Plank had died seventy years earlier, to the day. The noise, which sounded like a pitcher throwing to a catcher, continued nightly until March 31—the end of spring training—and then stopped.

The conclusion was obvious: The ghost of Eddie Plank was in the house, and warming up for the upcoming season. The enticing tale was picked up in several news outlets and is still well-known today. It would be a classic baseball ghost story except for one thing.

"I just made it up," Stitt says.

The ruse—which has never been revealed until now—started innocently enough: Stitt never intended to dupe anyone. "My original impulse was to spoof the ghost industry in Gettysburg," he says. "We have all these ghost tours, finding dead soldiers hanging around and stuff like that."

Stitt knew that Plank had built the house and died in it (something he later claimed to discover in city hall records while researching the "strange noises") and figured that was his best angle. "We had this real long space that went from the back wall to the front wall, so I paced it off and lo, it was about sixty-eight feet." Close enough to the sixty and one-half feet that separates the pitching rubber from home plate. "Then I said, 'I'm on my way!' I invented the noises with the dog, and it all fit together."

The piece was originally published in the *Gettysburg Review*, a literary magazine that Stitt edits. His tone throughout was ironic; he felt confident that the *Review*'s highbrow audience would get the joke, and they did.

"Then the editor of the alumni magazine at the college said, 'Hey, this is a great story because of all the tie-ins with Gettysburg College.'" Plank had been a student there; Stitt currently teaches there. The editor wanted to reprint the piece in the alumni magazine.

"He did a little editing and he took out two or three of my 'winks,'" Stitt says. The article now read like a much more earnest, straightforward ghost tale. It was this version that attracted ESPN and other media outlets. (Though the ESPN piece maintained its own tongue-in-cheek quality throughout, with the segment reporter making numerous ghost jokes along the way.)

Stitt enjoyed the attention. The skeptic in him had a good laugh at the hubbub his invented ghost created. "The whole thing was highly amusing," he says. "[ESPN] got these ghost people who bring in machines and this woman who walked around and could 'feel' things in certain corners."

Anyone who resents the hoax may take pleasure in knowing that Stitt did not emerge completely unscathed.

His original article spent a good deal of time talking about the house's previous owner, a wealthy elderly woman, thrice widowed. Stitt implied—jokingly—that she had likely killed all of her husbands for their money. When the piece ran in the alumni magazine, he got many letters from the deceased woman's friends—wealthy Gettysburg College alumni insulted at the insinuations and threatening to pull their funds from the school. Eventually the college president called and "I had to be very nice to a lot of rich people," Stitt says.

"But it worked out. There were no repercussions from it. To me it was obvious that it was all just good clean fun."

References

Abrams, Roger. *The First World Series and the Baseball Fanatics of 1903*. Boston: Northeastern University Press. 2003.

Allen, Jim. *Ichiro Magic!* Tokyo: Kodansha International. 2001.

"Angels Unplugged." *Los Angeles Times*, October 12, 2009. http://latimesblogs.latimes.com/angels_blog/2009/10/angels-red-sox-nick-adenhart-torii-hunter.html.

"Ballplayers Say Pfister Hotel Haunted." WISN.com, May 28, 2009. www.wisn.com/news/19586075/detail.html.

Barker, Barbara. "Gardner Revisits with Middle Island Bracelet Girl." *Newsday*, June 12, 2009.

Barone, Don. "Seeking Some Baseball Spirit." ESPN. com. http://sports.espn.go.com/espn/page2/story?page=barone/051031.

Belanger, Jeff. "Most Famous Phenomenon." Ghostvillage .com. http://www.ghostvillage.com/resources/2008/features_10082008.shtml.

Bjarkman, Peter C. *Baseball with a Latin Beat*. Jefferson, NC: McFarland & Company, Inc., Publishers. 1994.

Blum, Ronald. "Yankees Monitoring Wind, Tickets at New Ballpark." Associated Press, May 12, 2009.

Bollman, Andrew, and Thomas M. Keppeler. "Dorm Legends Spook Some Students." *The Daily Free Press*, October 30, 1998.

Bradford, Rob. "Product Has Red Sox Collared: Phiten Has Convinced Key Players." *Boston Herald*, June 20, 2008.

Bradley, Mickey, and Dan Gordon. *Haunted Baseball: Ghosts, Curses, Legends & Eerie Events*. Guilford, CT: The Globe Pequot Press. 2007.

Brother Gilbert and Harry Rothgerber. *Young Babe Ruth: His Early Life and Baseball Career, From the Memoirs of a Xaverian Brother*. Jefferson, NC: McFarland & Co. 1999.

Cool, Kim. *Ghost Stories of Clearwater & St. Petersburg*. Venice, FL: Historic Venice Press. 2004.

———. *Ghost Stories of Tampa Bay*. Venice, FL: Historic Venice Press. 2007.

Creamer, Robert. *Babe: The Legend Comes to Life*. New York: Pocket. 1976.

Dawson, Mike. "A Legend at the Lake." *Times-Herald Record*, May 11, 2006.

del Rosario, J. A. "Bewitched in Guayama." *Puerto Rico Herald*, March 19, 2004.

DeLuca, Chris. "MLB Talks to White Sox About Playing with Dolls in Clubhouse." *Chicago Sun-Times*, May 7, 2008.

DePorter, Grant, Elliott Harris and Mark Vancil. *Hoodoo: Unraveling the 100-Year Mystery of the Chicago Cubs*. Rare Air Books. 2008.

DiGiovanna, Mike. "Angels Play for Nick Adenhart's Memory." *Los Angeles Times*, September 29, 2009.

Doyle, John, Chuck Bennett, and Jeremy Olshan. "High 'Jinx' Hits Yankees." *New York Post*, April 11, 2008.

Dropkick Murphys. Liner Notes to *Tessie* (EP). Hellcat Records. 2004.

Edes, Gordon. "Sweeping in Seattle: Boston Finishes the Job after Long Day's Work." *Boston Globe*, July 24, 2008.

"Ed Thorp Shows Babe Ruth Art of Basketball Playing." *New York Times*, January 7, 1921.

Feinsand, Mark, Christina Boyle, and Corky Siemaszko. "Jason Giambi and His Magic Gold Thong." *The New York Daily News*, May 17, 2008.

Fine, Larry. "Gardner Comes Through After Getting Good-Luck Bracelet." Reuters, May 16, 2009.

Francis, Bill. "Roberto Clemente Jr. Shares Memories of His Legendary Father." June 9, 2006. www.baseballhall offame.org/news/2006/060609.htm.

Frethem, Deborah. *Ghost Stories of St. Petersburg, Clearwater and Pinellas County*. Charleston, SC: The History Press. 2007.

Gagne, Matt. "Tampa Bay Rays See Difference in Yankee Stadium's New Atmosphere." *New York Daily News*, June 6, 2009.

Garfield, Curtis F. *Sudbury 1890–1989: 100 Years in the Life of a Town*. Sudbury, MA: Porcupine Enterprises. 1999.

Gmelch, George, ed. *Baseball Without Borders*. Lincoln, NE: University of Nebraska Press. 2006.

Hartman, Steve. "Modern Day 'Pride of the Yankees.'" *CBS Evening News*, July 10, 2009.

Hern, Dylan. "Dodgers' Easy Win Comes with a Scare." *Los Angeles Times*, April 27, 2008.

———. "Dodgers' Shuffled Lineup Is a Big Hit." *Los Angeles Times,* April 22, 2008.

Herrman, Mark. "Larger-than-Life Ruth Built This House." *Newsday*, June 24, 2008.

Hime, Chris. "Yanks' Gardner Got Power Boost from Heart Patient." *New York Times*, June 13, 2009.

Hoekstra, Dave. "Conjuring a Cub." *Chicago Sun-Times*, March 26, 2008.

———. "Like a Bolt from the Blue," *Chicago-Sun Times*, March 26, 2008.

Holmes, Dan. "70 Years Later: The Hall of Fame's 'First Five.'" *Memories and Dreams: Commemorative Induction Ceremony Program*, July 30, 2006.

Holway, John B. *The Baseball Astrologer and Other Weird Tales*. Kingston, NY: Total/*Sports Illustrated*. 2000.

House, Tom, Ken Rosenthal and Nolan Ryan. *Nolan Ryan's Pitcher's Bible*. New York: Simon & Schuster/Fireside. 1991.

Hudson, Marilyn. "Dodgers Replacement Grass Goes on Road." *Los Angeles Times*, June 18, 1993.

"Ichiro's Bats More Than Pieces of Wood." ESPN.com, July 1, 2002. http://assets.espn.go.com/mlb/columns/caple_jim/1400915.html.

Jacobsen, Lenny. "Charles Murphy." The Baseball Biography Project. Society for American Baseball Research. http://bioproj.sabr.org/bioproj.cfm?a=v&v=l&pid=16915&bid=912.

Japan Today, "Colonel Sanders Statue and His Curse Lifted from Dotonbori River in Osaka," March 11, 2009. www.japantoday.com/category/national/view/colonel-sanders-statue-and-his-curse-lifted-from-dotonbori-river-in-osaka.

Jenkinson, Bill. *The Year Babe Ruth Hit 104 Home Runs.* New York: Carroll & Graf Publishers. 2007.

Kakinoki, Michiko. "Ups and Downs in the Life of Kuidaore Taro." *Nihon Keizai Shimbun,* May 29, 2008.

Kavanaugh, Jennifer. "Babe Ruth Really Slept Here." *Metrowest Daily News,* October 24, 2004.

Kawakami, Tim. "Dodgers—Last 10-Game Streak a Faded Memory." *Los Angeles Times,* May 30, 1993.

Kennedy, Kostya. "A Big Hit: The Good Deeds of Emerging Big League Star Matt Stairs Have Made a Hero in Navojoa, Mexico, His Winter League Baseball Home." *Sports Illustrated,* December 29, 1997.

Kepner, Tyler. "Once a Baseball Cathedral in Detroit, Now Neglected and Decrepit." *The New York Times,* July 10, 2005.

Kernan, Kevin. "Giving Up the Ghosts at Yankee Stadium." *New York Post,* September 21, 2008.

Kider, Terry. "For Yankees, Squirrel's Visit May Be Omen (a Bad One)." *The New York Times,* August 30, 2007.

Klinkenberg, Jeff. "Thanks, Babe." *St. Petersburg Times,* March 21, 2004.

Komura, Noriko. "People: Hideki Matsui." *Chopsticks NY,* October 2009.

Kornacki, Steve. "Visiting Granddaughter Touches Base with Babe's Old Haunts." *Tampa Tribune*, September 18, 2008.

Leiker, Ken, ed. *Jinxed: Baseball Superstitions from Around the Major Leagues*. New York: Ballantine Books. 2005.

Lemire, Jonathan. "Babe's Old Haunt Is Suite Memory." *New York Daily News*, October 13, 2003.

Leung, Diamond. "Dodgers Lose Again Missing Jones, Lowe and gnome." *The Press-Enterprise*, April 22, 2008.

Long, Karen Haymon. "War, the Depression No Match For Plant's Dream." *Tampa Tribune*, November 17, 2004.

Maraniss, David. *Clemente*. New York: Simon & Schuster. 2006.

Marquard, Bryan. "Faraway Faithful: Across US, It Sounds Like Red Sox Nation." *Boston Globe*, August 23, 2007.

Masur, Louis P. *Autumn Glory: Baseball's First World Series*. New York: Hill and Wang. 2003.

Matsuse, Manabu. "A Soul Lives in Tools." Mizuno Ballpark: Shodo Craftsman Column, Chapter 5. March 2, 2009. www.mizunoballpark.com/takumi/column/past/kubota05/index02.html.

McClatchy, Kevin M. *Babe Ruth in Florida*. Haverford, PA: Infinity Publishing. 2002.

Michaels, Will. "St. Petersburg's Passion—Baseball!" *Northeast Journal,* March 2005.

Michaels, Will, and Linda Ruth Tosetti. "Babe Ruth in St. Pete: A Soft Spot for Kids." *Northeast Journal,* May/June 2009.

Los Angeles Times, "Dodgers' Shuffled Lineup Is a Big Hit," April 22, 2008.

Liang, Fengrong. "Chengqing Hu Quichang Yu Lingyi Chuanqi" [Chengqing Stadium Has Mysterious Stories]. *Min Sheng Bao,* April 25, 2000.

Montefinise, Angela, Brad Hamilton, Alex Ginsberg, and James Fanelli. "Hammering the Hex." *New York Post,* April 13, 2008.

Montville, Leigh. *The Big Bam: The Life and Times of Babe Ruth.* New York: Bantam Books. 2007.

Moore, David Leon. "Star-crossed Angels Seek First Trip to Baseball Heaven." *USA Today,* October 3, 2002.

Murata, Masahiro. "The Truth about Ichiro: Testimony from Ichiro's Former Mentor Takeshi Nakamura." *Sankei News,* April 25, 2009. http://sankei.jp.msn.com/sports/mlb/090425/mlb0904250800000-n1.htm.

Nash, Peter J. *Boston's Royal Rooters.* Charleston, SC: Arcadia Publishing. 2005.

Nikkan Sports. "Purifying Toda Dorm for Yakult's Minor Leaguers." March 5, 2010. www.nikkansports.com/baseball/news/p-bb-tp0-20100305-602637.html

O'Leary, Ryan. " 'It Had to Be a UFO.' " *Northwest Indiana News*, August 2, 2003.

Olshan, Jeremy. "No. 1 Fan 'Bar' None." *New York Post*, April 15, 2008.

Olshan, Jeremy, Jason Nicholas, and Chuck Bennett. "'Under'miner A Bx. Traitor." *New York Post*, April 12, 2008.

Pearson, Kevin. "Dodgers Get 13 hits and Beat First-Place Arizona, 8–3." *The Press-Enterprise*, April 23, 2008.

Pirone, Dorothy Ruth. *My Dad, The Babe*. Boston: Quinlan Press. 1988.

Porrata-Doria, Adolfo. *Guayama: Sus Hombres y Sus Instituciones*. Barcelona: Jorge Casas. 1972.

Reeser, Tim. *Ghost Stories of St. Petersburg, FL*. St. Petersburg, FL: Ghostlore. 2004.

Reusse, Patrick. "Ghost Tales Get Go-going Out the Door." *Minneapolis Star Tribune*, June 14, 2008.

Ritter, Lawrence. *The Glory of Their Times: The Story of Baseball from the Men Who Played It*. New York: Macmillan. 1966.

Rocky Mountain News, "LA Finds Grass Isn't Always Greener As Streak Ends," May 31, 1993.

Rooters: The Birth of Red Sox Nation. DVD, Cooperstown Monument Co./Killswitch Productions, 2007.

Rouen, Ethan, and Bill Hutchinson. "Squirrel in Outfield Seems to Be Good Omen for Yankees." *The New York Daily News*, September 6, 2007.

Ruth, George Herbert, and Bob Considine. *The Babe Ruth Story, by Babe Ruth as Told to Bob Considine*. New York: E. P. Dutton & Co. 1948.

"Ruth and His Women." BaseballGuru.com. http://baseballguru.com/omi/ruthandhiswomen.htm.

Ryan, Bob. *When Boston Won the World Series*. Philadelphia: Running Press. 2002.

St. Petersburg Times, "Reopening of Belleview Casino Sparks Past Glories," January 28, 1945.

Sanborn, I. E. "Cubs Knock Off Drill a Day and Visit Catalina." *Chicago Daily Tribune*, March 8, 1920.

Saxon, Mark. "Teammate Lives in Angels' Hearts." *Orange County Register*, October 3, 2009.

Schwartz, Alan. "Some Players Hold Their Noses to Say Goodbye to Stadium." *The New York Times*, July 15, 2008.

Seattle Post-Intelligencer, "Dodgers Finally Lose Game, but Keep Good-Luck Grass Strip," May 31, 1993.

Spring Training Online Magazine, "Greetings from Catalina Island," September 29, 2006. http://www.springtraining magazine.com/history2.html.

Stewart, Wayne. *Babe Ruth: A Biography*. Santa Barbara, CA: Greenwood Press. 2006.

Stitt, Peter. "A Ghost of Gettysburg." *Gettysburg*. Vol. 88, no. 2, Summer 1997.

Stout, Glenn and Richard A. Johnson. *Red Sox Century*. Boston: Houghton Mifflin. 2000.

Swanson, Harry. *Ruthless Baseball*. Bloomington, Indiana: AuthorHouse. 2004.

Taylor, Phil. "Single Minded." *Sports Illustrated*, June 27, 2005.

The Curse of the Bambino. DVD, directed by George Roy. HBO Video, 2003.

"Tiger Stadium." www.ballparksofbaseball.com/past/TigerStadium.htm.

Tyler, Vanessa. "The Magic Bracelet?" WPIX.com, June 12, 2009.

Verducci, Tom. "Tough Customers." *Sports Illustrated*, August 20, 2001.

Verrell, Gordon. "Dodgers' Streak Falls Just Short of a Dozen." *Press-Telegram*, May 31, 1993.

Vitti, Jim. *The Cubs on Catalina*. Darien, CT: Settefrati Press. 2003.

Wasserman, Aaron. "Local Fan Pays $175,000 for Buried Sox Jersey." *The Milford Daily News*, April 25, 2008.

Whiting, Robert. *The Meaning of Ichiro*. New York: Warner Books. 2004.

Wittenmyer, Gordon. "The Rookie Curse." *Chicago Sun-Times*, March 30, 2008.

Wlodarski, Robert J., and Anne Nathan-Wlodarski. *Haunted Catalina: A History of the Island and Guide to Paranormal Activity*. West Hills, CA: G-Host Publishing. 1996.

Yumoto, Yuki. "[Team] Considering Exorcizing Toda Dorm Due to Strange Happenings." Nikkan Sports, January 11, 2010. www.nikkansports.com/baseball/news/p-bb-tp0-20100111-584599.html.

Index

Index

Horton, Willie, 33, 41
Hotel Carlos, Chicago, IL, 178–79
Hotel Principe, Venezuela, 174–75
Hough, Don, 101
Howard, Frank, 34
Hubbs, Ken, 189
Huck, Tim, 85
Hudson, Tim, 34
Huggins Stengel Field, St. Petersburg, FL, 89–90
Hughes, Paul, 75
Hunter, Torii, 24, 58–59, 60
Huyke, Woody, 101, 105–7, 171–72

I
Igawa, Kei, 127, 137
Ilitch, Mike, 35, 38

J
Jack Murphy Stadium, San Diego, FL, 190
Japan, 123–48
Jenkinson, Bill, 89–90
Jennings, Hughie, 32
Jeter, Derek, 24–25, 204
Johjima, Kenji, 134
John, Tommy, 189
Johnson, Walter, 32
Johnston, Kevin, 154
Jolley, Smead, 233
Jungle Hotel and Country Club, St. Petersburg, FL, 87, 96
Jurges, Billy, 178, 179–83

K
Kaline, Al, 32, 35
Kata, Matt, 249
Kato, Daisuke, 136, 141
Kelly, Lisa, 75
Kemp, Matt, 195, 197
Kennedy, Kevin, 65–66
Kenney, Crane, 183–85, 187
Key West Conchs, 191–94
Killebrew, Harmon, 34
Kintetsu Buffaloes, 124, 140

Kitoh, Makoto, 129, 130–31
Kiyohara, Kazuhiro, 142
Knorr, Randy, 174–75, 237
Koenig, Mark, 178–79
Koshien Stadium, Japan, 125–28
Kristinat, Rik, 179–83
Kruger, Lonny, 191
Kuehnert, Marty, 137
Kura, Yoshikazu, 127, 129, 131
Kyoto, Japan, 140

L
Lackawanna Station Hotel, Scranton, PA, 236–55
Landrum, Tito, 191
Lang, Stephen, 75–76
Latin-American ballplayers, 165–76
LaValle, Denise, 69–70, 72–73
Lazzeri, Tony, 228
Leach, Tommy, 214
Levin, Carl, 44
Levine, Randy, 26
Liefer, Jeff, 124, 243–44
Lincecum, Tim, 5–6
Lincoln, Eric, 192, 193
Loebel, Bob, 202
Lomasney, Steve, 241
Longoria, Evan, 26
Lopez, Yadira, 230, 231
Los Angeles Angels, 48–60, 63
Los Angeles Dodgers, 195–99
Lowe, Derek, 224
Lowe, Q. V., 193
Lowell, Mike, 223–24

M
Mack, Connie, 215
Mack, Shane, 134
Maddon, Joe, 51–52
Majewski, Gary, 244, 245
Malzone, Frank, 233
Mantle, Mickey, 24
Markusen, Bruce, 109, 110–11, 114
Martin, Russ, 195–98
Masterson, Justin, 223

Index

Index

About the Authors

Mickey Bradley and Dan Gordon coauthored the popular *Haunted Baseball: Ghosts, Curses, Legends & Eerie Events*. Bradley is a lifelong Yankee fan, named after the team's legendary centerfielder. He has been working as a freelance writer for more than fifteen years, both in Manhattan and Upstate New York. Gordon, who lives and dies with the Red Sox, is the author of *Cape Encounters: Contemporary Cape Cod Ghost Stories*. His writings on baseball have appeared in numerous publications, including the *Providence Journal* and *Fort Worth Star*.